A Collection Of

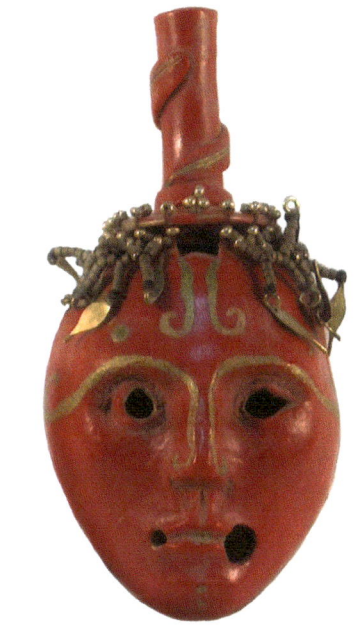

Polymer Clay Masks

Sarajane Helm

A Collection Of Polymer Clay Masks

Copyright ©2010 Sarajane Helm

All rights reserved.
No part of this book may be reproduced
in any form or by means electronic
or mechanical, including photocopying,
recording, or by an information storage
and retrieval system without
permission in writing from the publisher.

Photography by Sarajane Helm except as noted.

First published and printed as a paperback in
the United States of America in 2010
by PolyMarket Press

ISBN 978-0-9800312-2-5

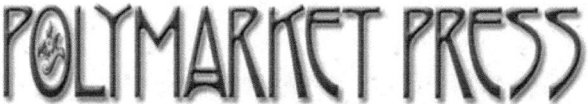

For more information about our books
and the authors and artists who create them,
please visit our website:
polymarketpress.net

Front Cover Mask: Katherine Dewey, *photo Katherine Dewey,*
Back Cover Masks: Sarajane Helm, Melanie West; Flyleaf Mask: Margaret Rheid

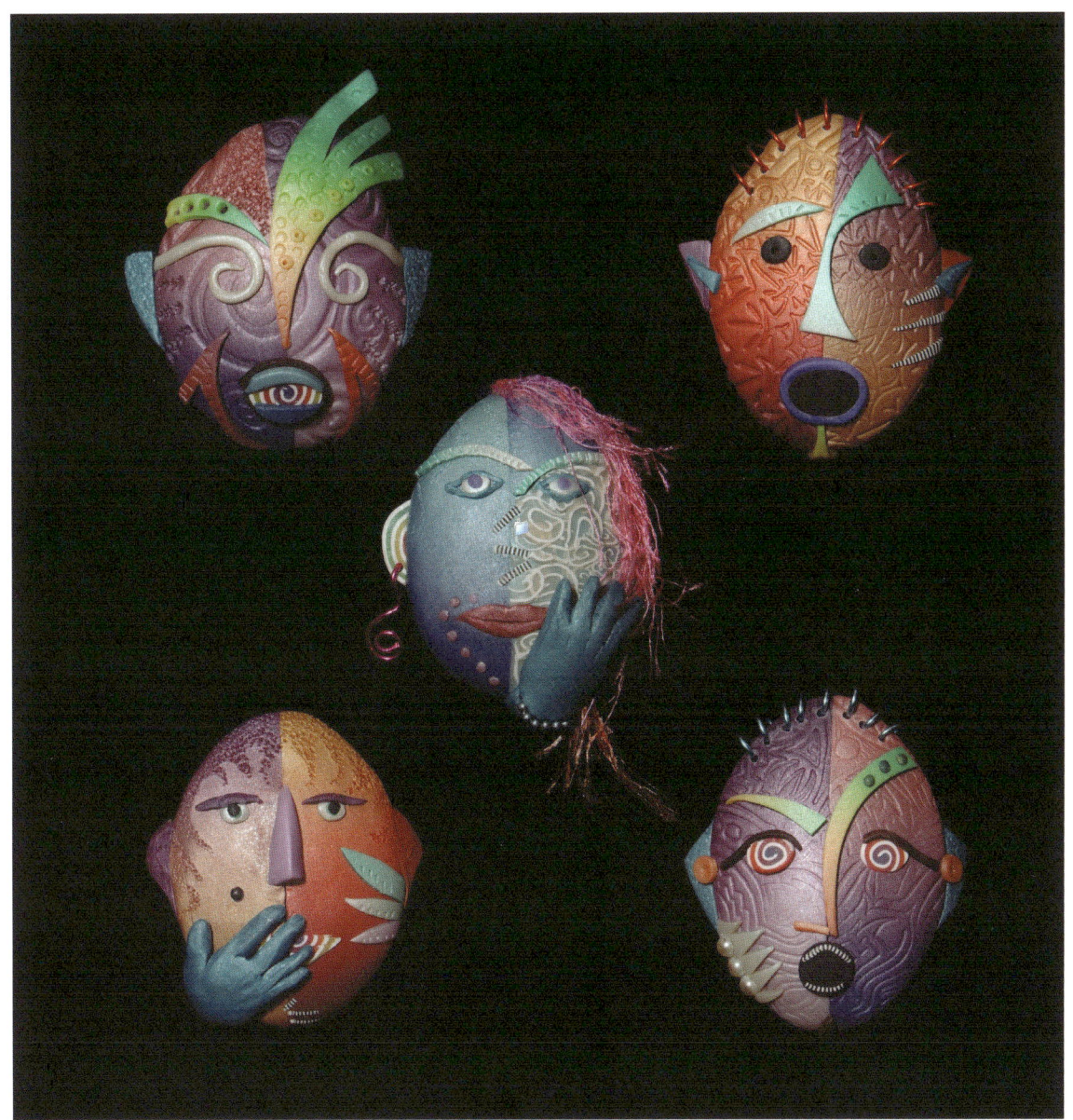

Dorothy Greynolds   *photo Dorothy Greynolds*

Faces are one of the first images that babies learn to recognize, and the ability to recognize facial expressions is a skill most of us learn very early in our infancy. How to hide our true expressions is our introduction to the power of a mask (and we've all heard some variation on "Don't you make that face at ME"). Whether it is mask we craft by controlling our own muscle shifts and movements, or an applied structure, masks have the profoundly alterative ability to display or conceal chosen emotional states, thoughts, and identities. My continuing interests in perception and communication have led me to study story telling and theatre in college and university courses, and on the world's wider stage. Masks were used in the original plays of the Greeks to transform the actors from mere mortals to beings who spoke for the gods; masks are used in rites and rituals in many cultures to enable viewers and participants to transcend mortal barriers and hear truths. What is hidden allows for revelation at another time.

Sarajane Helm

Masks allow us to present the faces we choose to paint for the world, and create and carry the illusions and realities we present to others. They can give to the wearer a sense of privacy and protection while in full public view. What we choose to hide says as much (or more) about who we are as what we choose to display. These idealized images and forms are distillations of our own perceptions, and yet are shared and valued from culture to culture in widely disparate times and places. When artisans create masks, there is often a strong element of personalization that occurs even in those forms that have been passed down throughout the centuries with loving care. There are parameters and outlines which are necessary for each characterization, but there is always room for personal decorative interpretation and detail.

In designing and creating costumes and props, I developed my creative and technical abilities while also learning a great deal about how people have adorned, hidden and presented themselves throughout recorded history. Since then I have made my living creating wearable and decorative art in many media, with textiles and a love of color, texture and pattern recurring elements in my work. When I began working with polymer clay in 1986, I immediately was hooked by the way I could create small mannequins for me to costume. Dolls are much easier to organize and keep around than groups of actors and they never complain if you make them look fat!

I have learned from what others do, developed and taught techniques of my own, and spent many happy, creative, productive years. Though the polymer clay has changed some in its chemical makeup since its early use in the 1930s, what is truly astounding are the unlimited number of ways it can be used for different decorative effects. As more and more artists got it into their hands they incorporated their own favorite tools, materials and ways of doing things from other media, and shared what they discovered with others. Techniques spread like wildfire in creative cooperation, and polymer clay is amenable to almost all of them! Make it look like metal, stone, wood or fabric, a baby's skin or leather hides, mold it, model it, carve or stamp it. The options of what to do with it fill many books (including a few I've written) and yet the surface of what can be done has only been slightly uncovered.

This creative cooperation between artists is particularly nurtured in the worldwide polymer clay community, and there are many very active guilds, organizations, and online groups where information is shared and friendships are made as well. Sometimes there are common interests in kinds of items, such as beads, artist trading cards, or in a particular technique like millefiore cane work, stamping, or faux finishes. "Swaps" are often held, in which participants all make a certain number of items and then they trade among themselves within groups to build collections. A "swapmeister" is the central management point that receives, sorts, and sends out the items to the group members. When Sherry Bailey initiated the polymer clay miniature mask swap in 1997, it mingled my love of costumes, faces, and the endless array of looks that are possible with polymer clay. I started to collect them and haven't stopped yet. I owe a giant debt of thanks to all that have participated in making these masks, and to my husband Bryan for years of his help in the sorting, shipping, and cataloguing of all the pieces. He's spent many an hour at the post office shipping boxes of masks back to swappers! And we've built a wonderful collection over the years.

In the pages of this book you will find hundreds of masks made by 150 different artists. Many are large enough to wear, and have their sizes and photographer listed in the captions. Most of them are sized to fit in a 3 inch square and are often shown at, or very close to, their actual size. Taken all together they form a sampler of polymer clay techniques and decorative styles as well as a large miniature collection of expressive art. It's just astounding, how much can be communicated with a mask!

August 24, 2010
Sarajane Helm

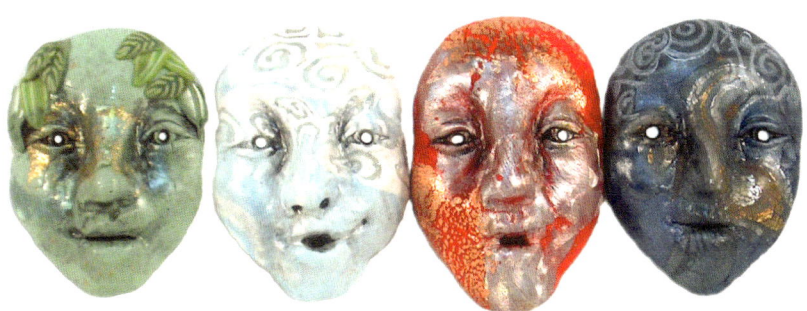

Sarajane Helm

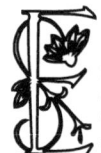Emerson said: "Society is a masked ball, where every one hides his real character, and reveals it by hiding," and I couldn't agree more. We all wear so many masks throughout our lives; oftentimes we use them as a behavioral façade that we put on to hide our insecurities and fears.

If one ventures into the criminal museum in Rothenburg ob der Tauber, Germany one can see a more visceral use of masks. From the 14th through 18th century masks were often used as a penalty of shame or dishonor. If you were the town gossip you may have been forced to walk through town in an iron mask with a large tongue or lips. A mask of a large nose might be worn if one was meddling into the affairs of others, or a pig's snout if one was treating women poorly. A bad musician might even be forced to wear a mask of a flute extending from his face to show he needed to practice. Indigenous cultures throughout the world have embraced masks as effigies to gods and deities, often worn to embrace their spirits or personal characteristics. Yet in modernity we often frown about such behavior as being inhuman or idolatrous.

I would argue that we have not evolved much past these times. As a behavioral scientist, my area of specialty is the study of human behavior. I am fascinated by how human resilience challenges us to reinvent and rebrand ourselves as a means of survival, likewise in how the labels of society serve to trap and confine us. All too often we disguise our true nature behind a mask, and yet society still seems to enjoy the humility suffered by shame.

Today's masks are more intangible, and figurative, but if we look closely we can see them. The ageing woman hides behind the mask of botox, insecure about her fading youth, the mask of fame and success that is flaunted on the red carpet. The mask of privilege and power that some individuals hide behind to disguise their unethical behavior is yet another residual from ancient days. These masks surround us and are often used to highlight character or to shame.

My love of masks began in childhood when my father would bring them to me from his many business travels. It evolved over the years to mesh with my passion for psychology. As a feminist artist, my love of nature, women, and the human condition drew me to Sarajane. Her ability to capture the soul of women in her faces touched me and inspired me to embrace my own love of clay and masks. Once that seed was planted…the rest is developing.

August 12, 2010
Rebecca Wells Stout

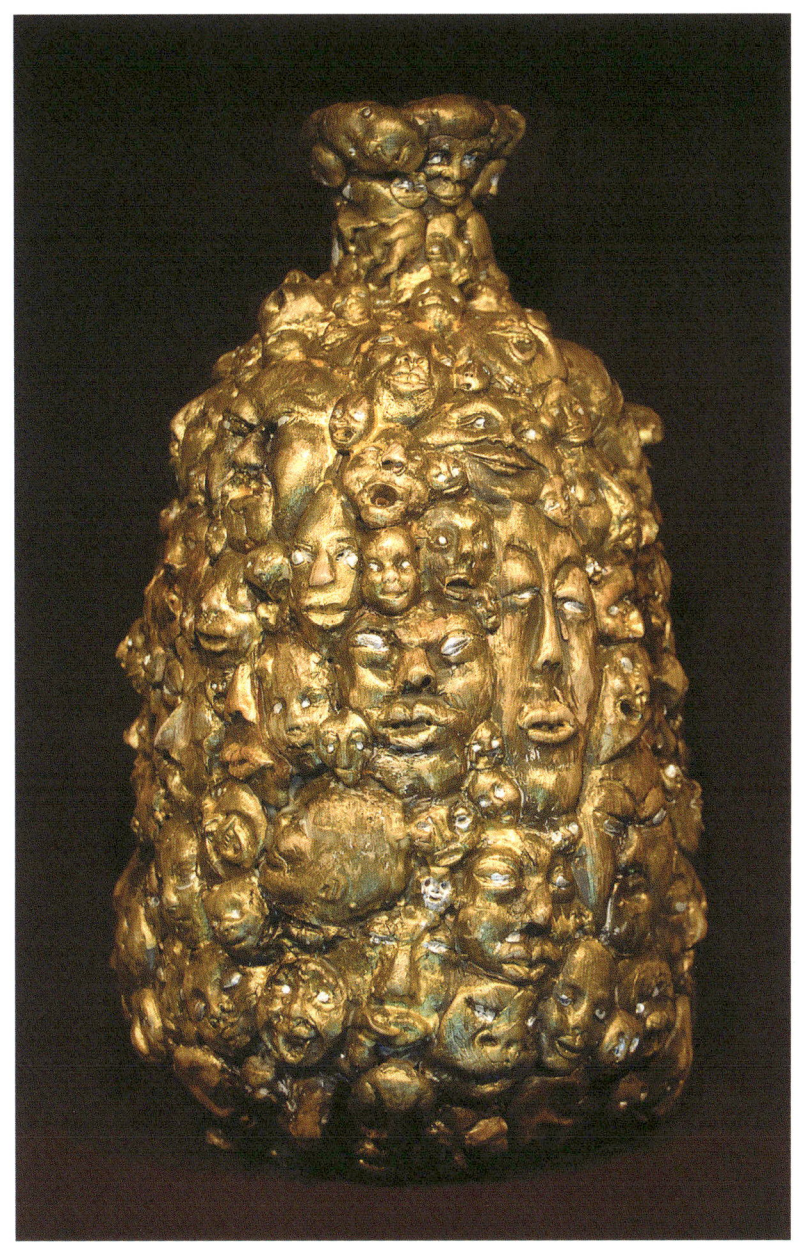

Rebecca Wells Stout   *photo Mark Stout*   22"x18"

I have always loved masks, from the whimsical to the tribal to the ceremonial, and have wondered about the anthropological stories behind them. I also love small things, dollhouse miniatures and slightly bigger representations of things usually seen larger. One day it hit me that a fun swap would be miniature masks of all kinds!

In my mind, I envisioned a collection of similarly sized relatively flat faces that could be hung from a chain in a grouping to make a "charm bracelet" style necklace, or maybe a group of pins to wear. In order to make this possible, I determined that each mask needed to fit within a three inch square. I also requested that each one either arrive with a pin back or with some kind of loop for hanging as a pendant, in case that's how the recipient wanted to use it. I believe I may have also asked that eye holes be included to discriminate masks from small faces, but perhaps that was optional.

Sherry Bailey

I posted the swap, got a lot of interest, and forged ahead. I learned a lot of things from hosting the first miniature masks swap. First, I am not alone in my love of representations of the face (human or other). Second, in any given swap, somebody ignores the rules! Masks arrived that were very amazing, but bigger than any jewelry most people would wear. So the idea of making a shadow box display was born, and subsequent mask swaps have mainly considered that the logical end result—after all, how many pins or pendants does anyone need, anyhow?

When Sarajane picked up the torch and became mistress of miniature mask swapping, I was delighted that people still wanted to play that particular game! It was and is a creative challenge that provides an unusual number of options for the creative clayer.

March 19, 2007
Sherry Bailey

(Editor's Note: Sherry made her masks for the original 1997 swap in book form and they each contained pictures of the other masks in the swap!)

Sherry Bailey

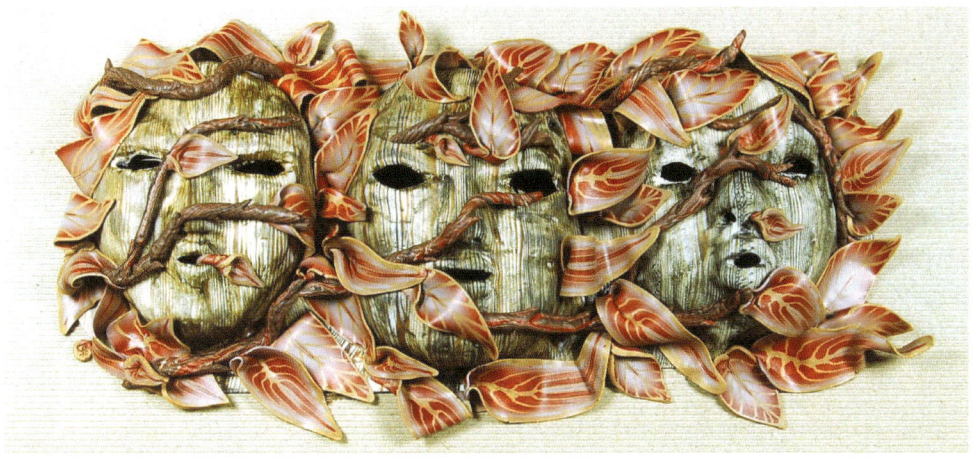

Rebecca Wells Stout   photo Mark Stout   22" x 6"

"Man is least himself when he talks in his own person. Give him a mask, and he will tell you the truth."
~Oscar Wilde

"Without wearing any mask we are conscious of, we have a special face for each friend."
~Oliver Wendell Holmes

"No mask like open truth to cover lies, As to go naked is the best disguise."
~William Congreve

"Although I know it's unfair I reveal myself one mask at a time."
~Stephen Dunn

"Pride is the mask of one's own faults."
~Jewish Proverb

"Sometimes people carry to such perfection the mask they have assumed that in due course they actually become the person they seem."
~William Somerset Maugham

"Year by year, the monkey's mask reveals the monkey."
~Matsuo Basho

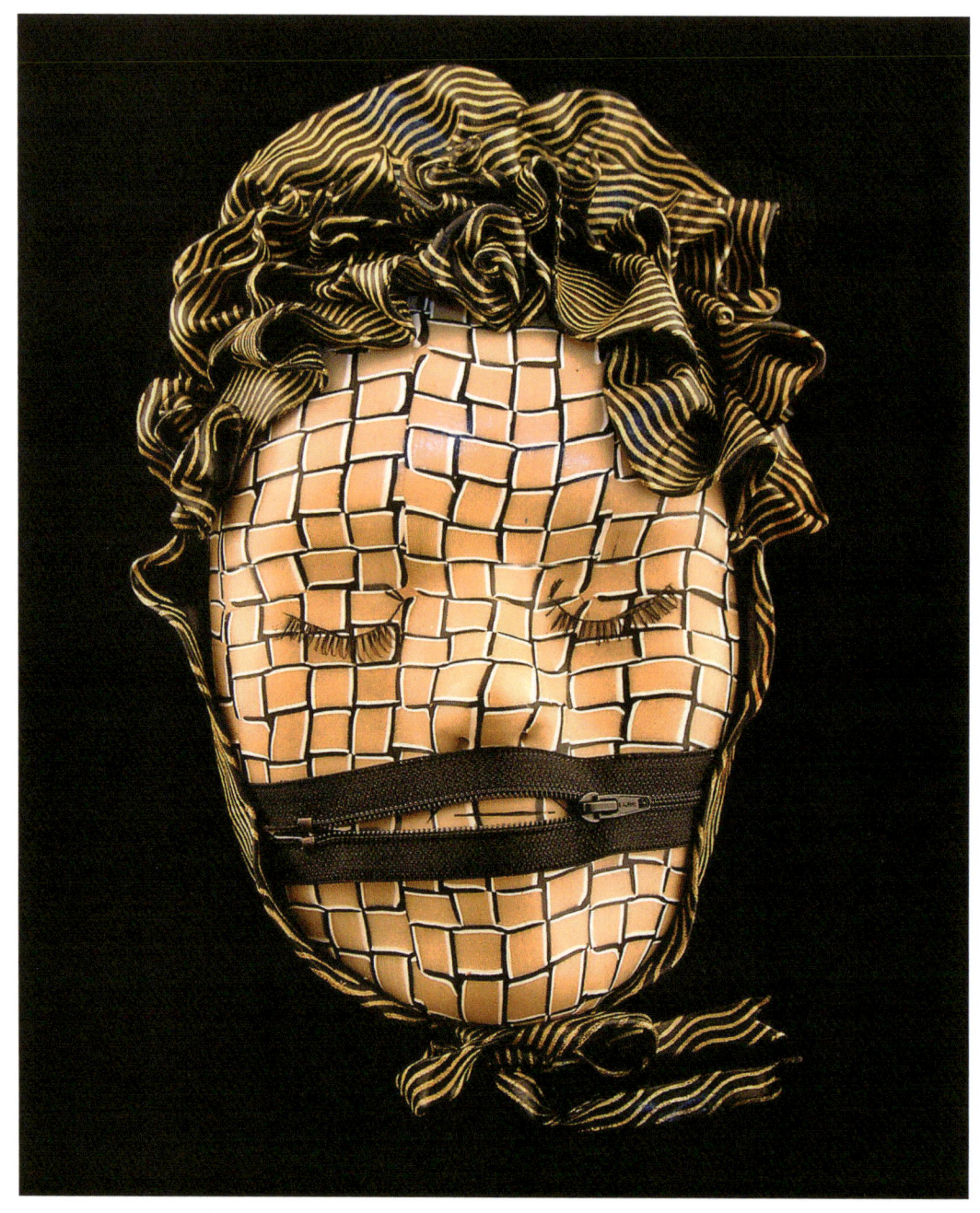

Rebecca Wells Stout   *photo Mark Stout 6" x 6"*

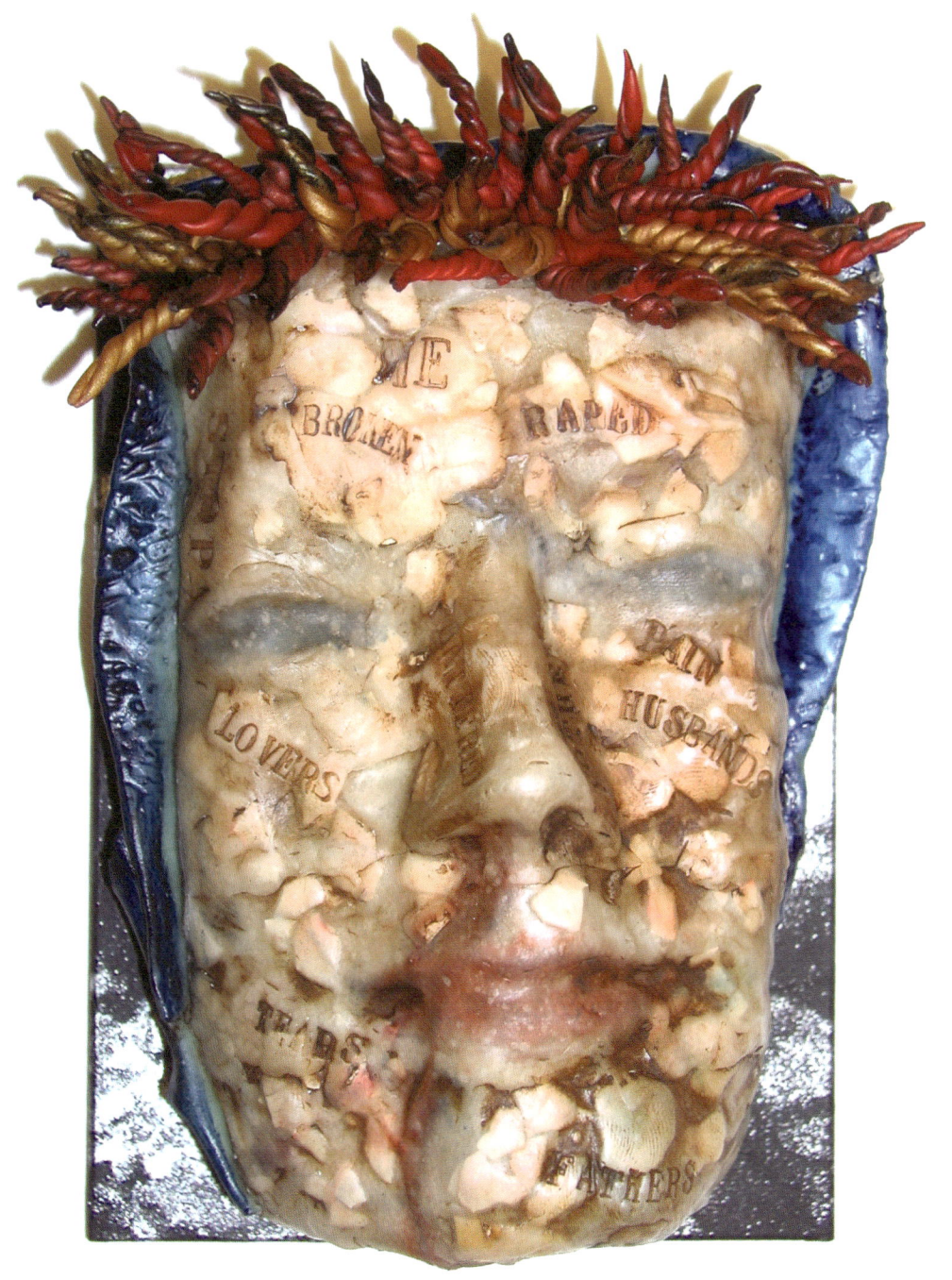

Christopher Knoppel   *photo Christopher Knoppel   7" x 5"*

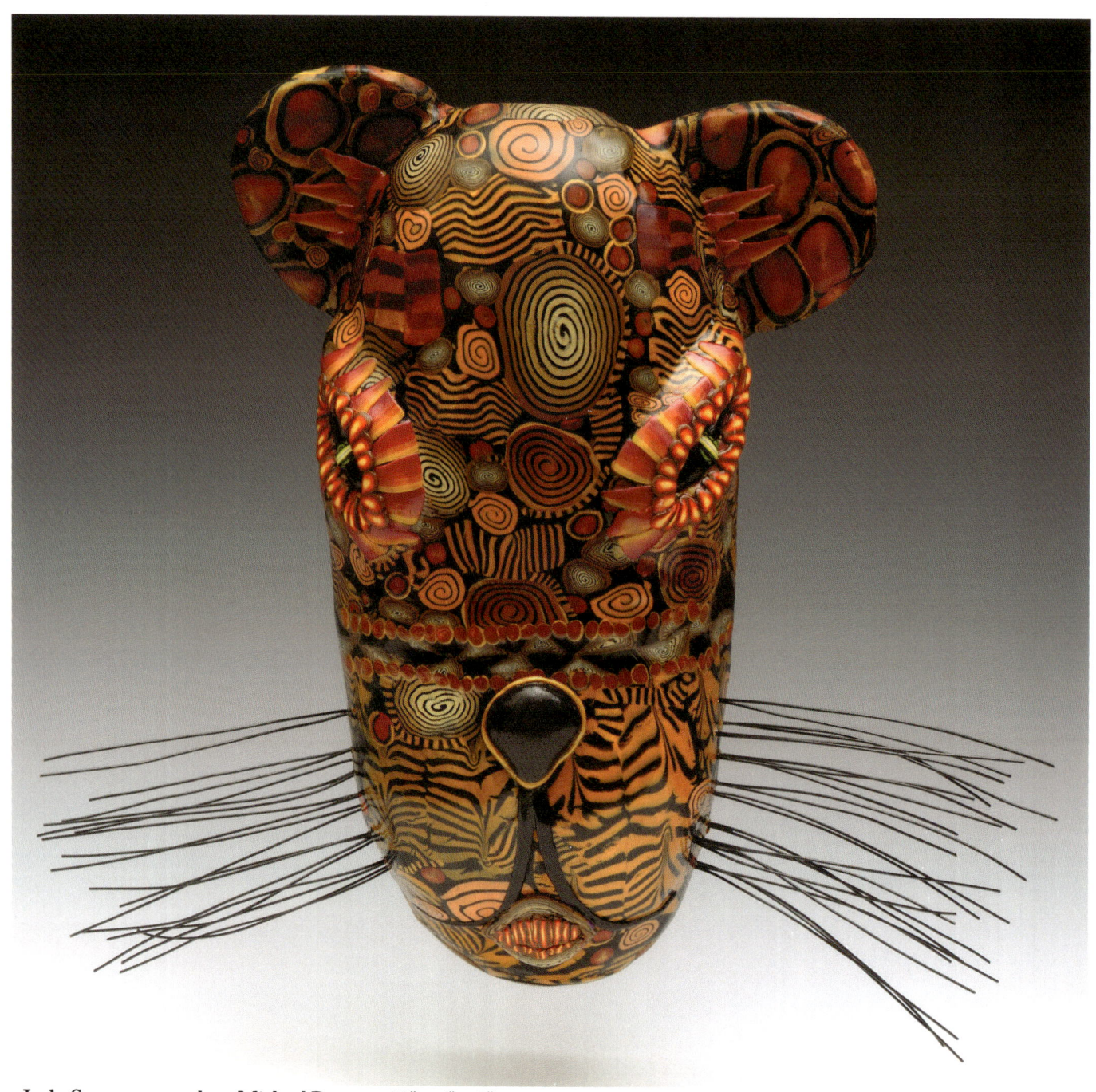

Judy Summer   *photo Michael Doogan 18" x 6" x 3"*

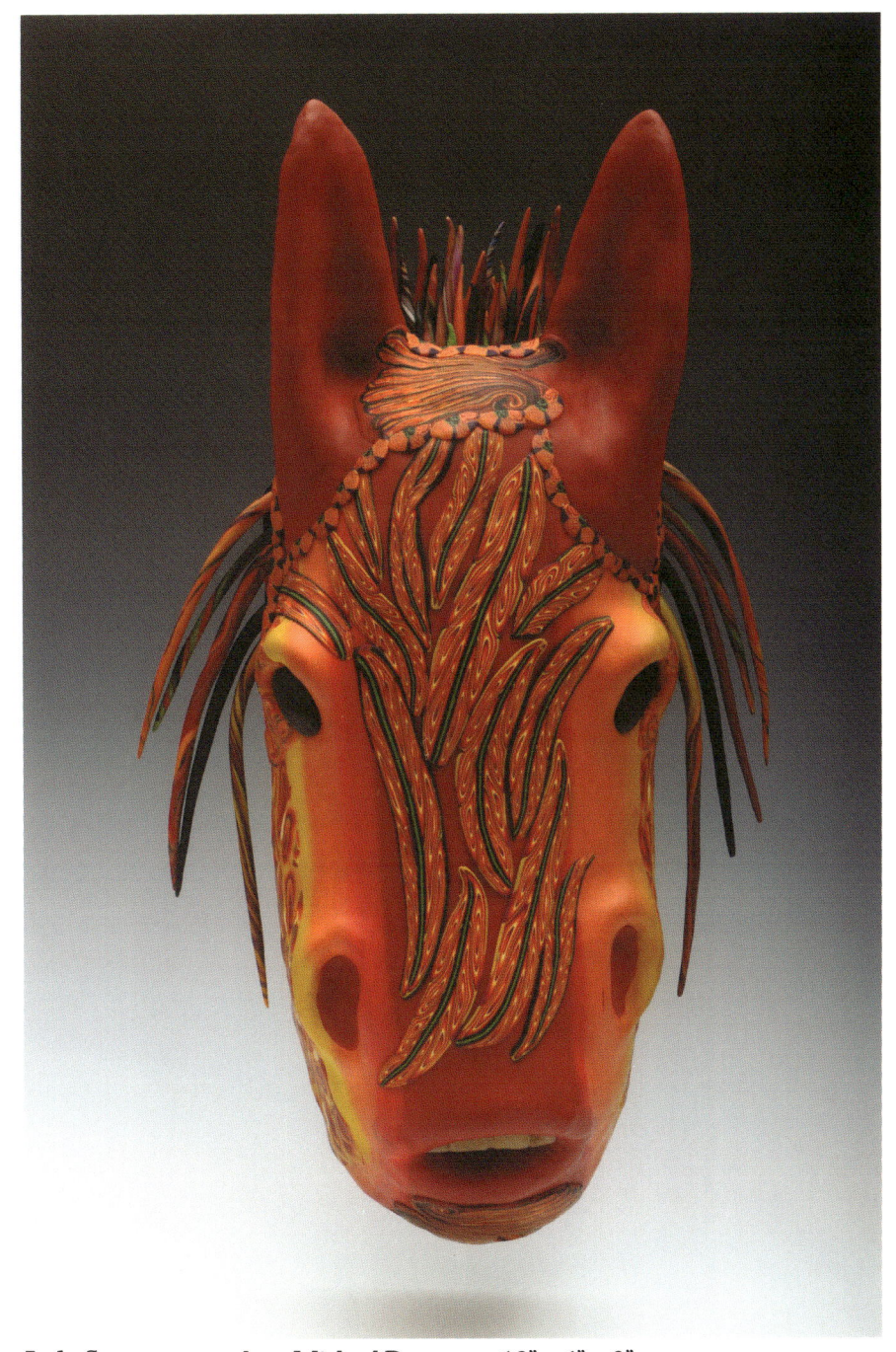

Judy Summer   *photo Michael Doogan*   18" x 6" x 3"

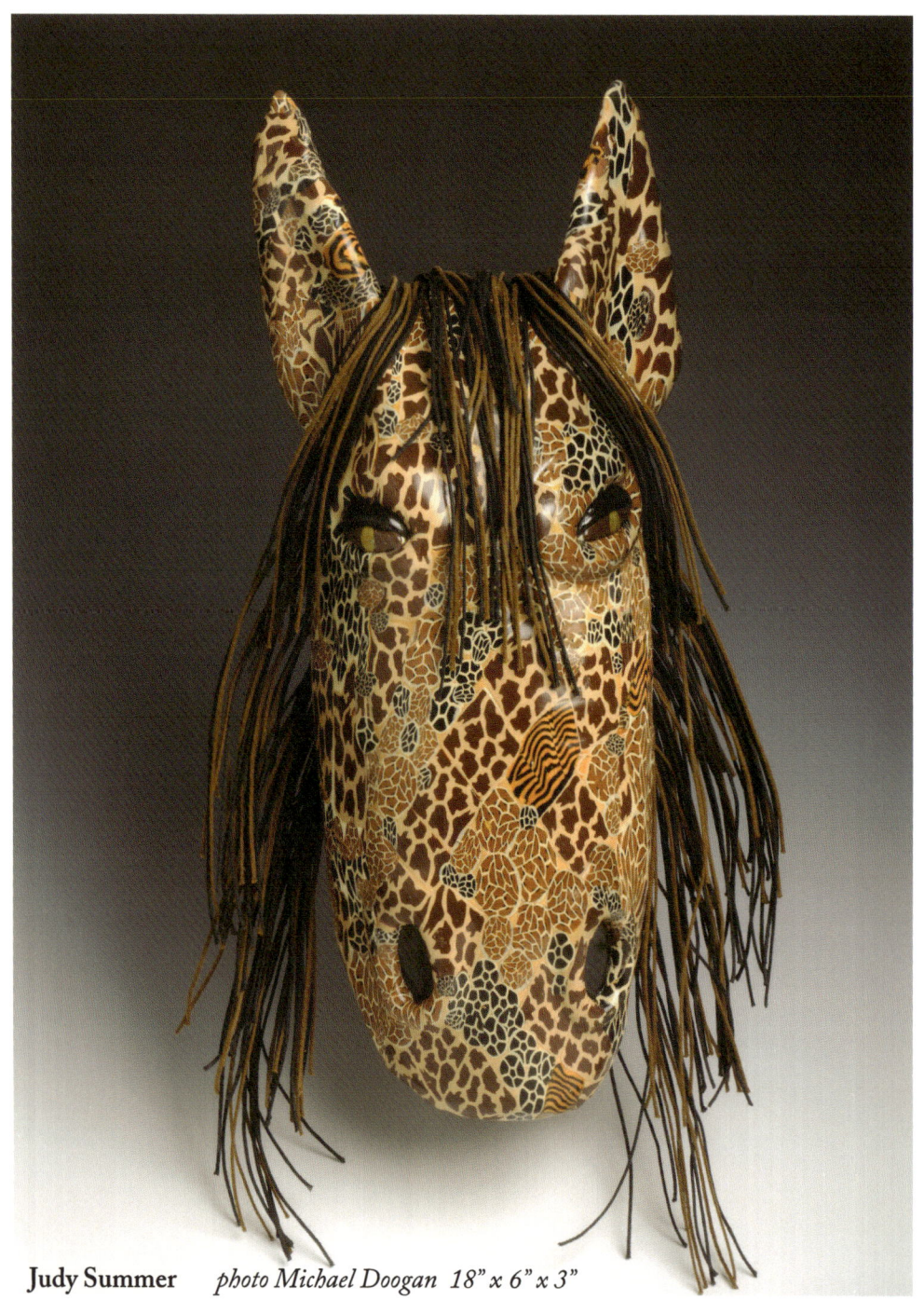

Judy Summer   *photo Michael Doogan 18" x 6" x 3"*

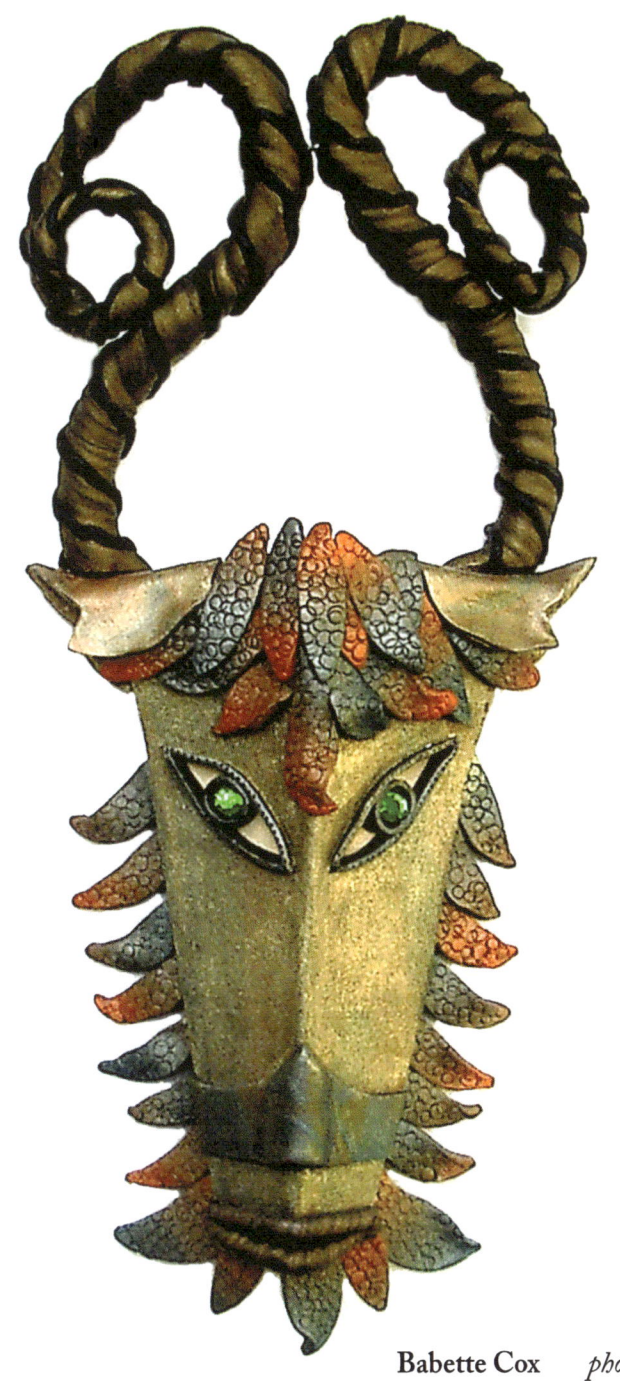

Babette Cox *photo Babette Cox* 13" x 6"

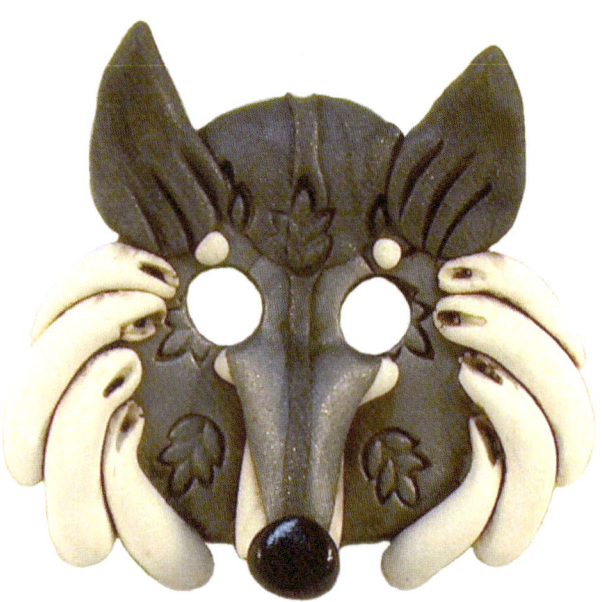

Patricia Edmonds

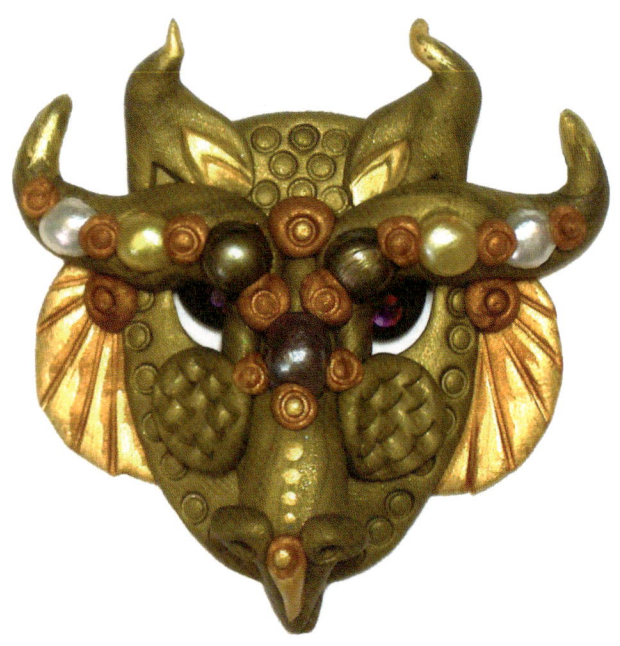

Patricia Edmonds

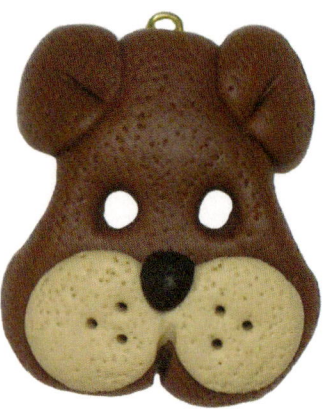

Carolyn Sherman

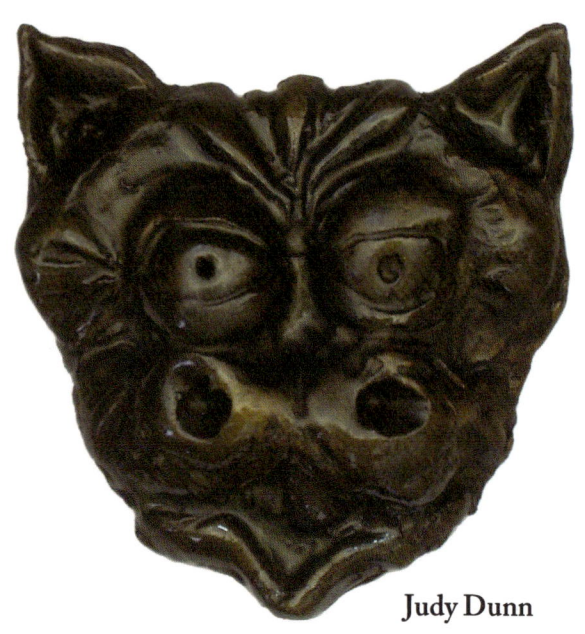

Judy Dunn

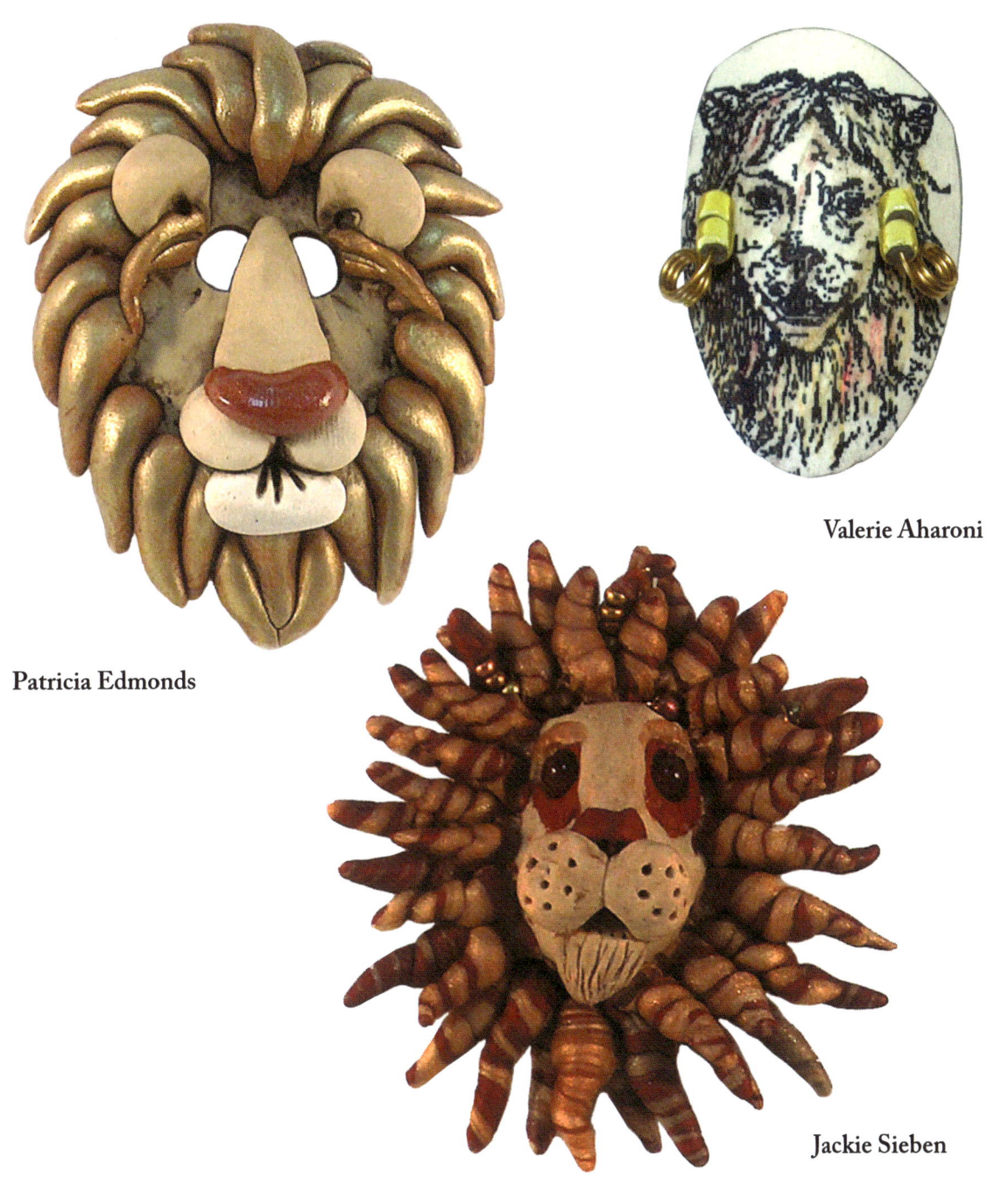

Patricia Edmonds

Valerie Aharoni

Jackie Sieben

PolyMarket Press

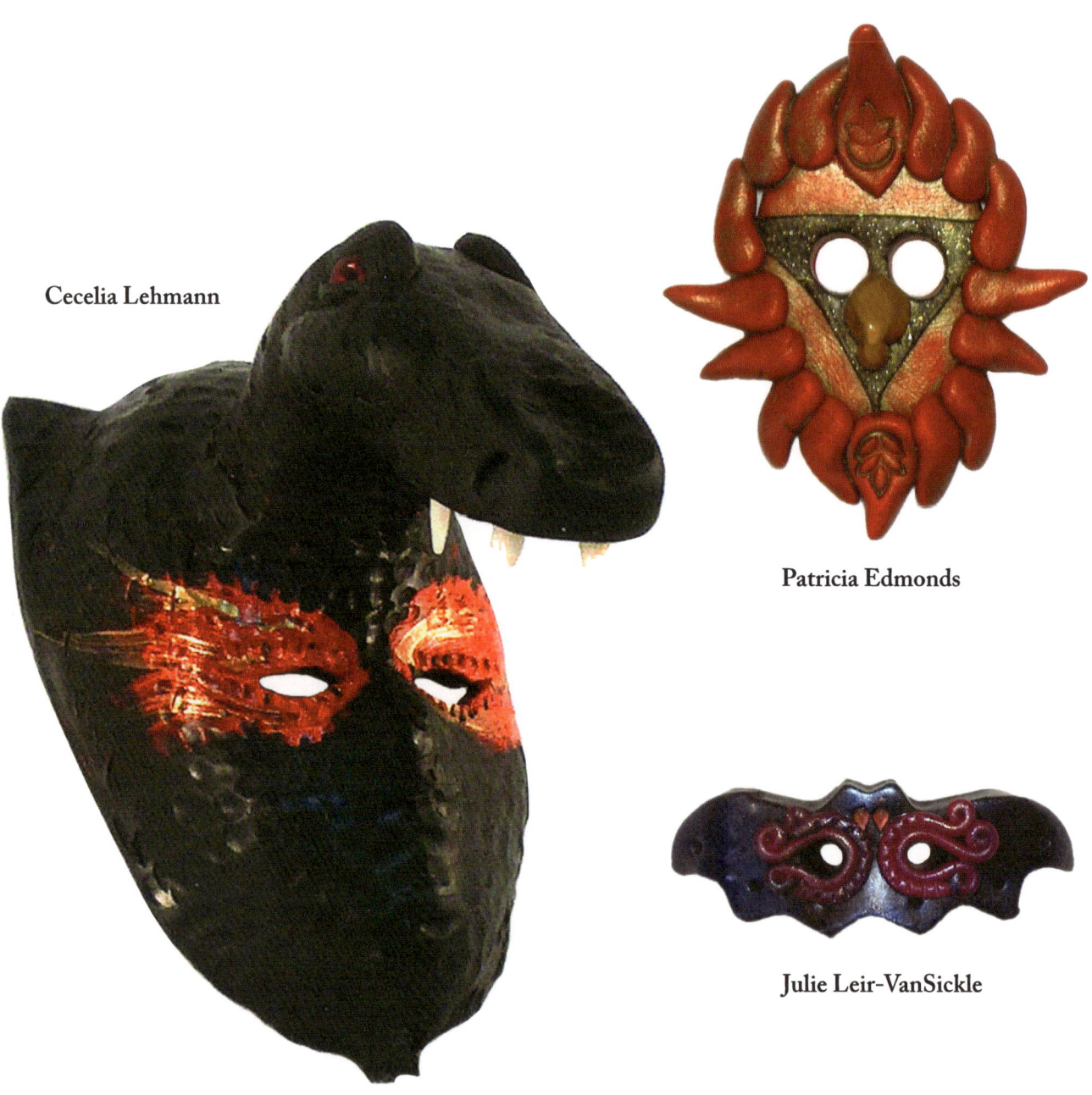

Cecelia Lehmann

Patricia Edmonds

Julie Leir-VanSickle

A Collection Of Polymer Clay Masks

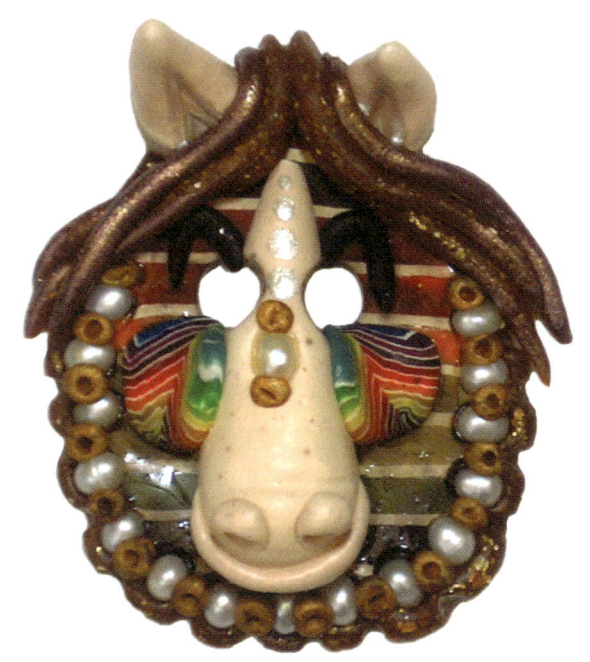

Patricia Edmonds

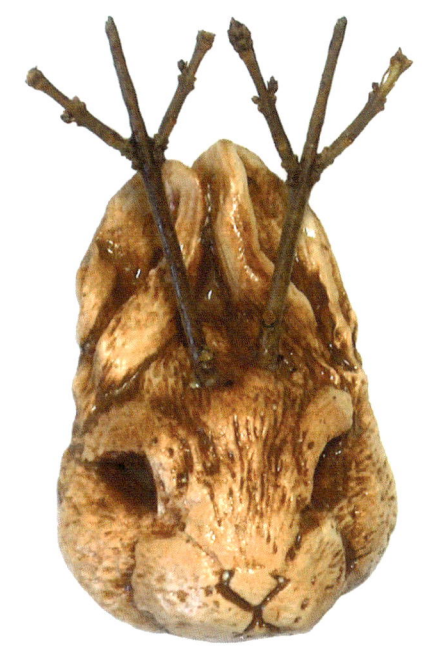

Marie-Therese

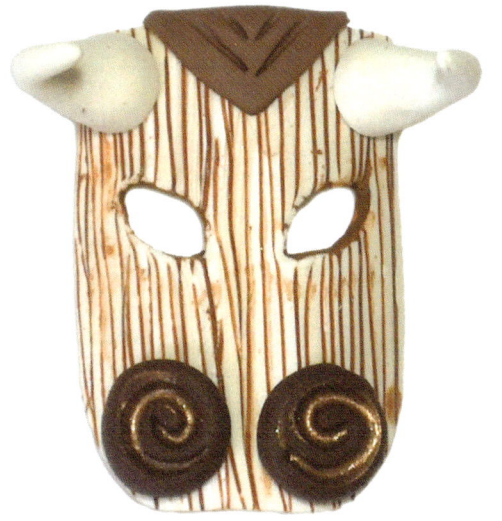

LynnDel Newbold

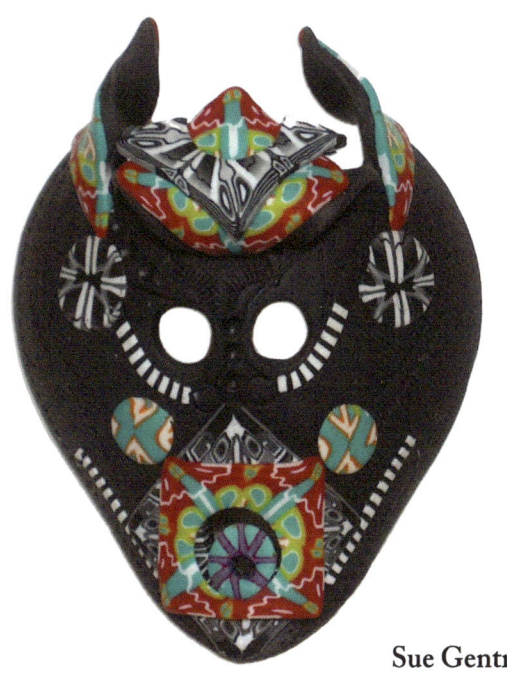

Sue Gentry

PolyMarket Press

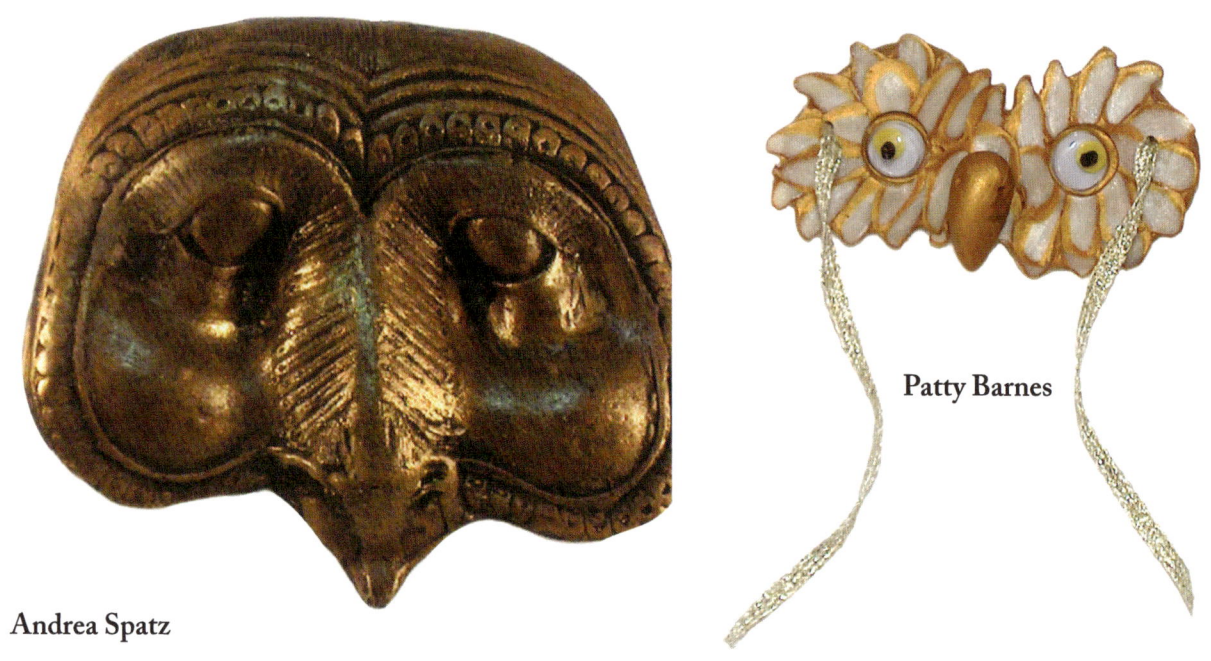

Andrea Spatz

Patty Barnes

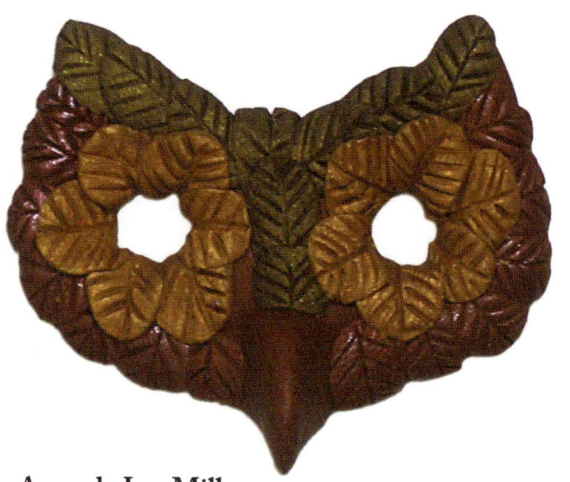

Amanda Lee Miller

A Collection Of Polymer Clay Masks

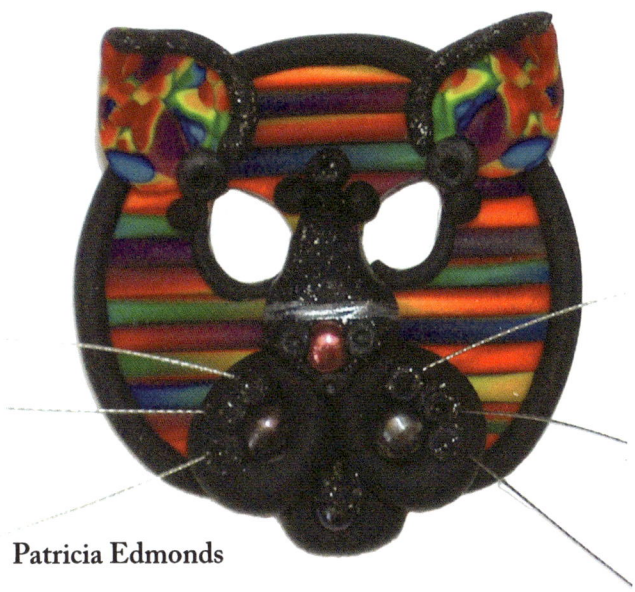

Patricia Edmonds

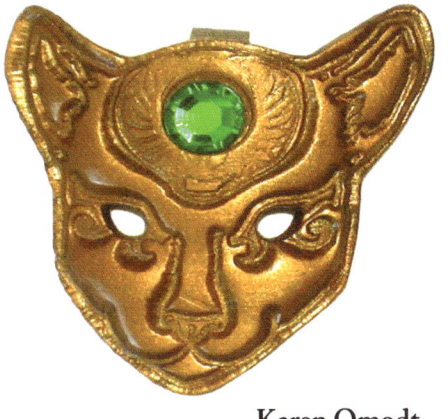

Karen Omodt

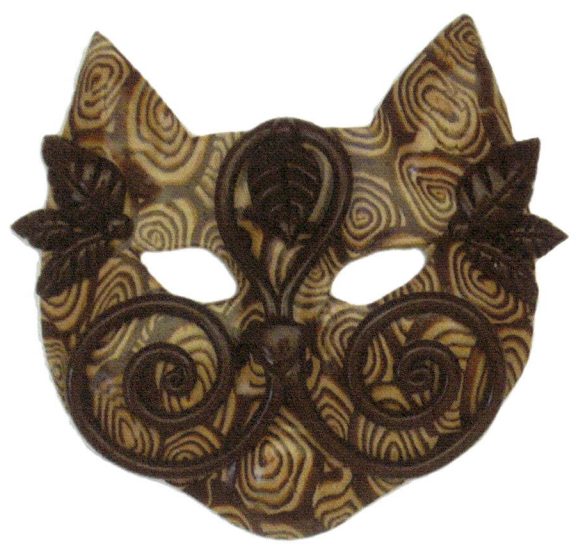

Susan Wrisley

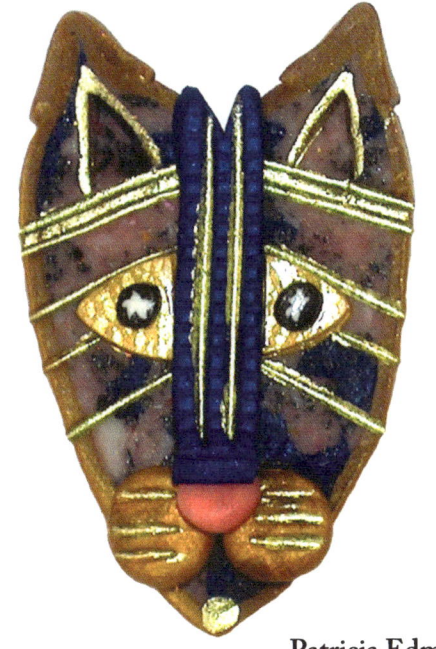

Patricia Edmonds

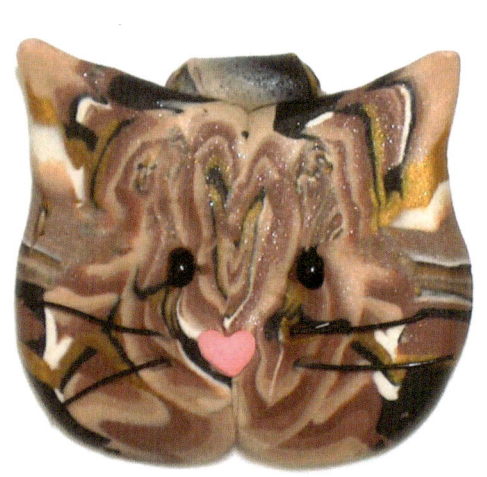
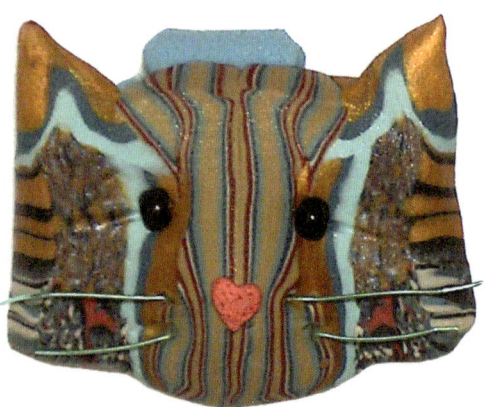

Sarajane Helm

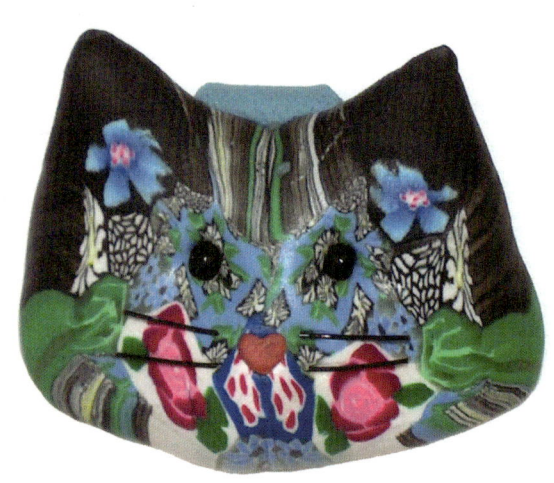

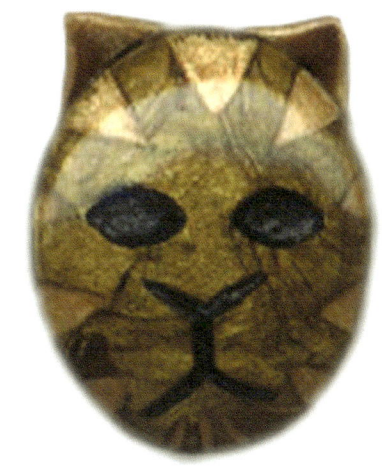

Tonja Lenderman

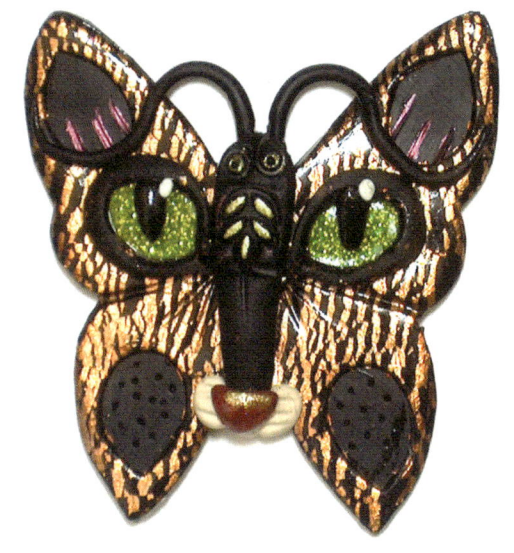

Patricia Edmonds

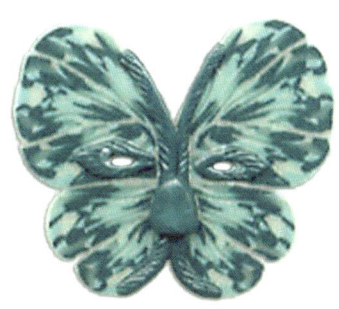

Lisa Carlson

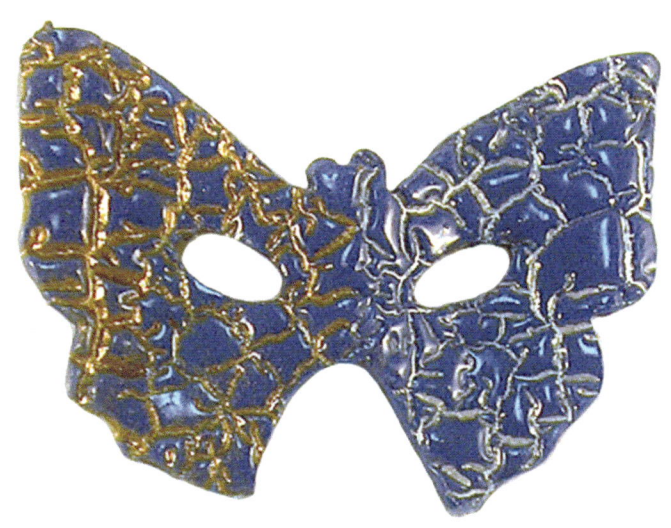

Greta Fry

Lynne Ann Schwarzenberg

Rebecca Wells Stout

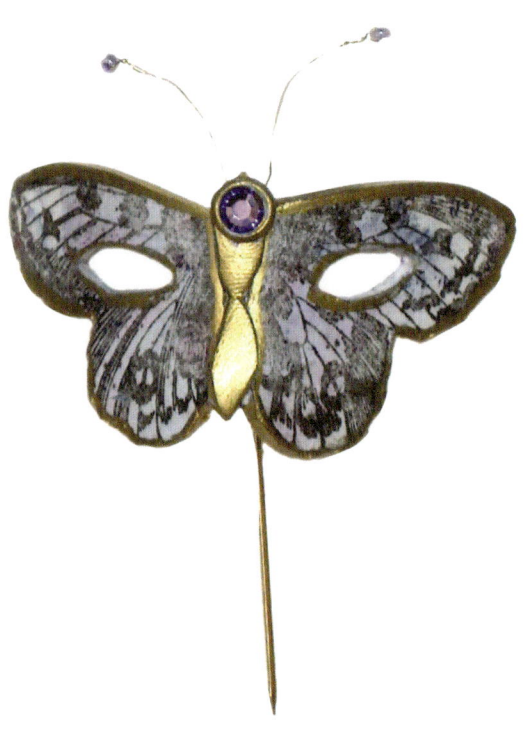

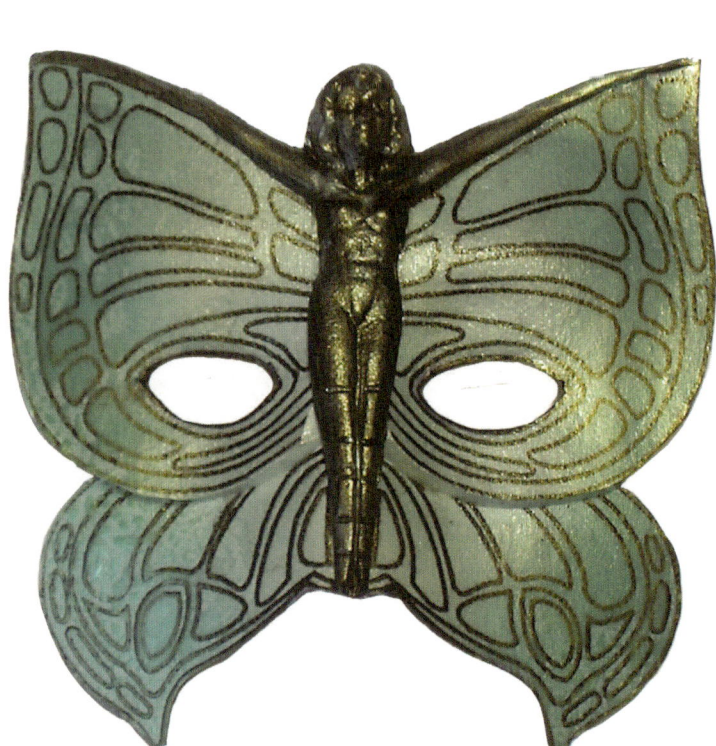

Robert Houghtaling

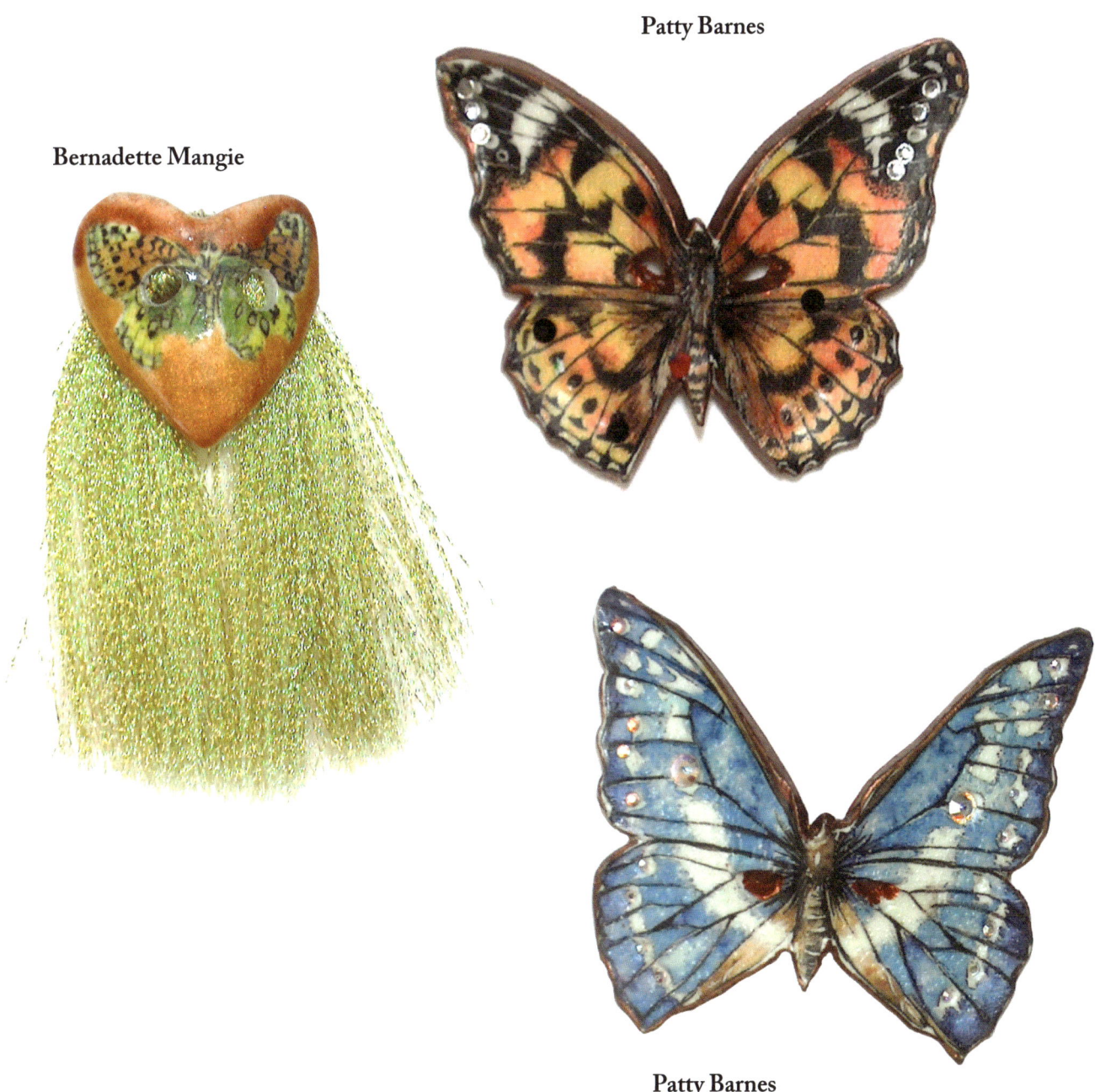

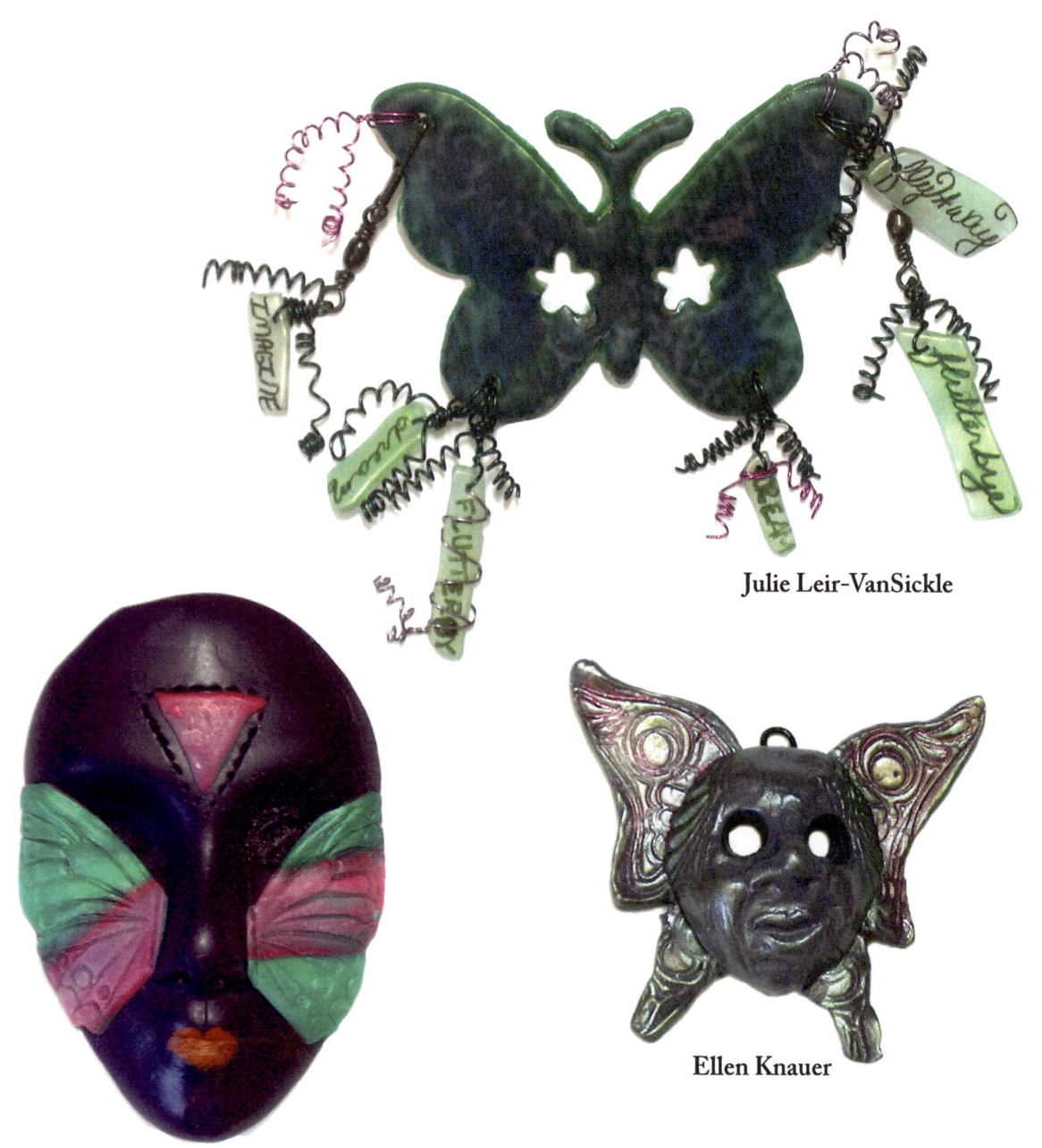

Julie Leir-VanSickle

Evelyn Gibson

Ellen Knauer

A Collection Of Polymer Clay Masks

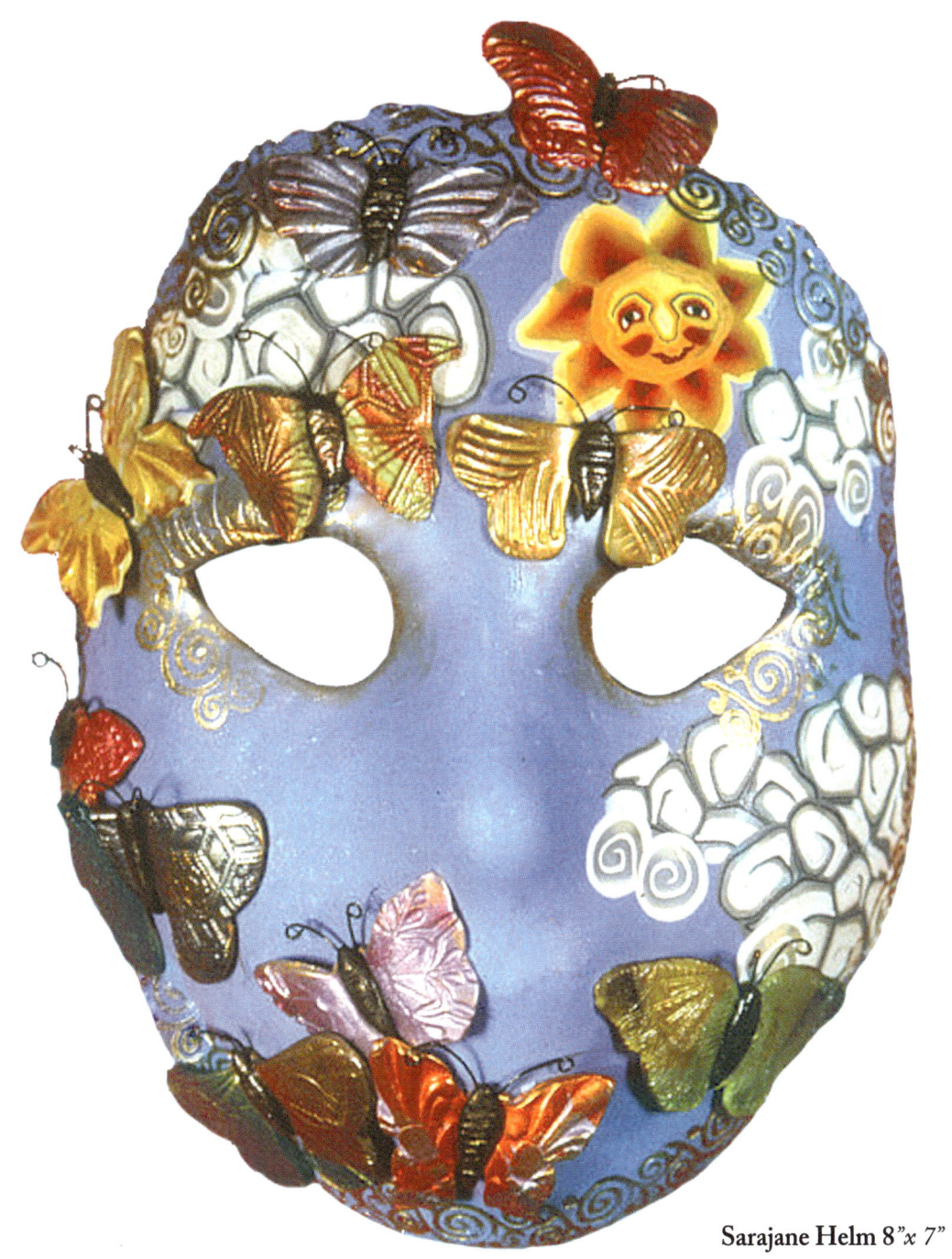

Sarajane Helm 8"x 7"

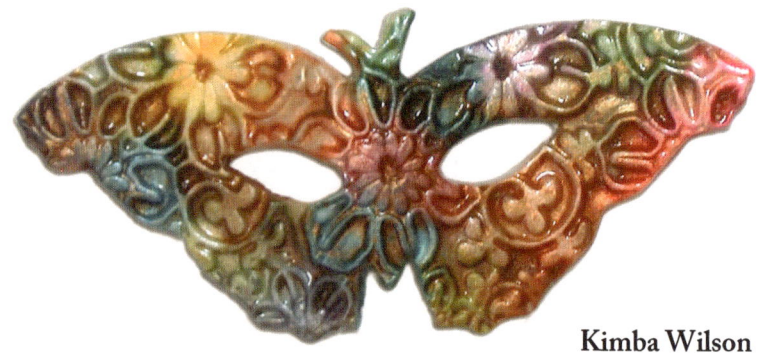

Kimba Wilson

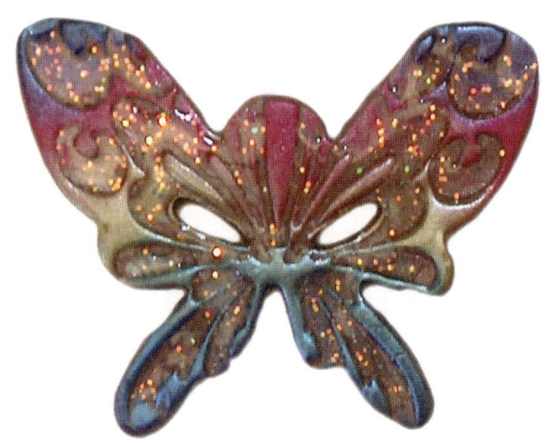

Tonja Lenderman

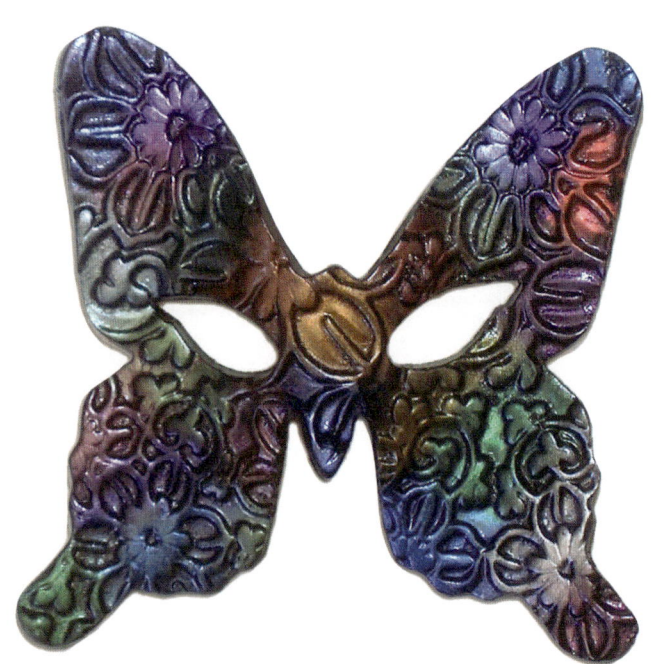

Kimba Wilson

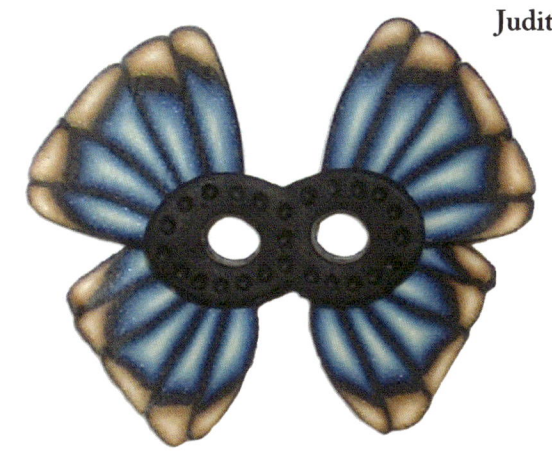

Judith Skinner

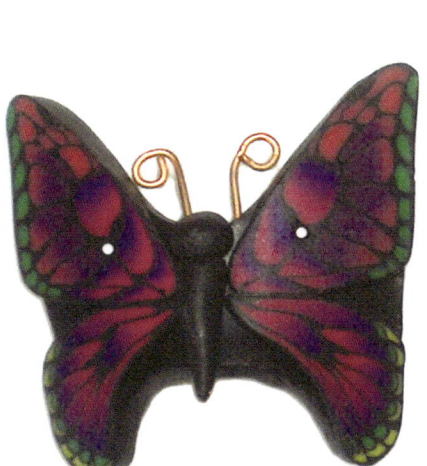

Rita Seale

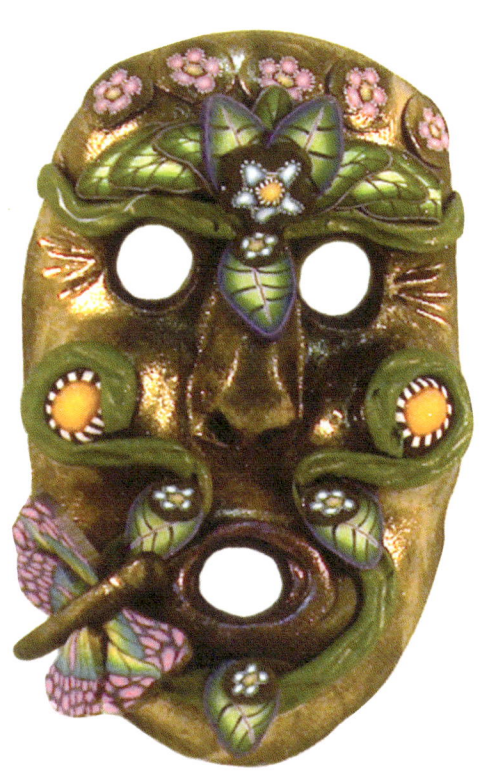

Diane MacCallum

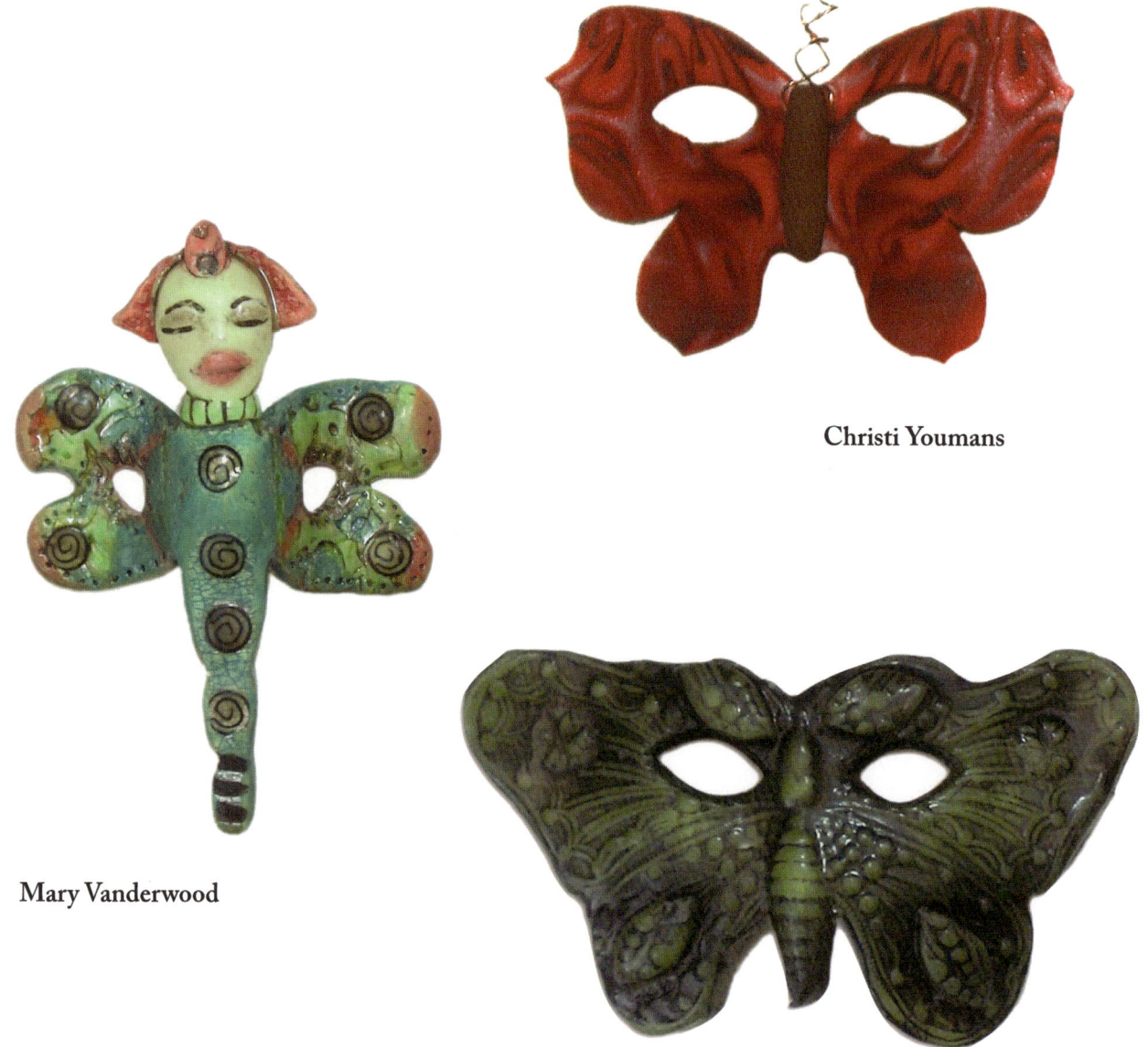

Christi Youmans

Mary Vanderwood

Laurel Steven

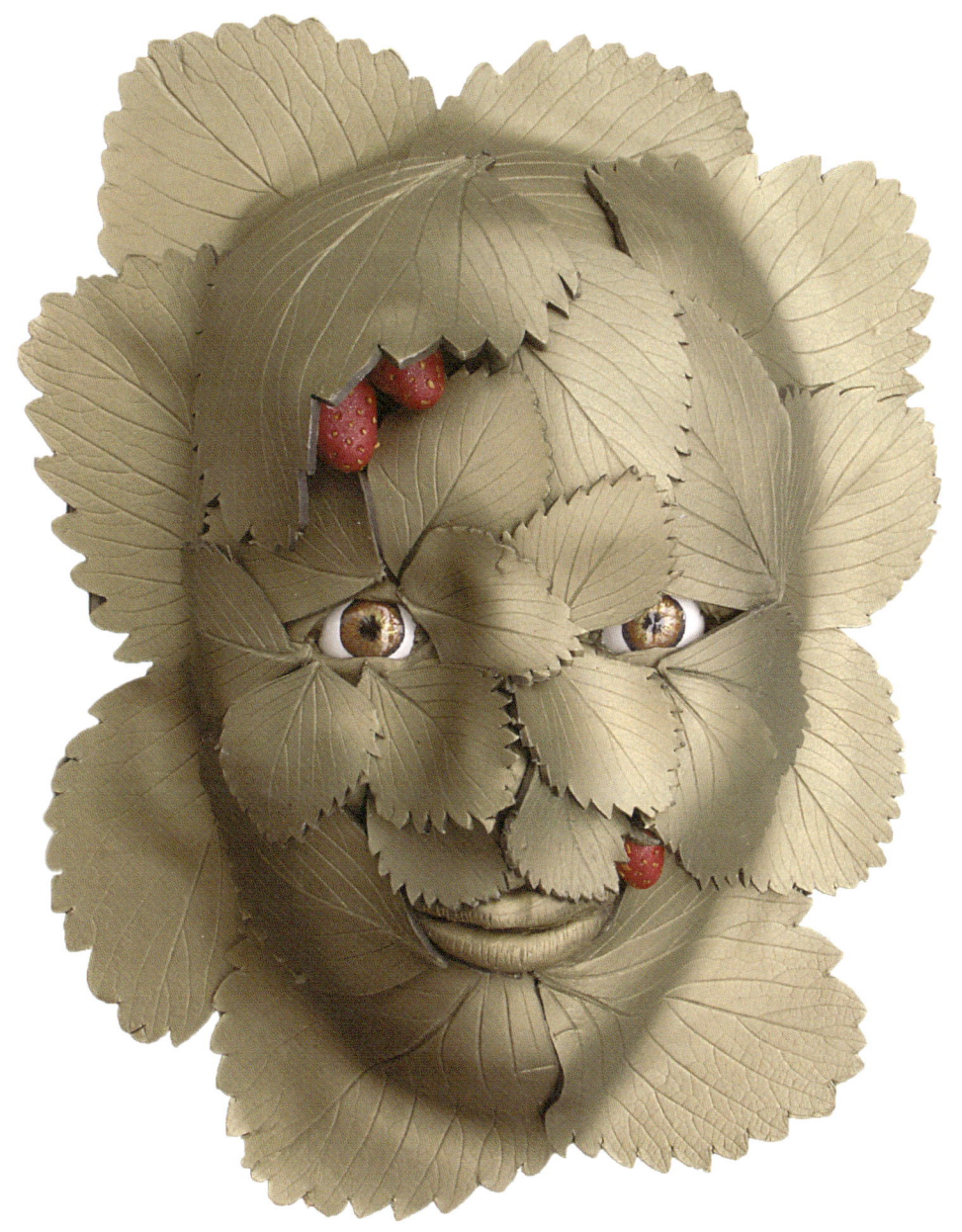

Cecelia Lehmann *photo Cecelia Lehmann 9" x 8"*

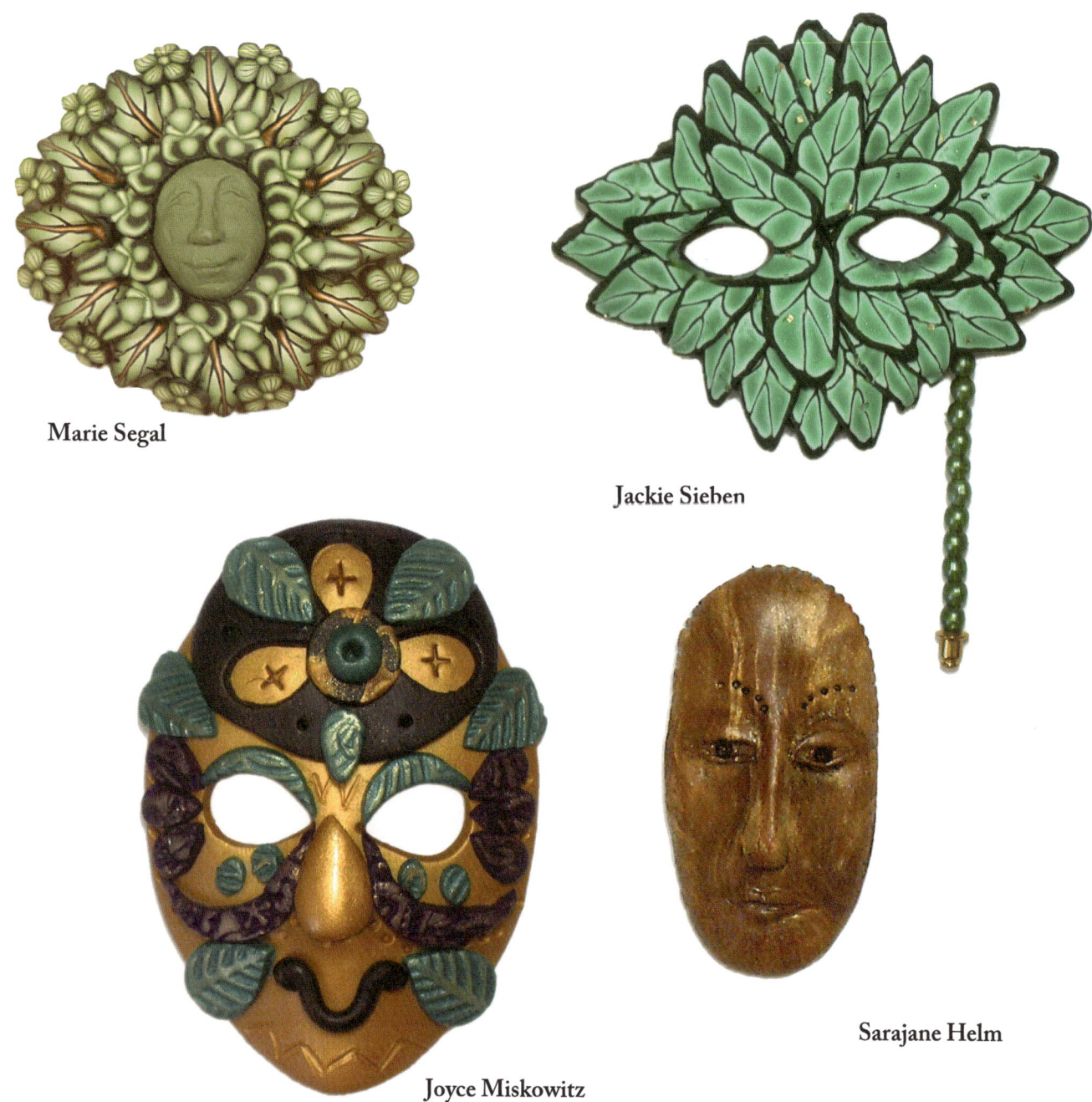

Marie Segal

Jackie Sieben

Joyce Miskowitz

Sarajane Helm

A Collection Of Polymer Clay Masks

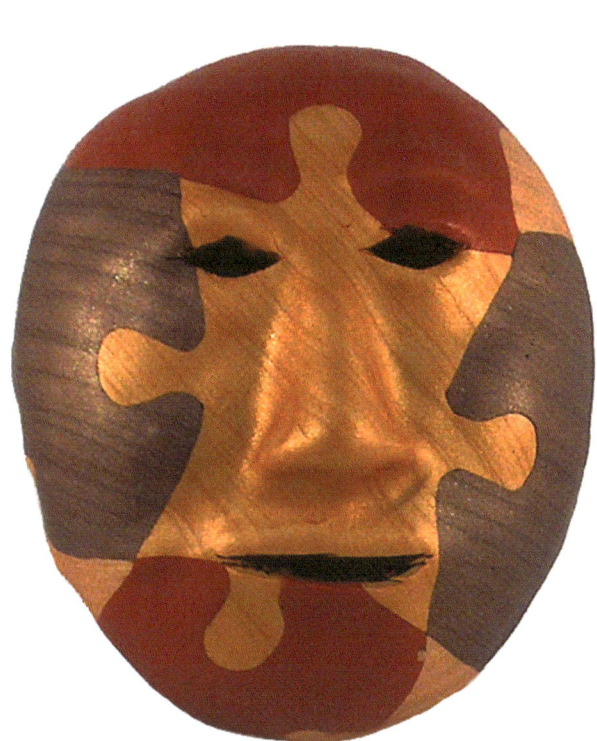

Robert Wiley

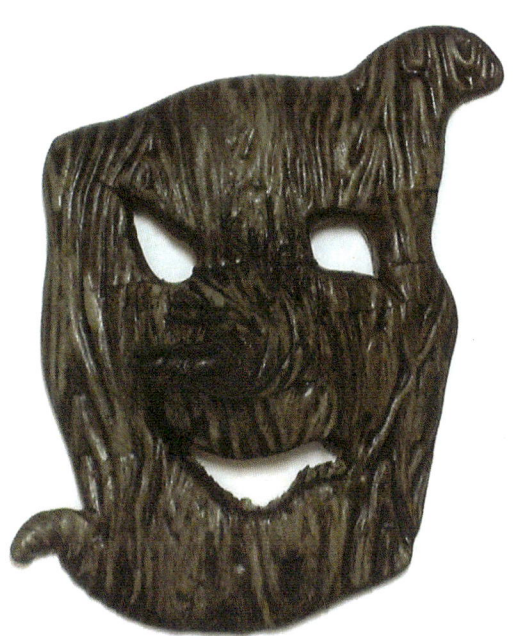

Chris Rutter

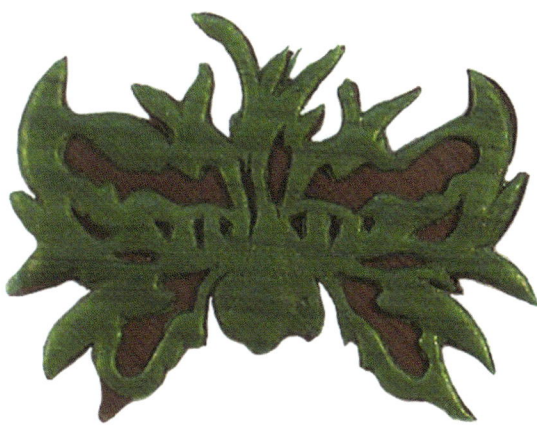

Robert Wiley

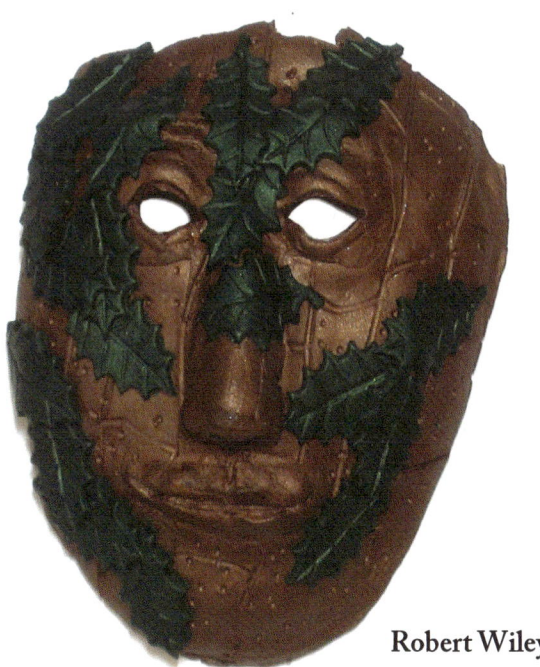

Robert Wiley

PolyMarket Press

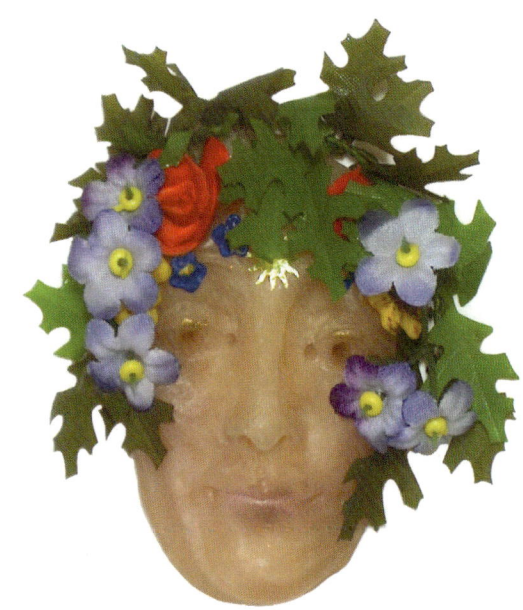

Sherry Bailey

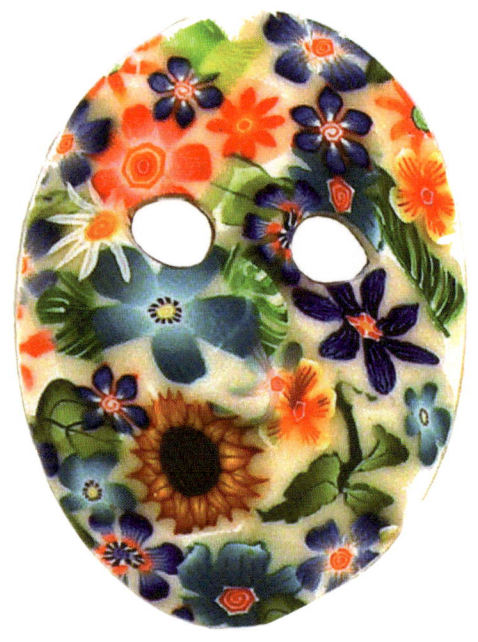

Karen Scudder

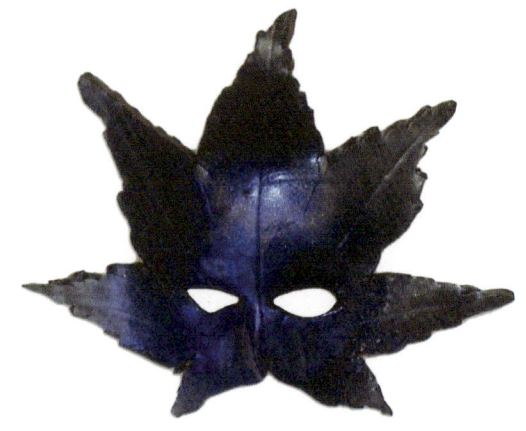

Cecelia Lehmann

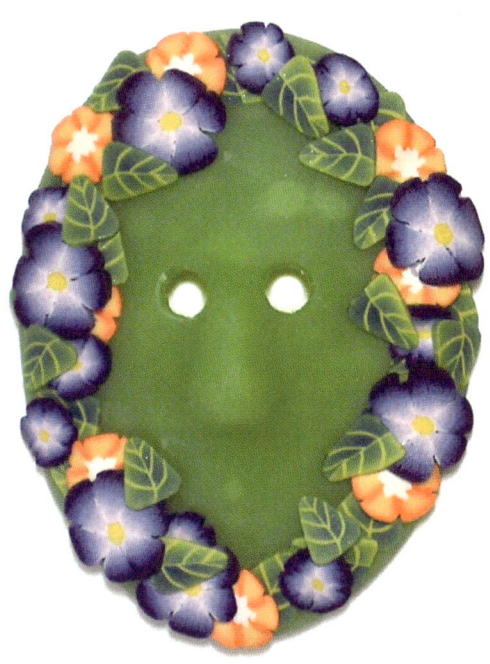

Karen Scudder

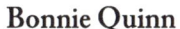

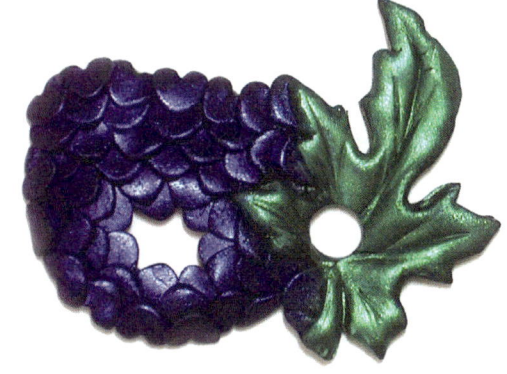

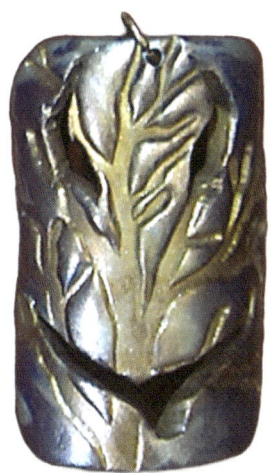

Denise Standifer

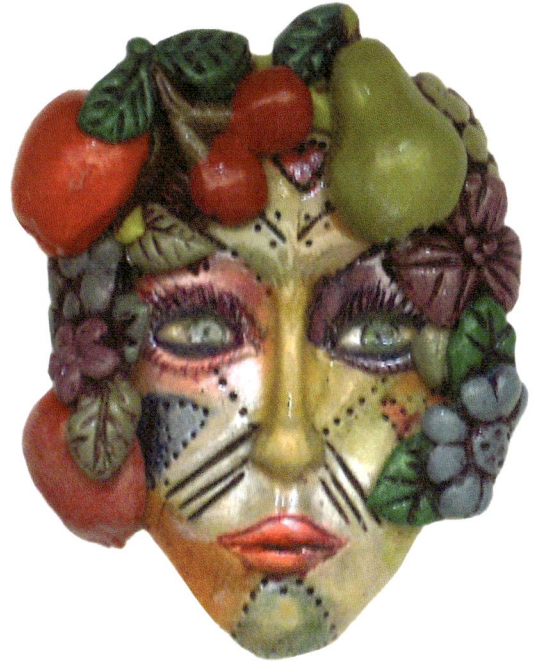

Mary Vanderwood

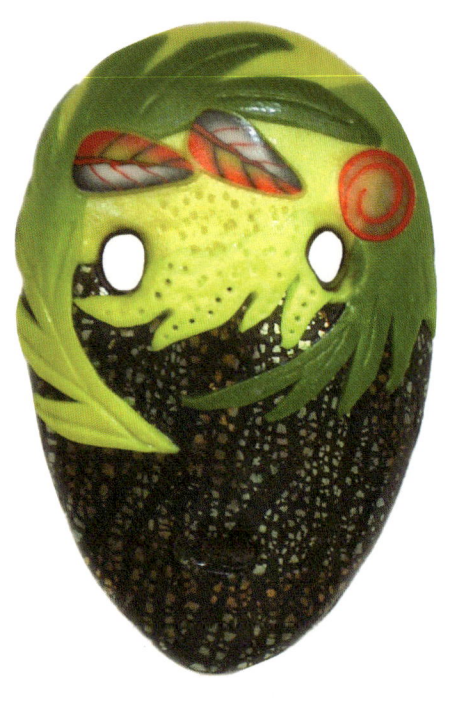

Patsy Monk

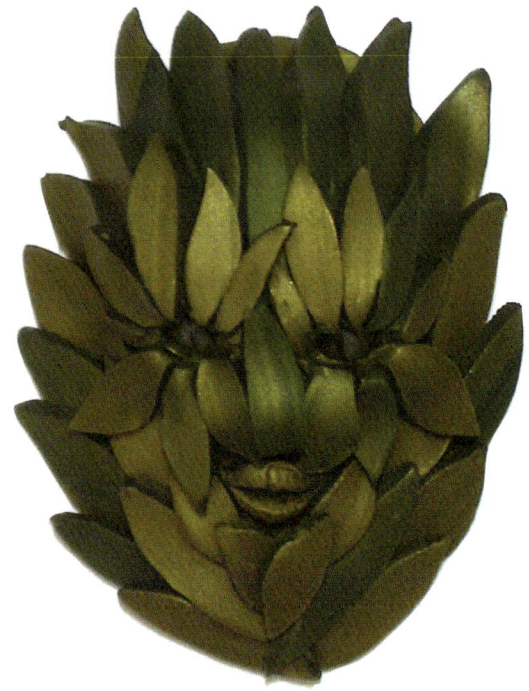

Cecelia Lehmann

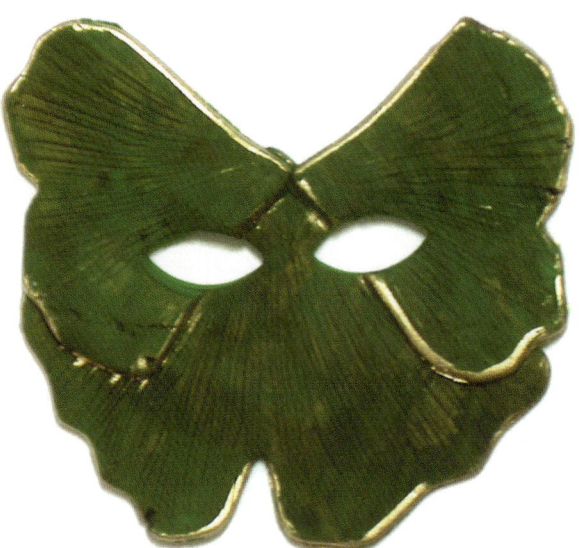

Helen Jacob

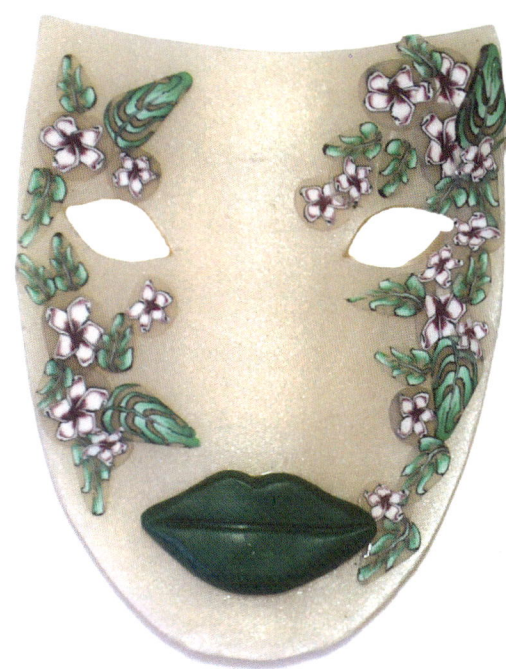

Tonja Lenderman

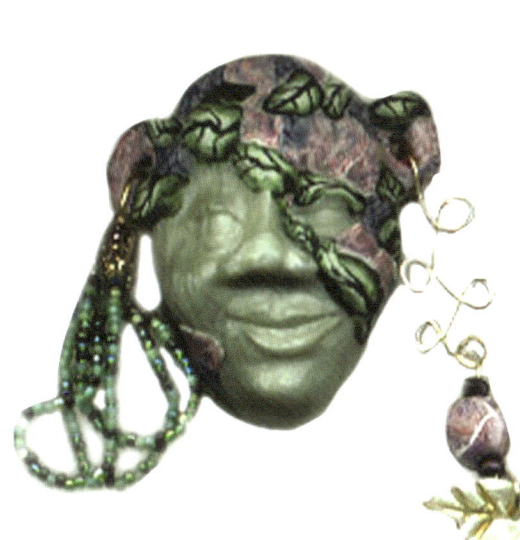

Jane Olson Phillips

Ellen Knauer

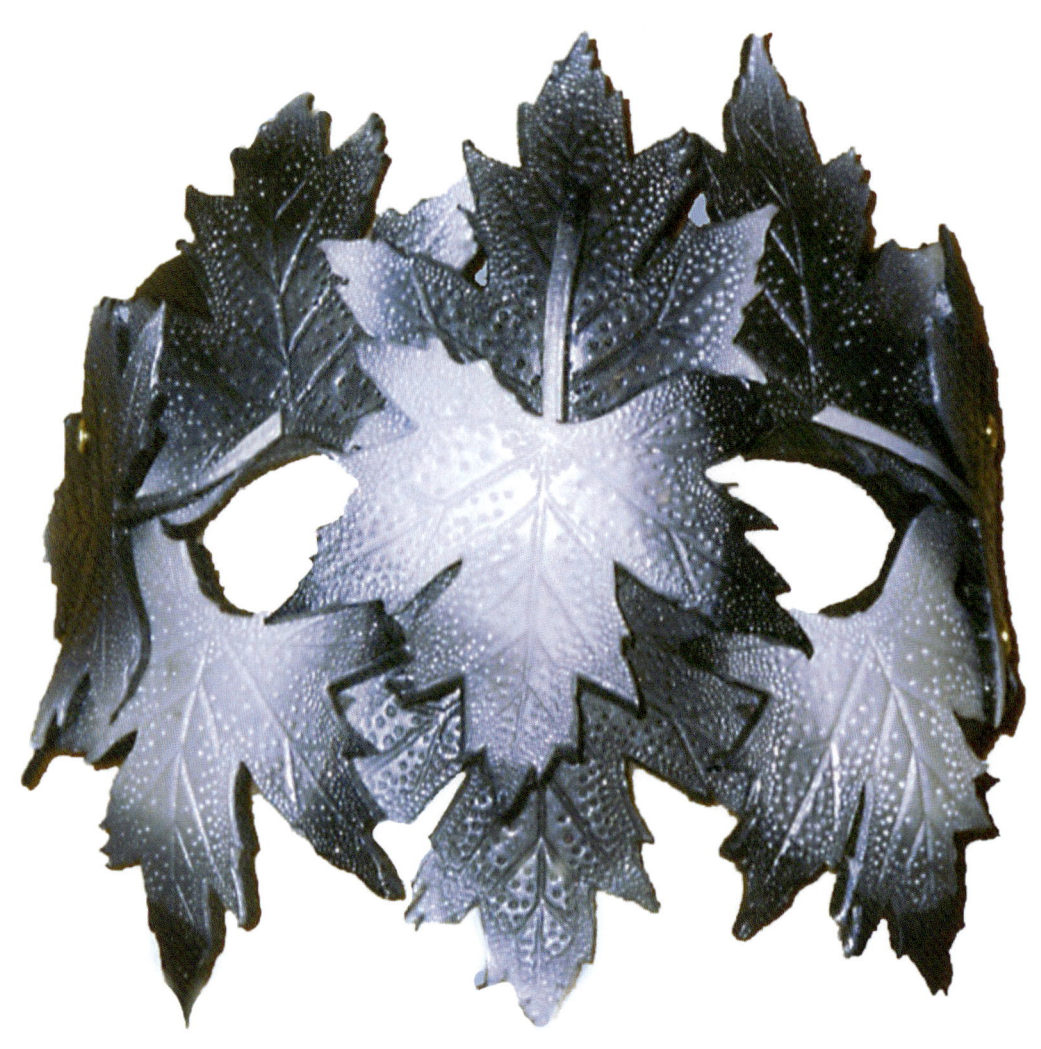

Charles Reed *photo Charles Reed*   *4.5" x 7.75"*

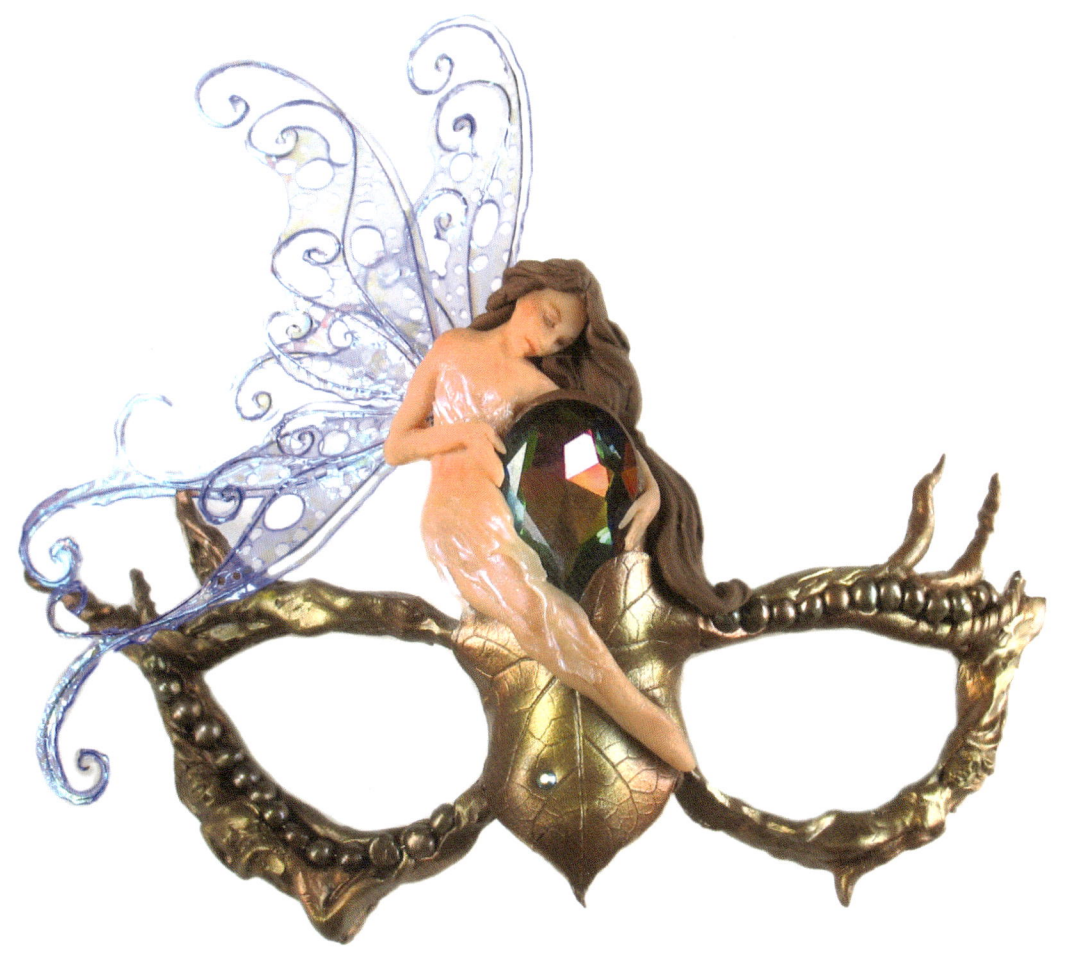

Lori O Follett *photo Lori O Follett*   5.5" x 7"

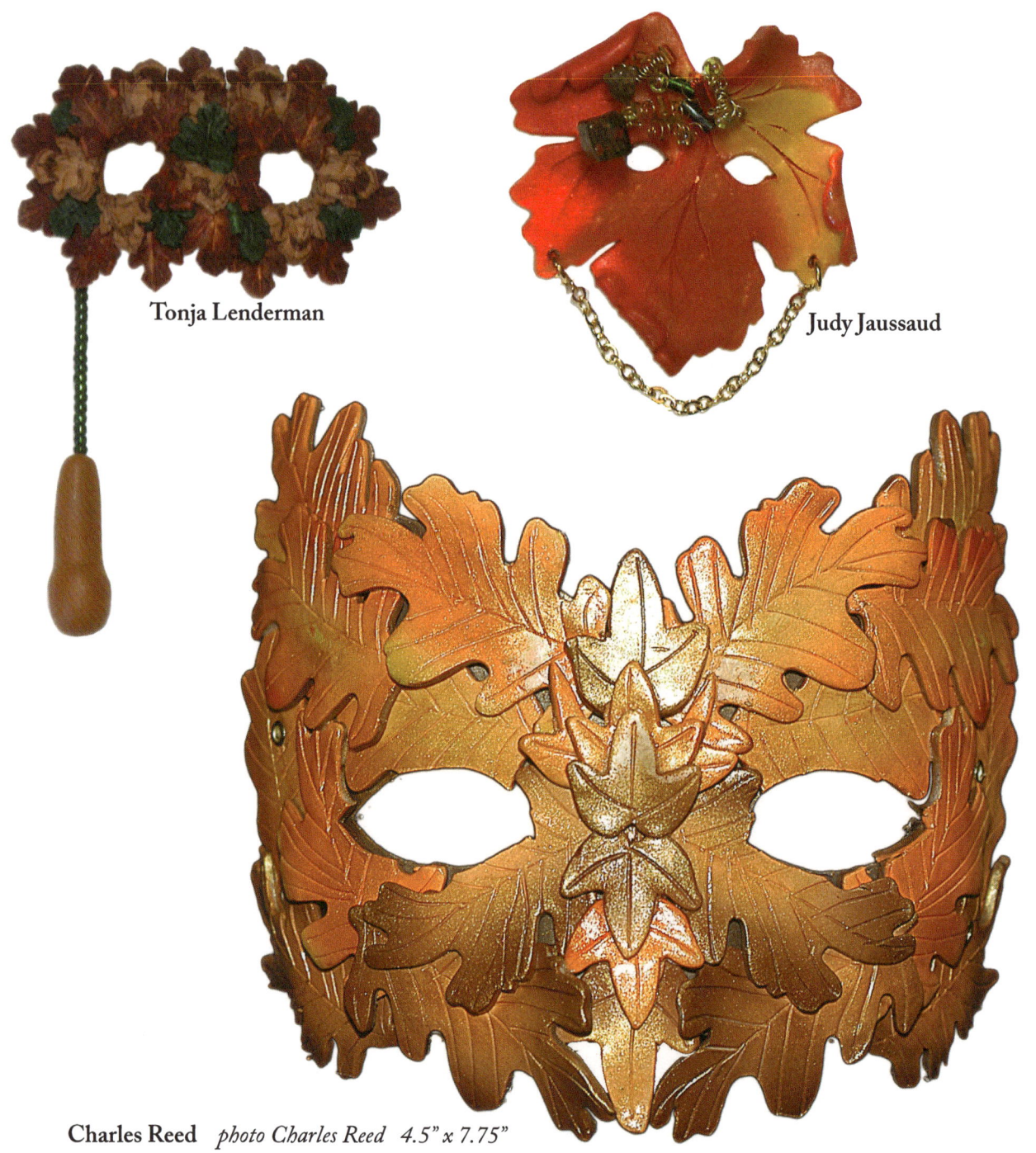

Tonja Lenderman

Judy Jaussaud

Charles Reed *photo Charles Reed* 4.5" x 7.75"

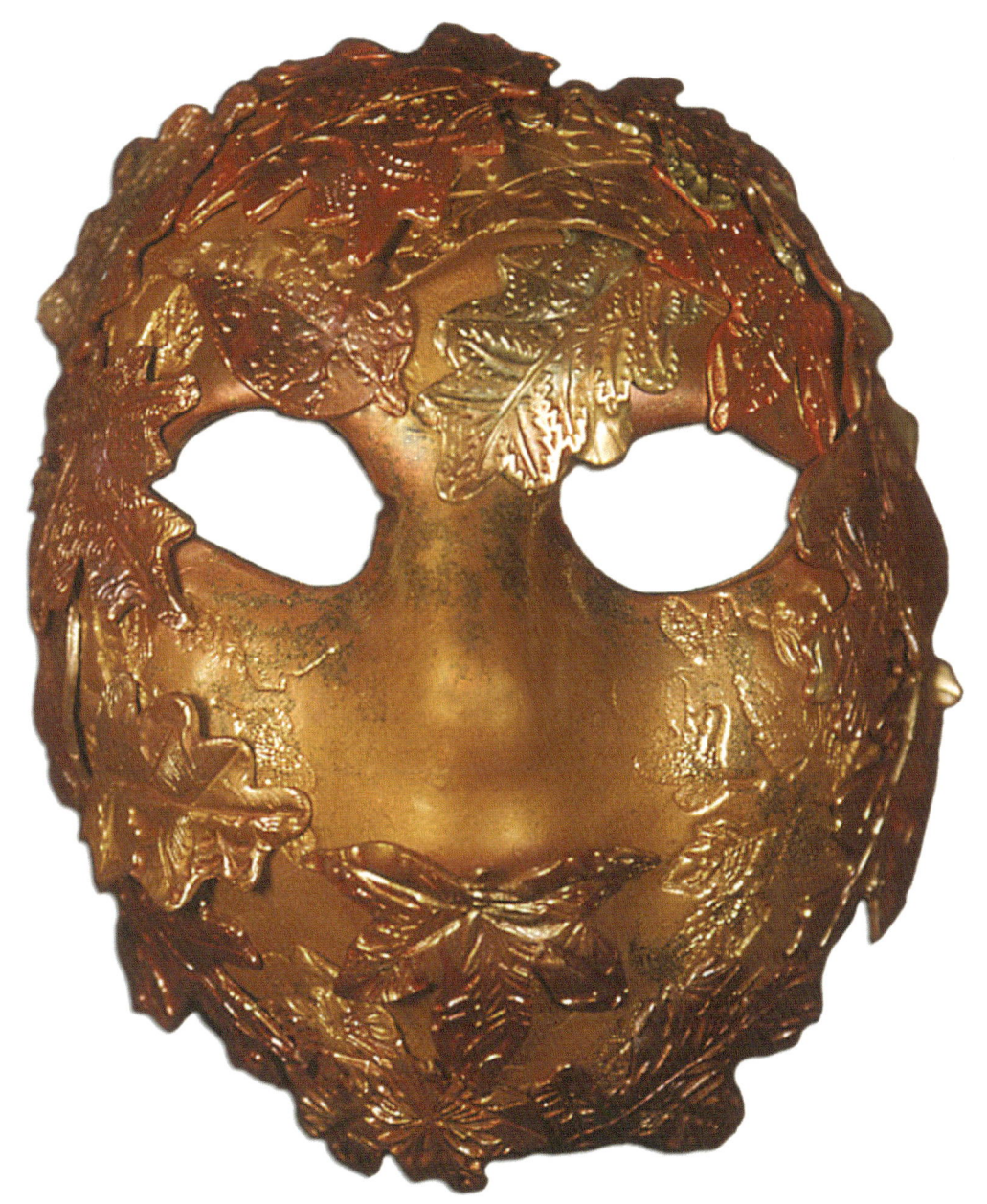

Sarajane Helm   *8" x 6"*

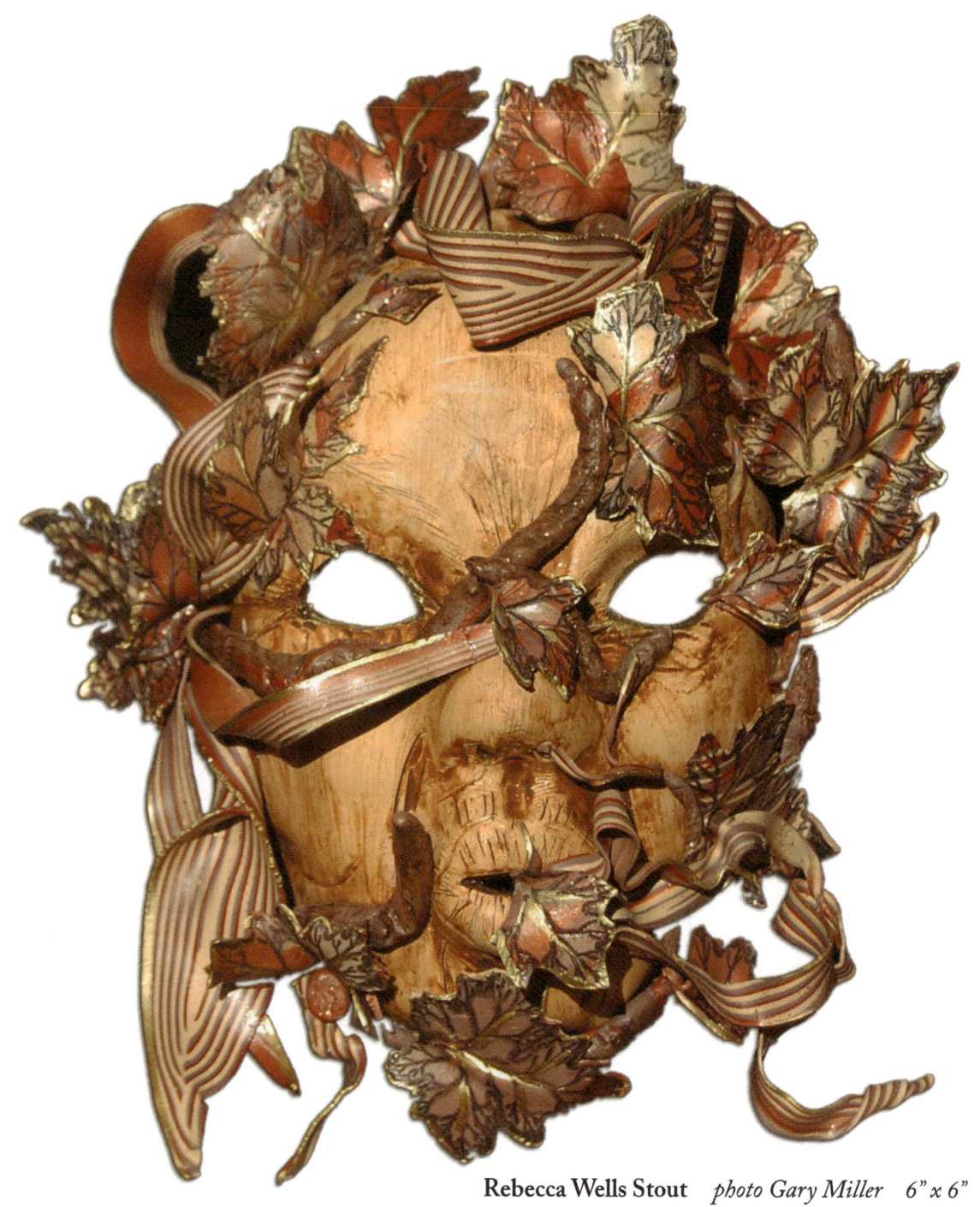

Rebecca Wells Stout   *photo Gary Miller*   6" x 6"

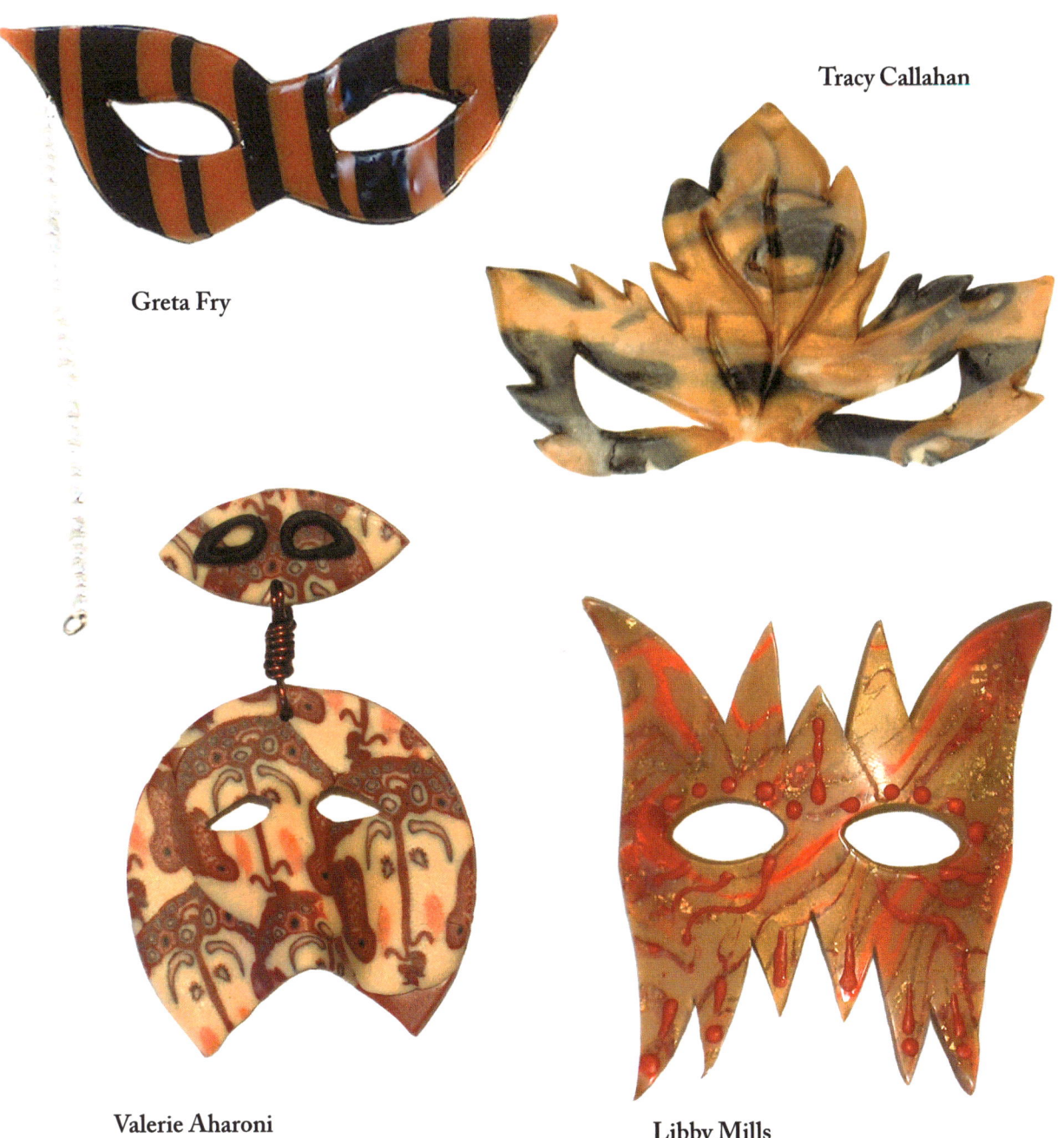

Tracy Callahan

Greta Fry

Valerie Aharoni

Libby Mills

PolyMarket Press

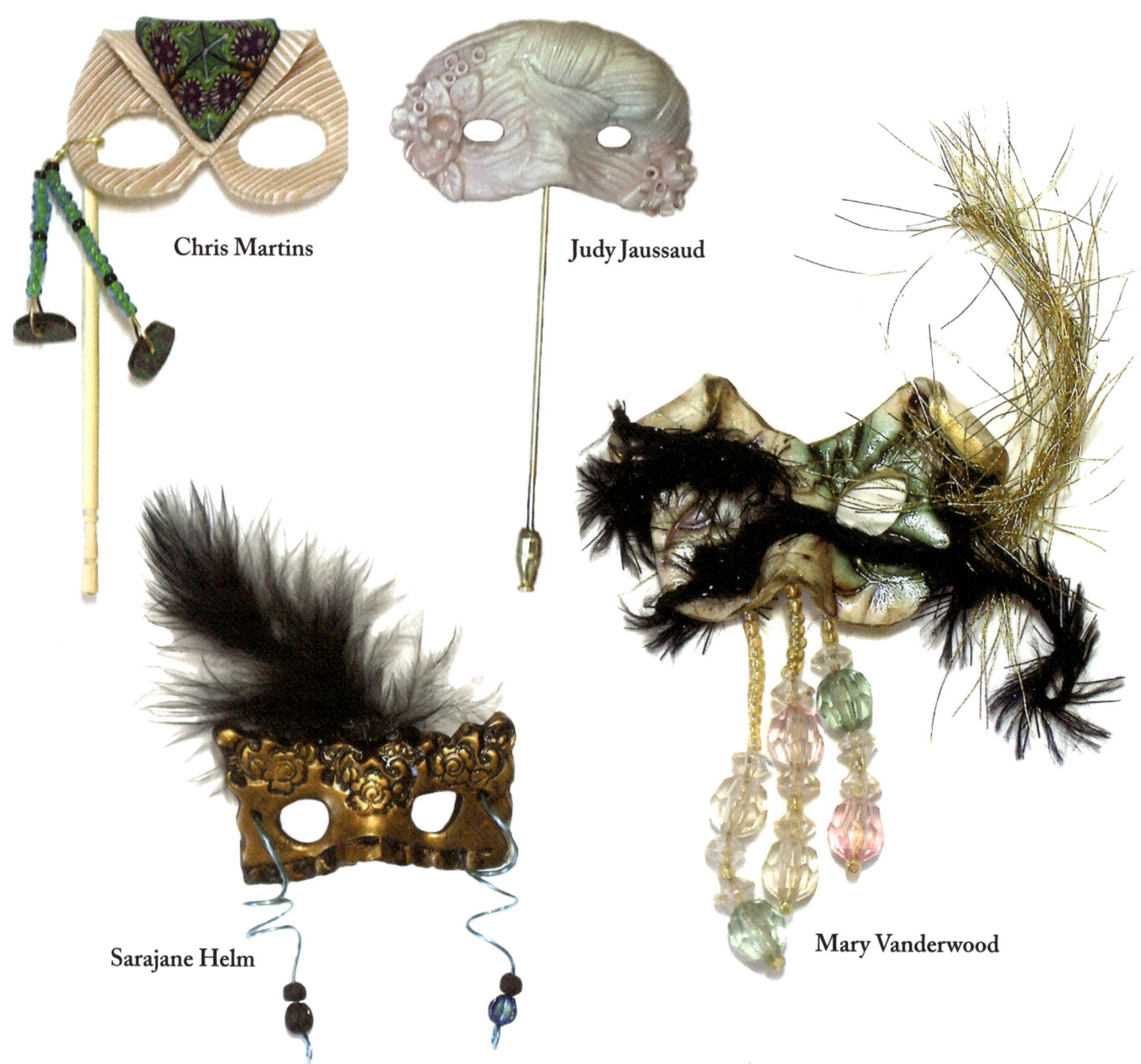

Chris Martins

Judy Jaussaud

Sarajane Helm

Mary Vanderwood

A Collection Of Polymer Clay Masks

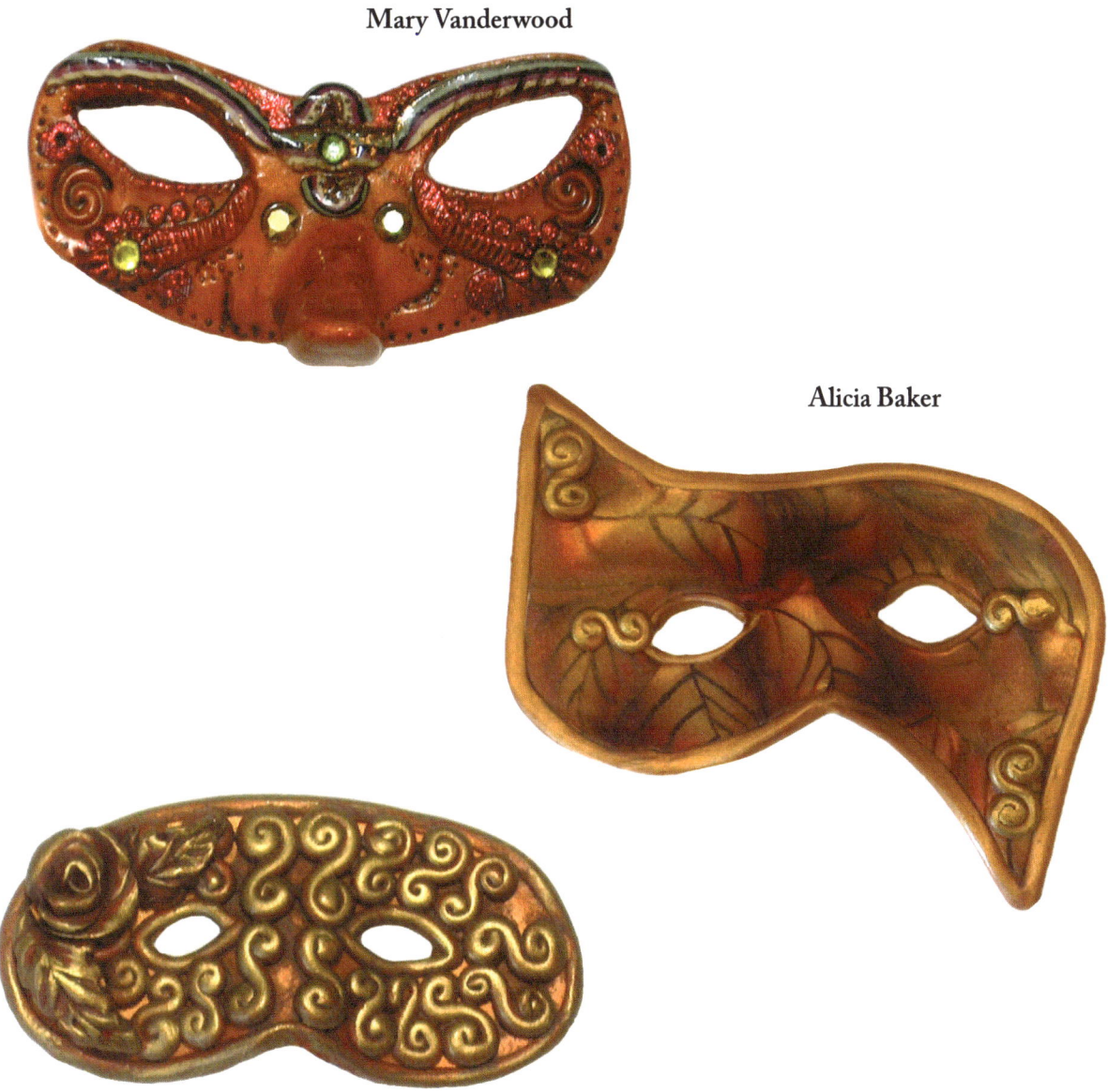

Mary Vanderwood

Alicia Baker

Alicia Baker

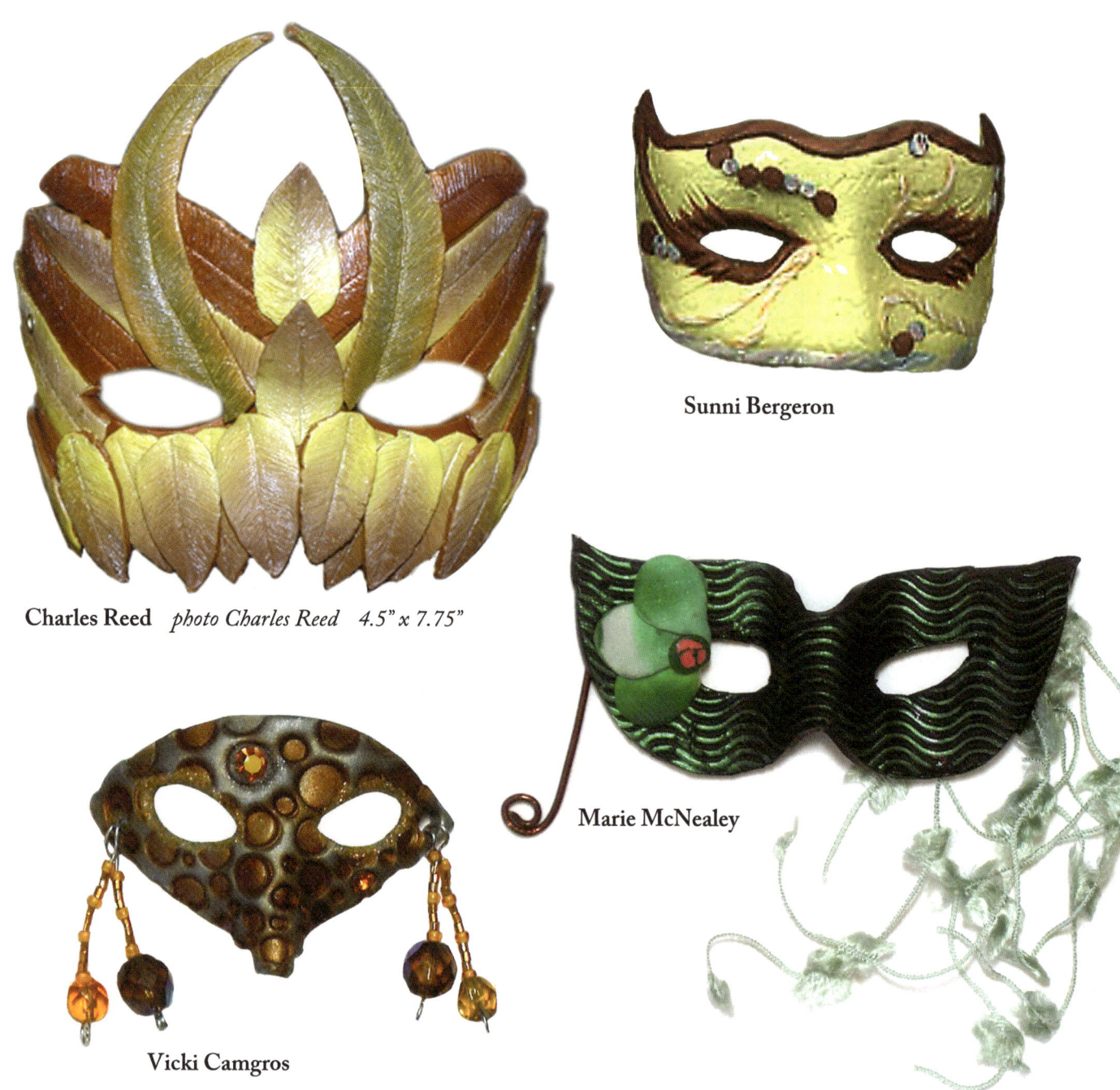

Charles Reed *photo Charles Reed* 4.5" x 7.75"

Sunni Bergeron

Marie McNealey

Vicki Camgros

A Collection Of Polymer Clay Masks

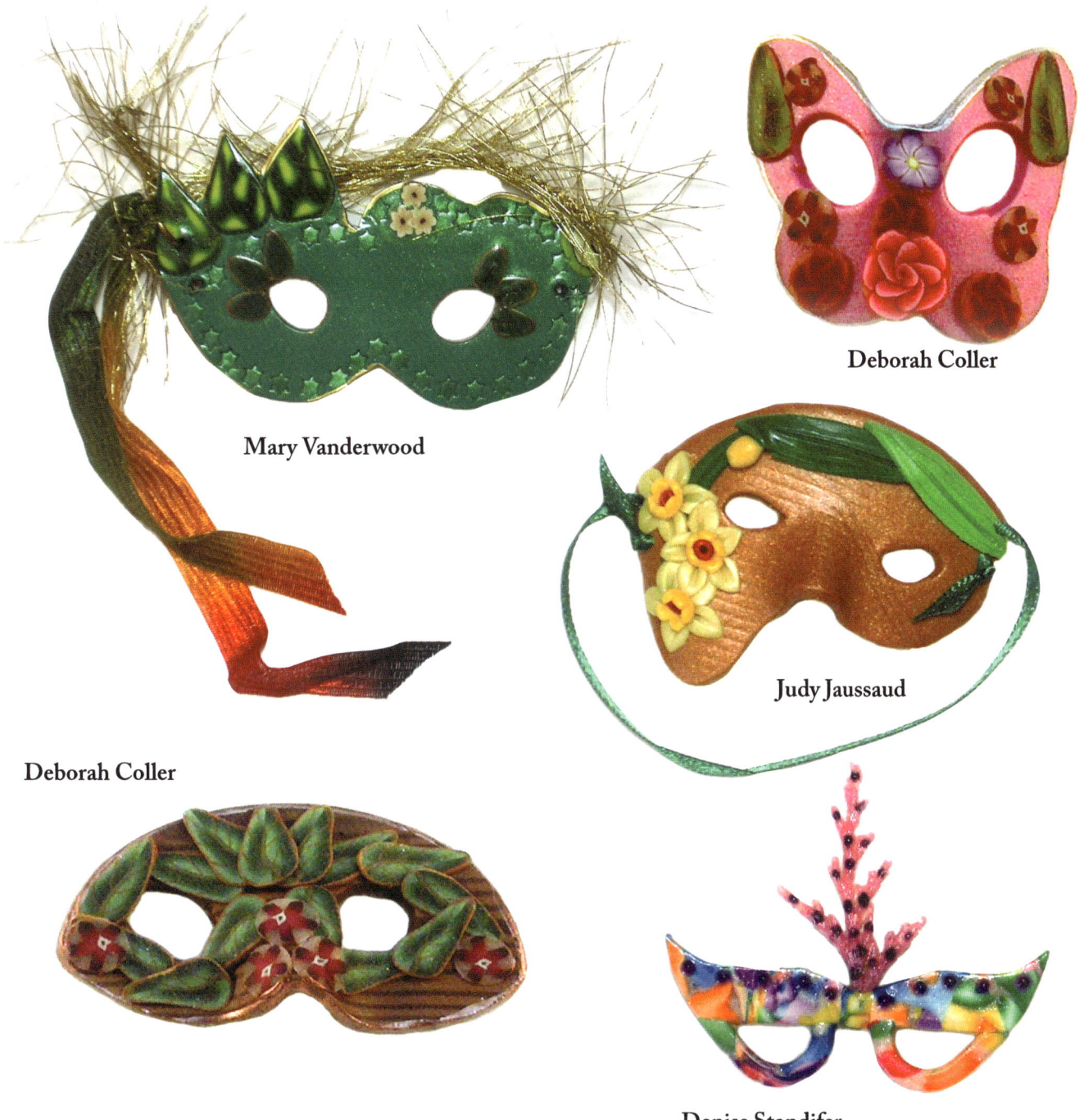

Mary Vanderwood

Deborah Coller

Judy Jaussaud

Deborah Coller

Denise Standifer

PolyMarket Press

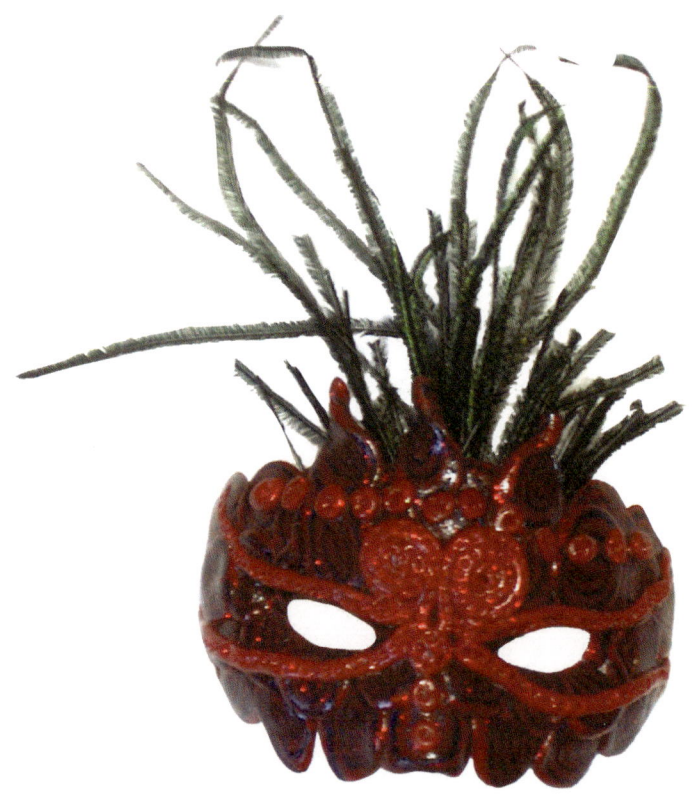

(artist not known)

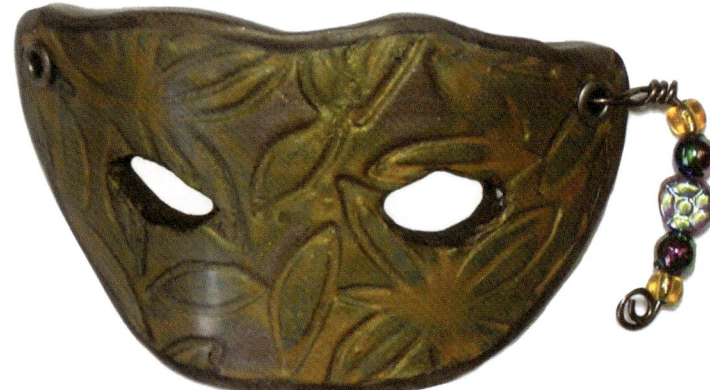

Pat Osmundson

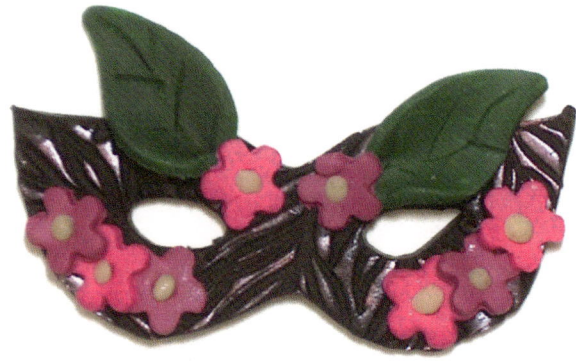

Marie McNealey

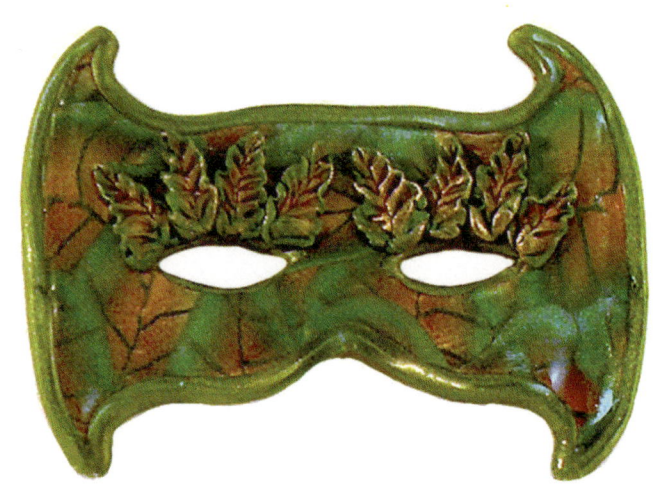

Alicia Baker

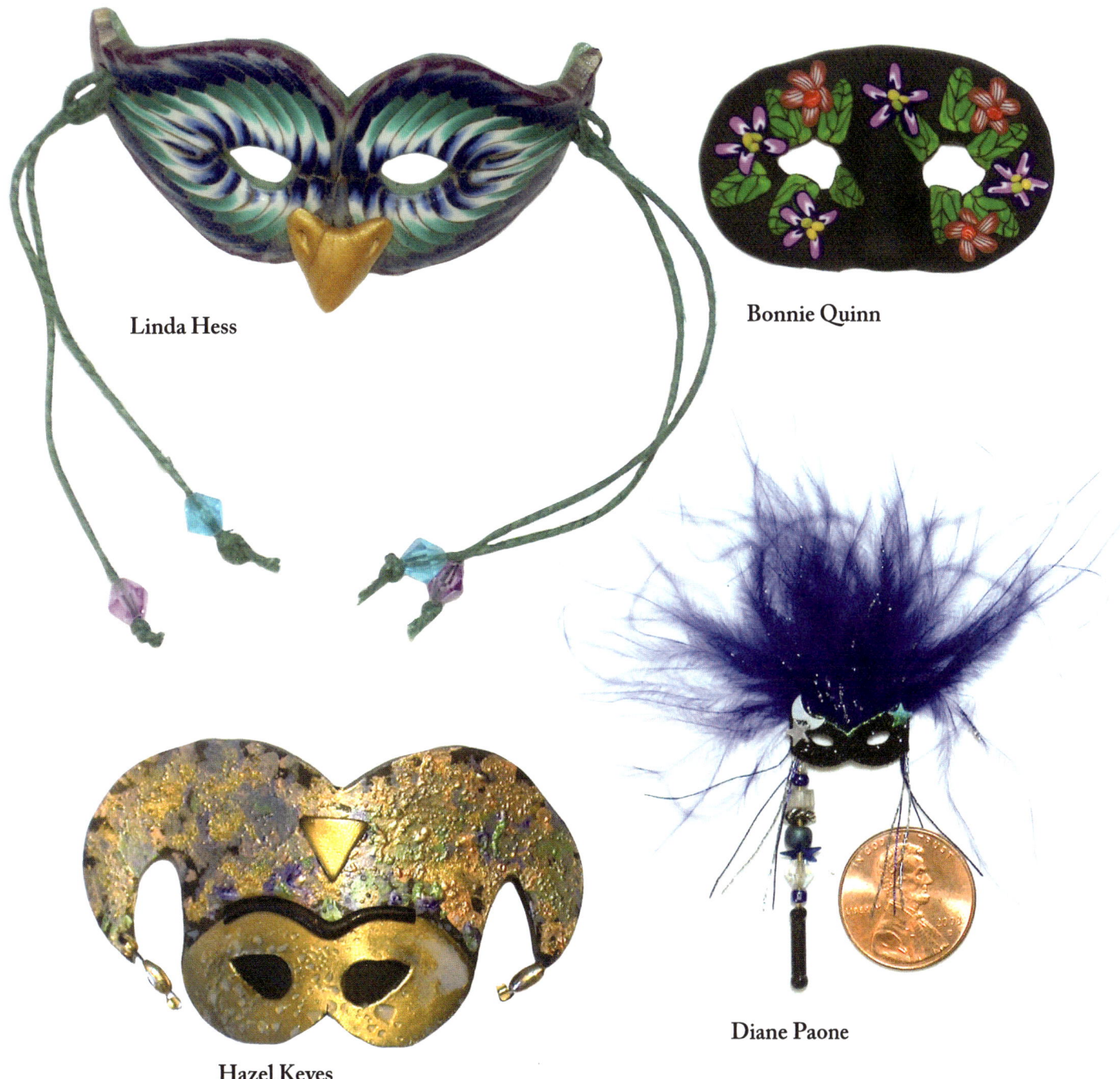

Linda Hess

Bonnie Quinn

Hazel Keyes

Diane Paone

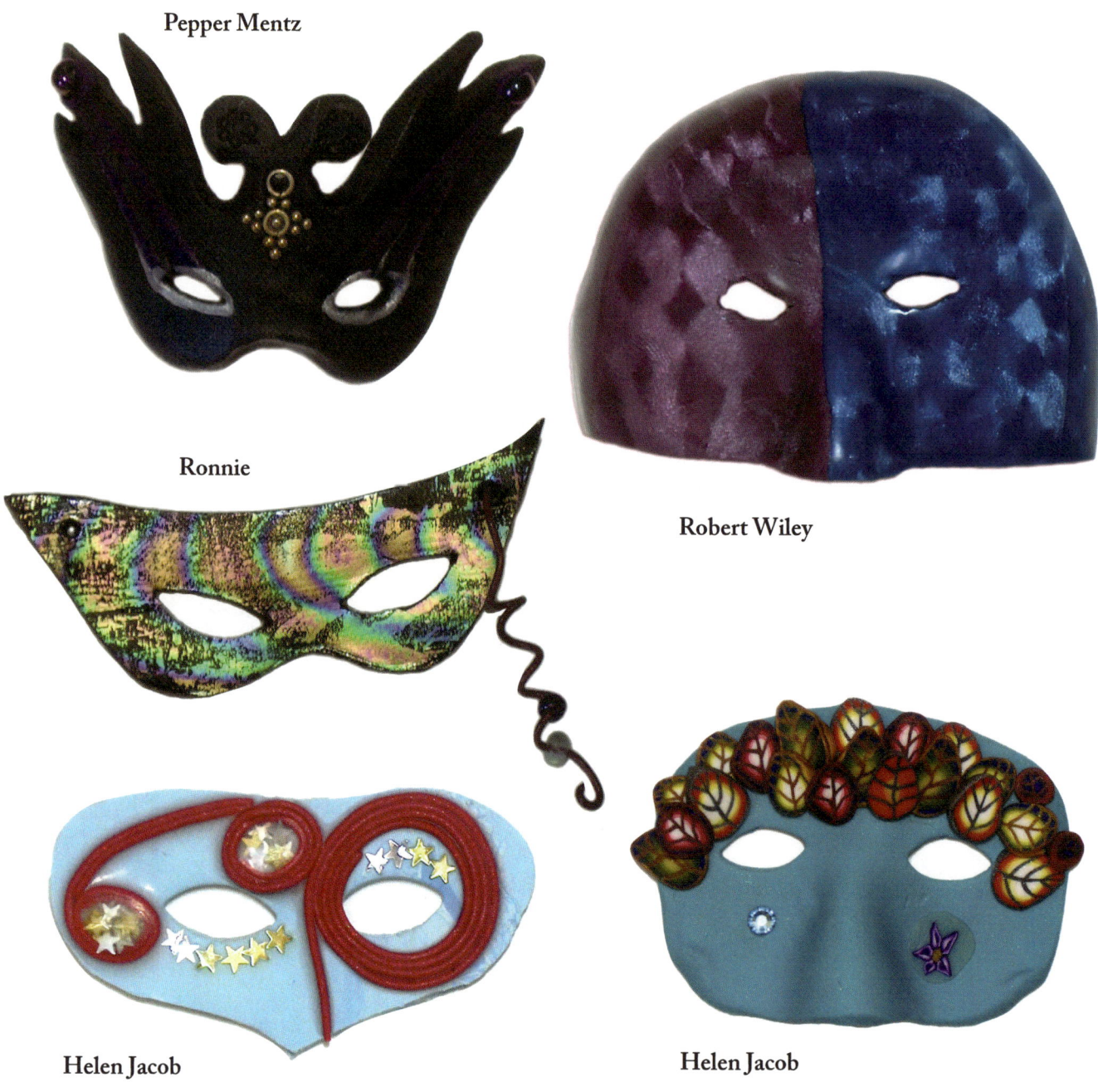

Pepper Mentz

Robert Wiley

Ronnie

Helen Jacob

Helen Jacob

A Collection Of Polymer Clay Masks

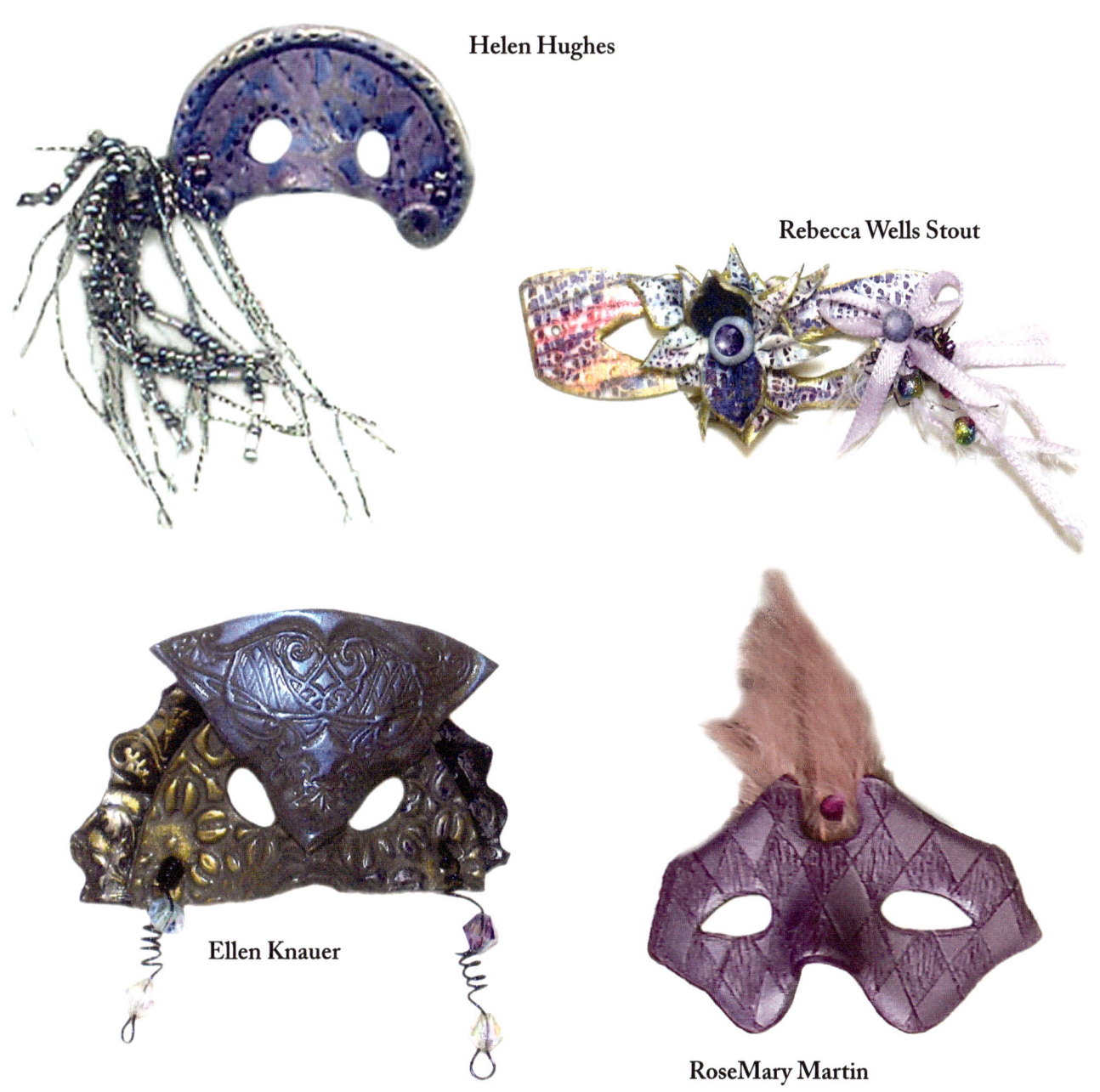

Helen Hughes

Rebecca Wells Stout

Ellen Knauer

RoseMary Martin

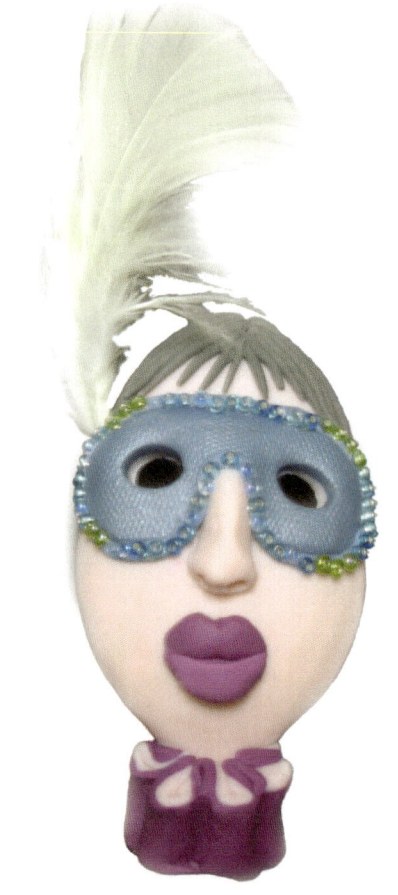

Eileen Mackin

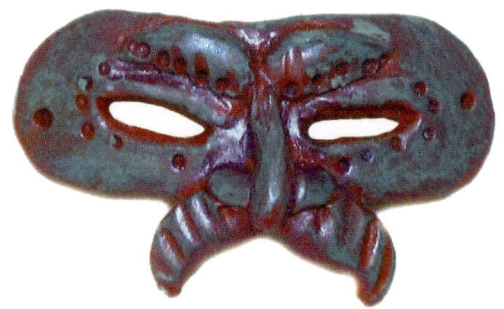

Ulrika O'Brian

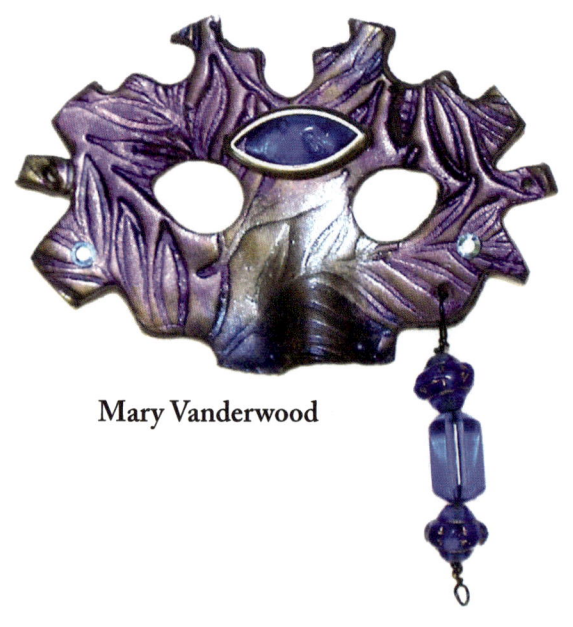

Mary Vanderwood

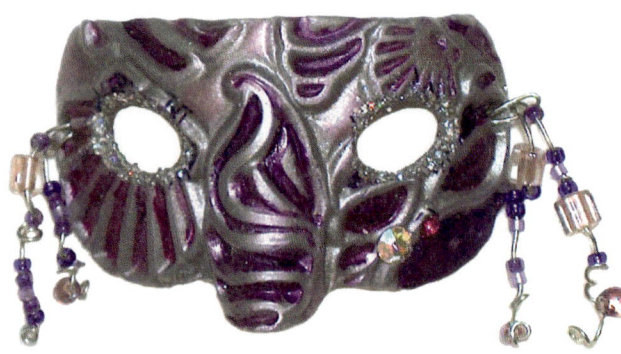

Vicki Camgros

A Collection Of Polymer Clay Masks

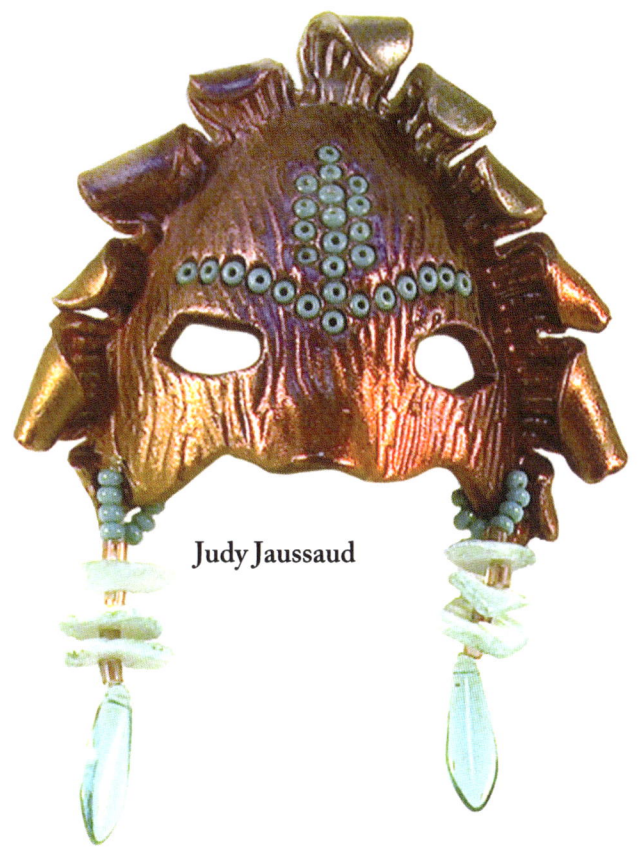

Judy Jaussaud

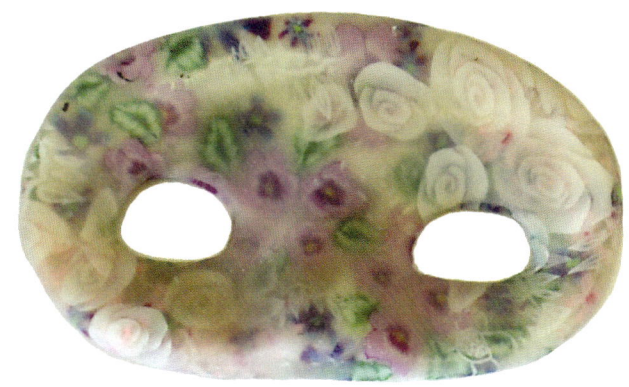

Marla Frankenberg

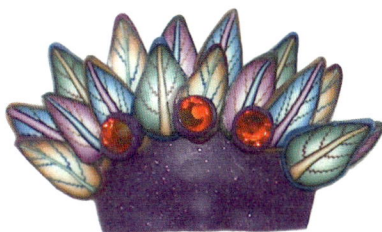

Beth Ackley

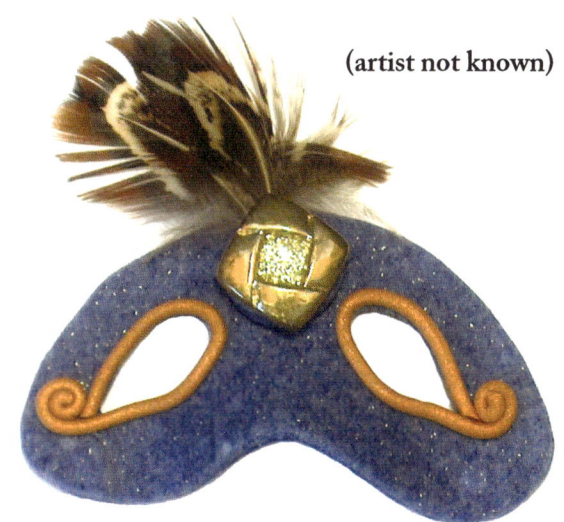

(artist not known)

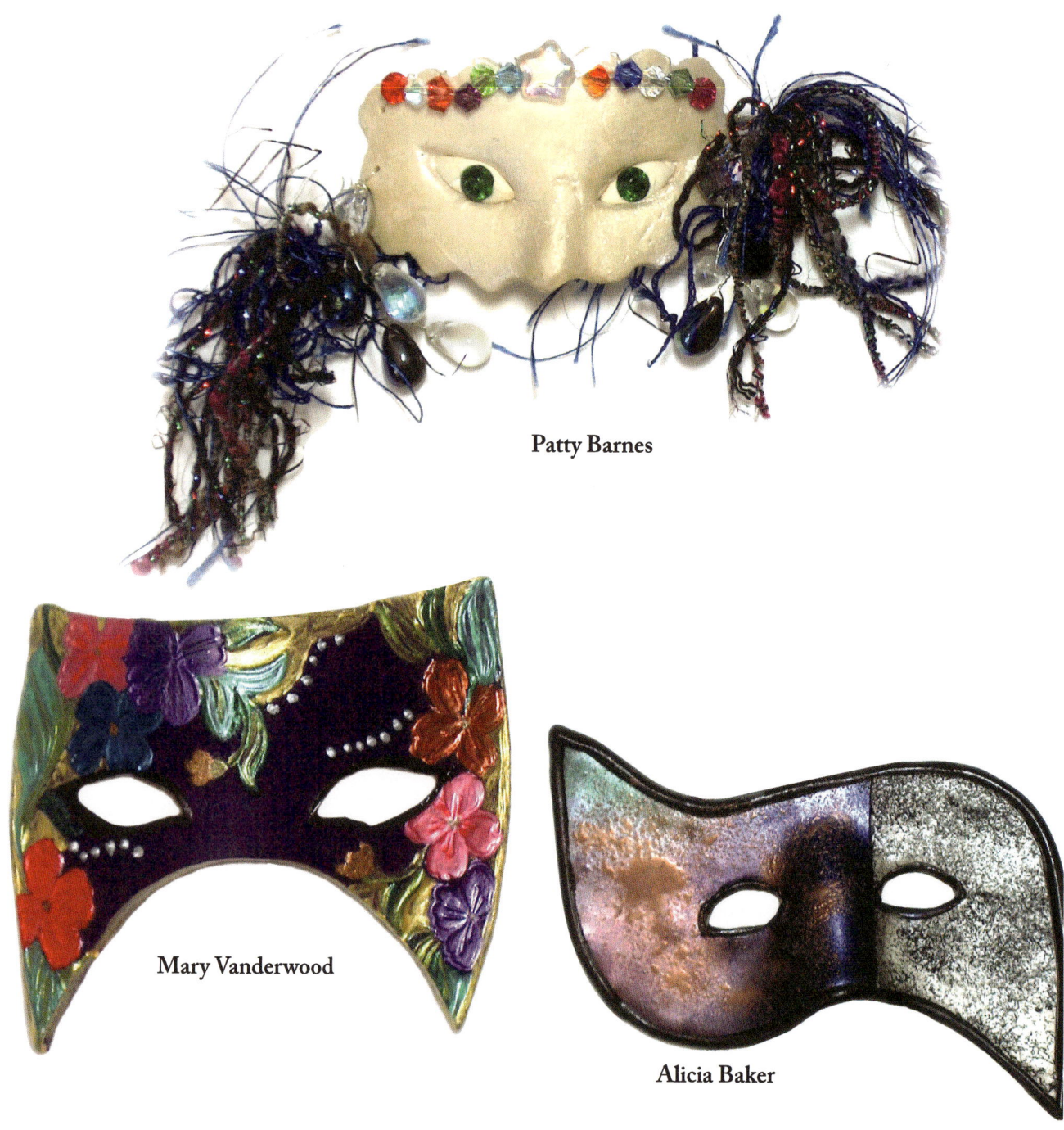

Patty Barnes

Mary Vanderwood

Alicia Baker

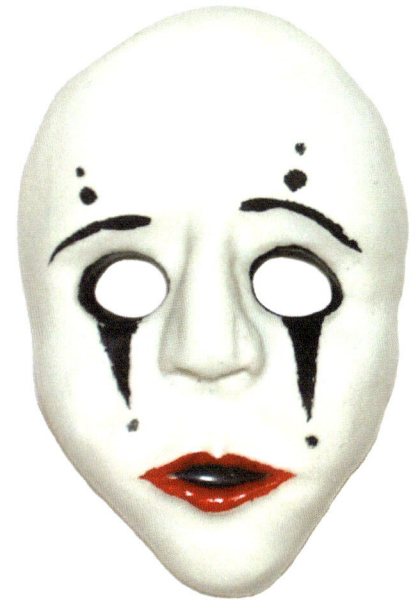

Judy Dunn

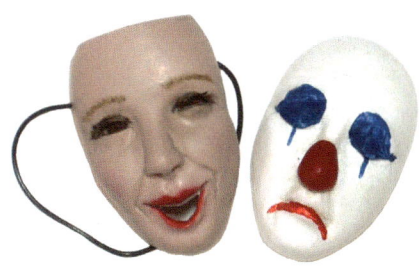

Lynne Ann Schwarzenberg

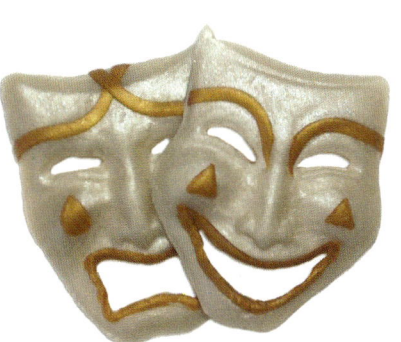

Robert Wiley

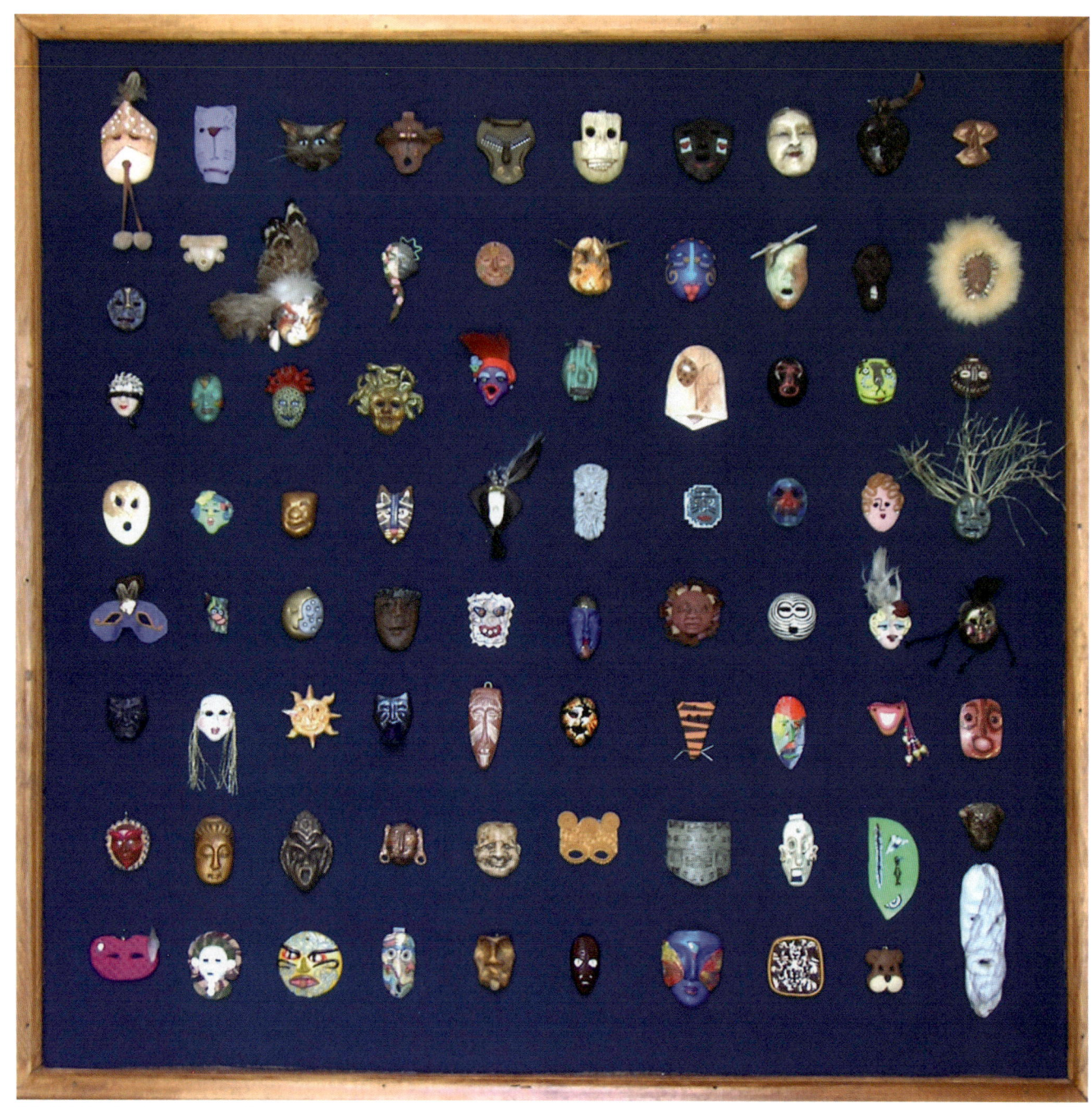

Multiple Artists   3 x 3'

A Collection Of Polymer Clay Masks

Tess Gunnell

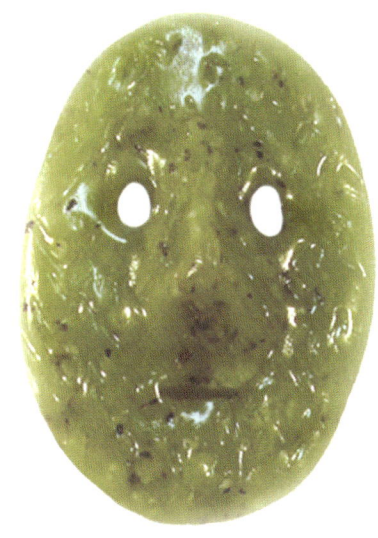

Ellen Rumsey Bellenot

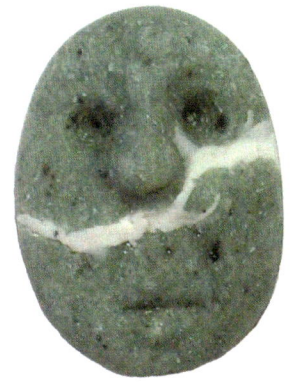

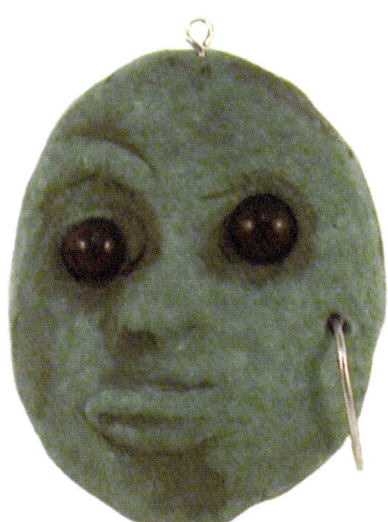

JoAnn Thomas

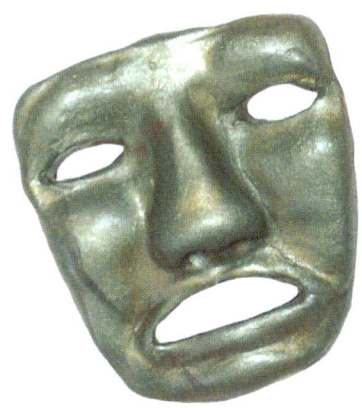

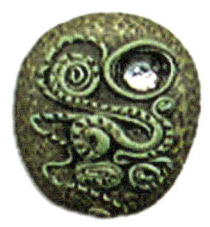

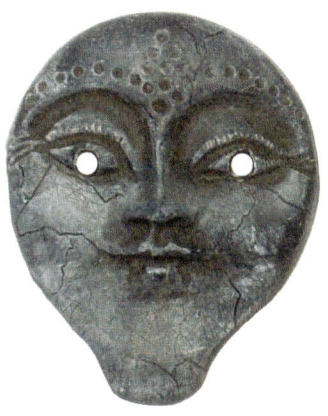

Alicia Baker

Julie Leir-VanSickle

Tommie Howell

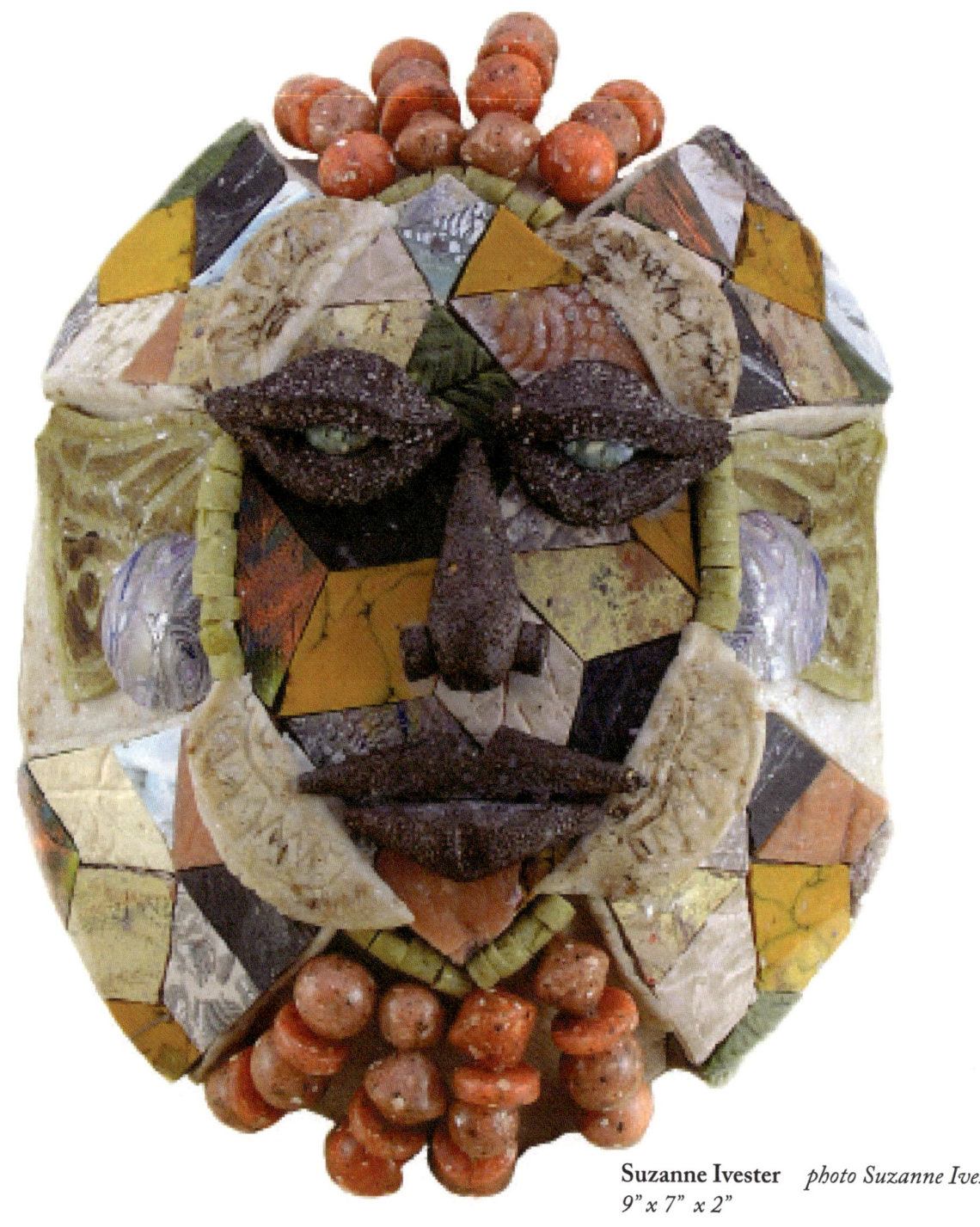

Suzanne Ivester   *photo Suzanne Ivester*
9" x 7" x 2"

Ronnie   Alicia Baker

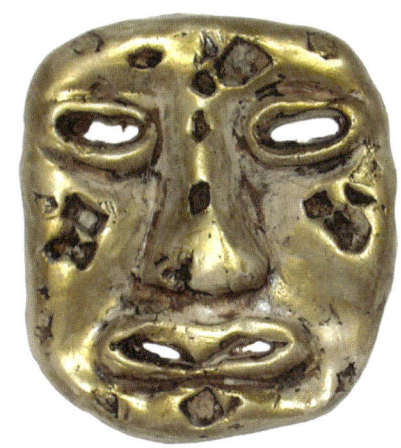

Lynne DeNio   Jeanean Wendland

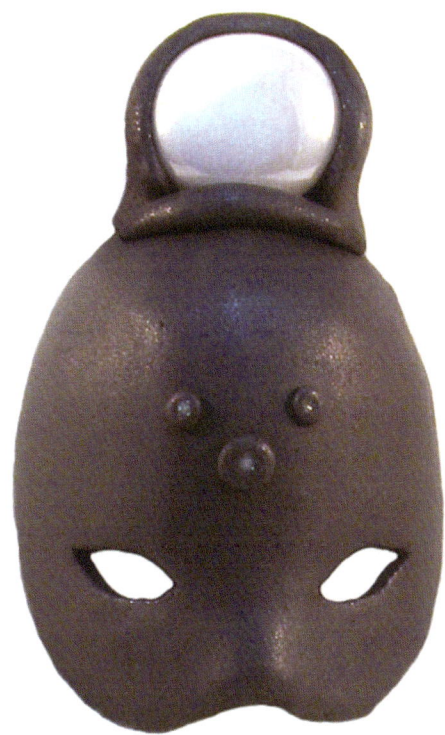

Cecelia Lehmann

RoseMary Martin

Janet Hoy

Denise Standifer

60

A Collection Of Polymer Clay Masks

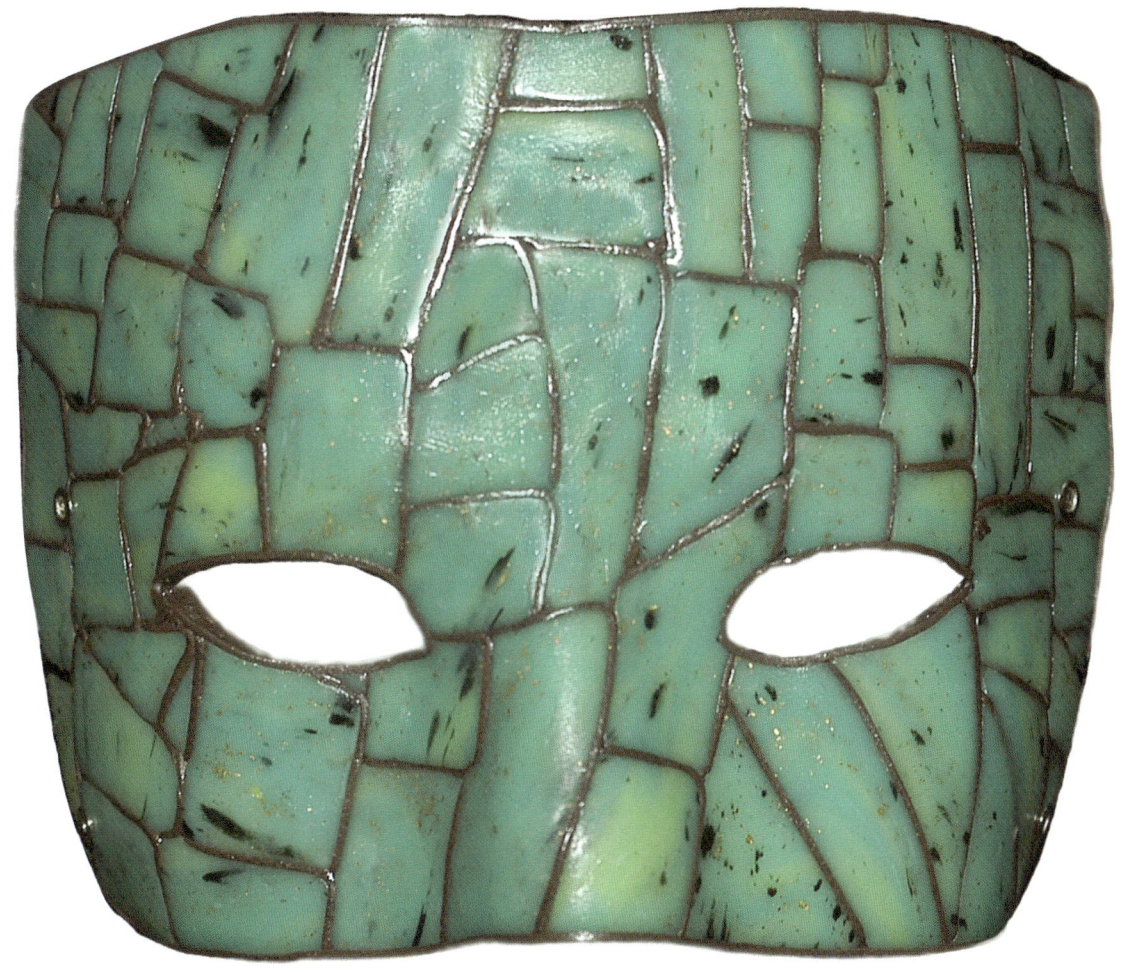

Charles Reed *photo Charles Reed* *4.5" x 7.75"*

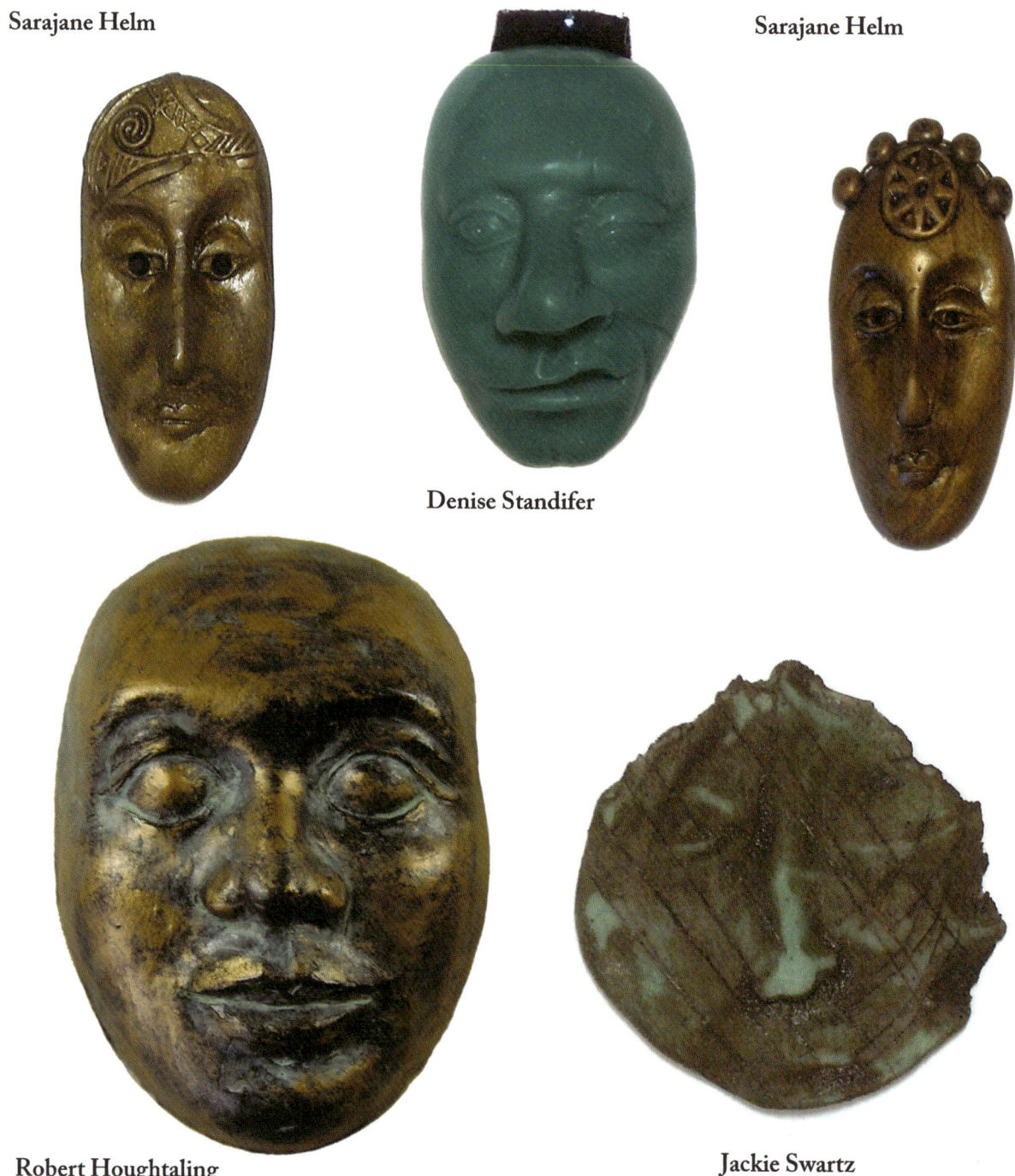

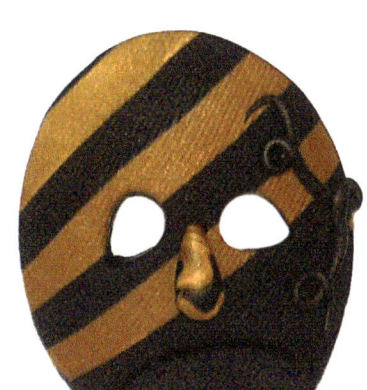
Helen Hughes

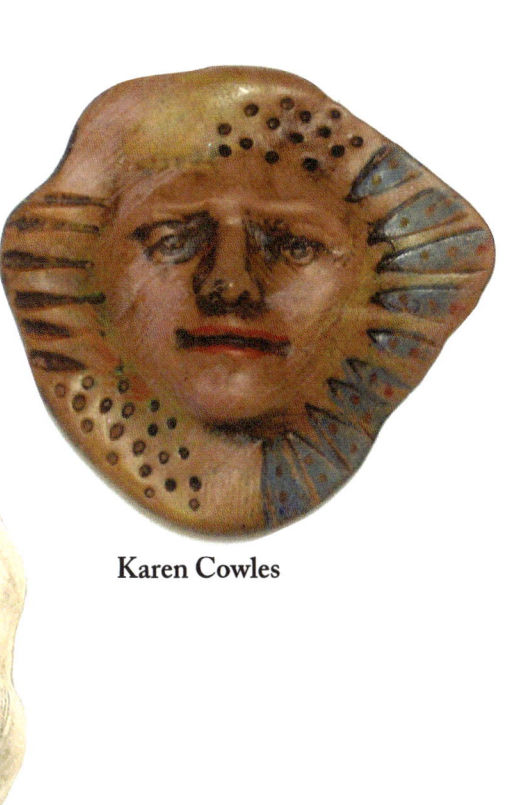
Karen Cowles

Sarajane Helm

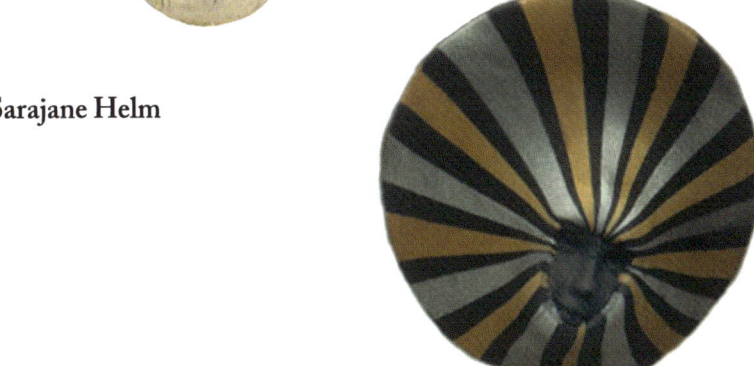

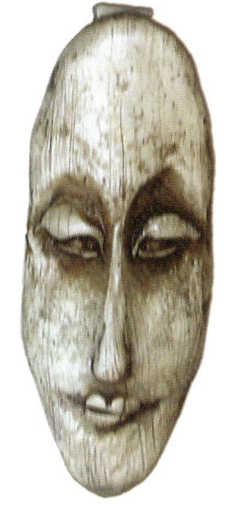

Judith Skinner

Sarajane Helm

PolyMarket Press

Sherry Bailey

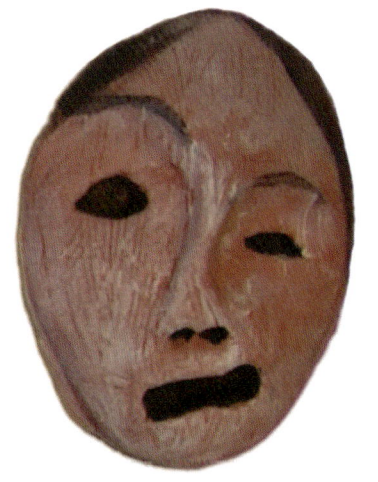

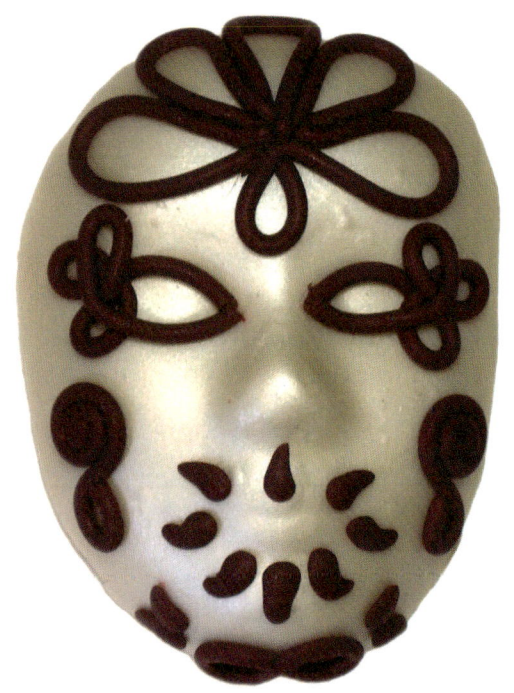

Cecelia Lehmann

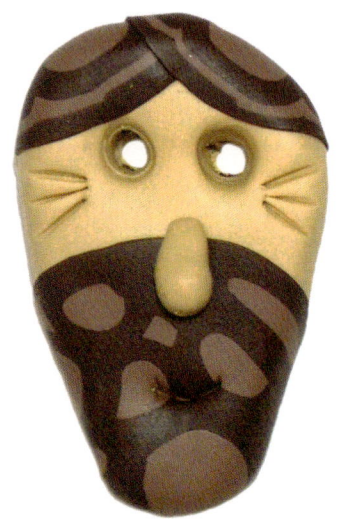

Marie McNealey

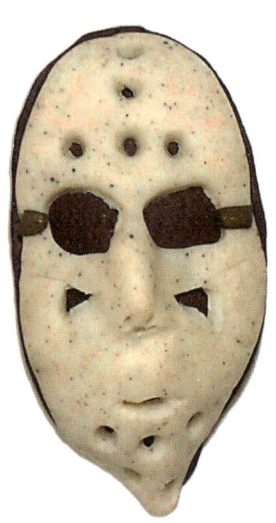

Julie Leir-VanSickle

A Collection Of Polymer Clay Masks

Karen Scudder

Jen Santoro

Jackie Swartz

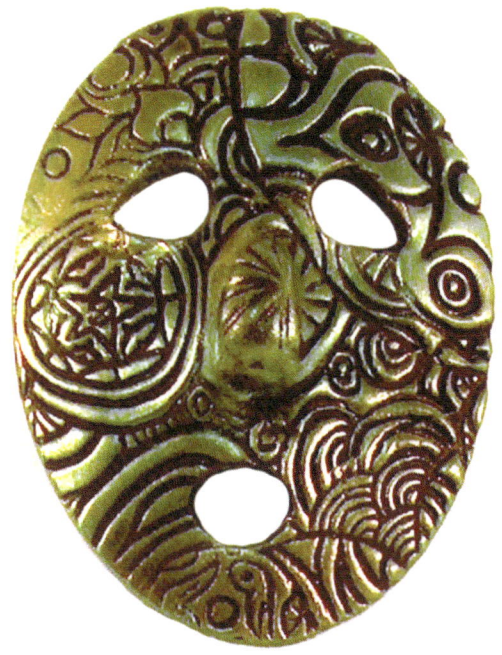
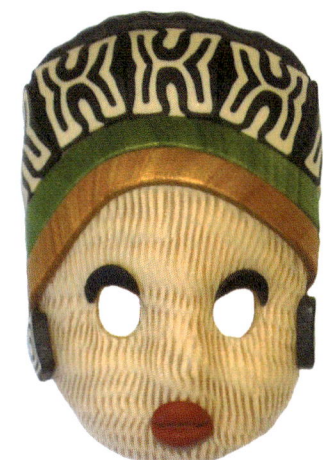
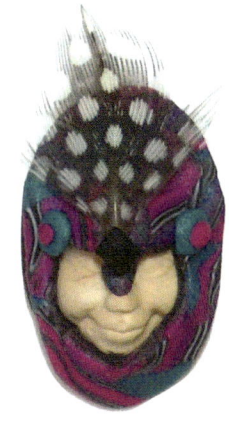
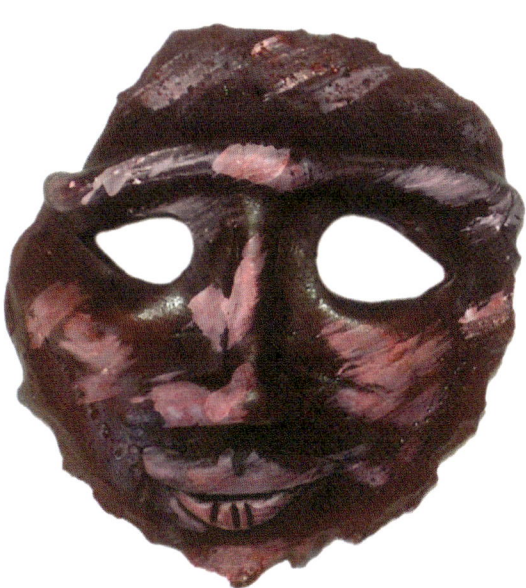

Jen Santoro

Jackie Swartz

Rebecca Wells Stout

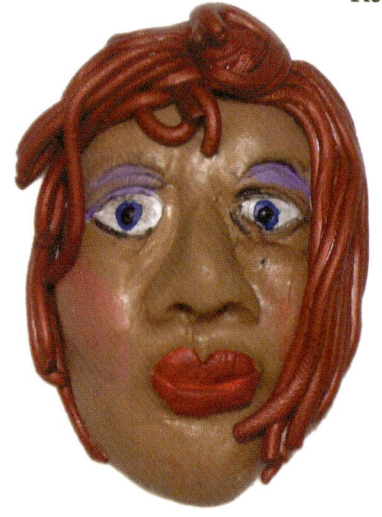

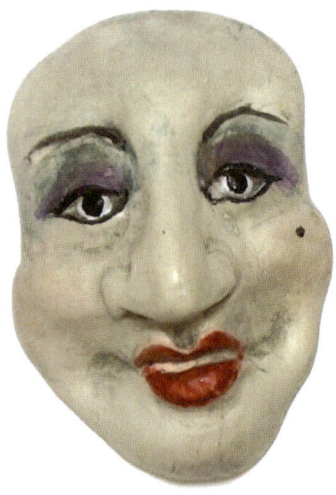

Sarajane Helm

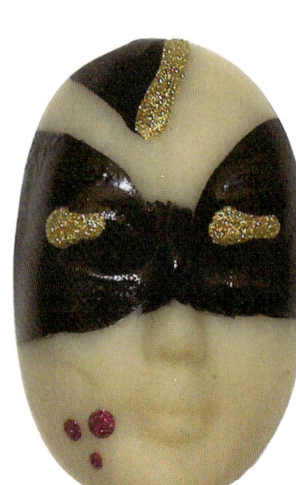

Andrea Spatz

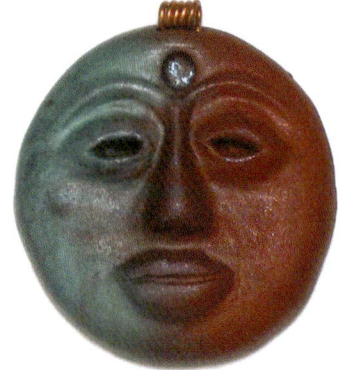

Tonja Lenderman

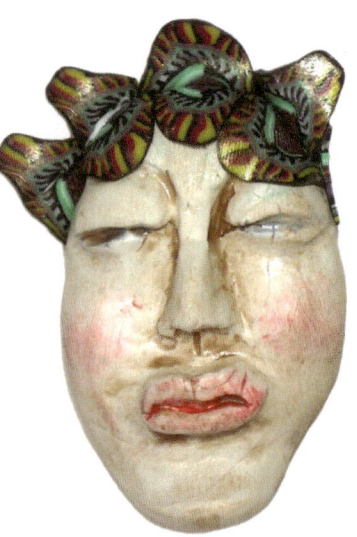

Rebecca Wells Stout

A Collection Of Polymer Clay Masks

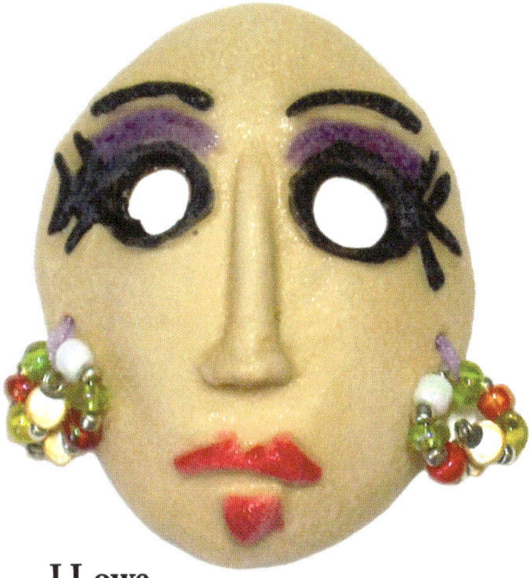

J Lowe

Connie Pelkey
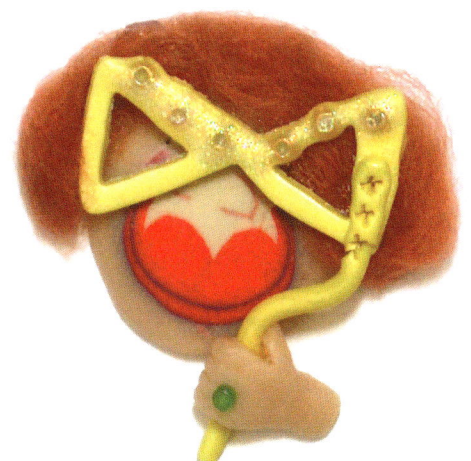

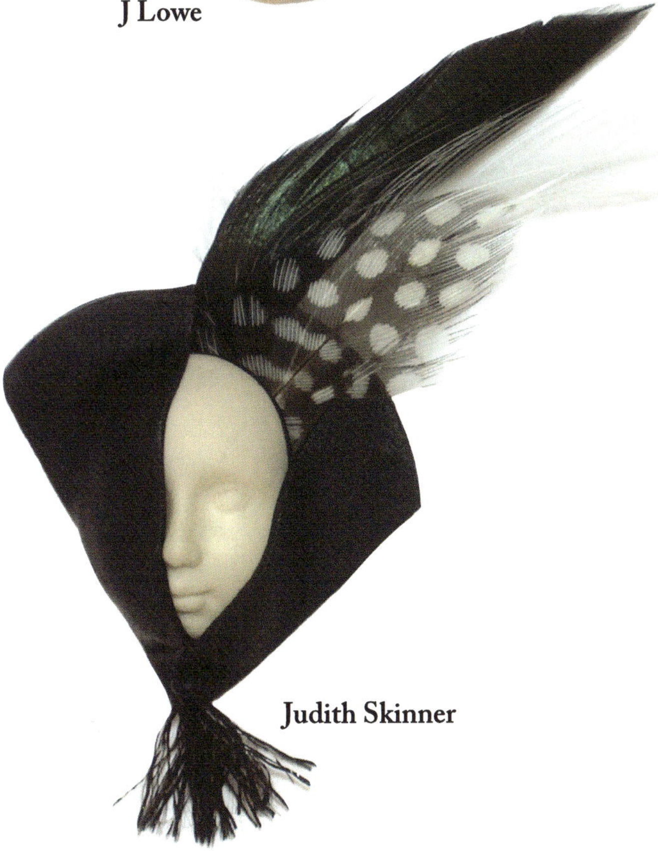

Judith Skinner

Helen Bradley
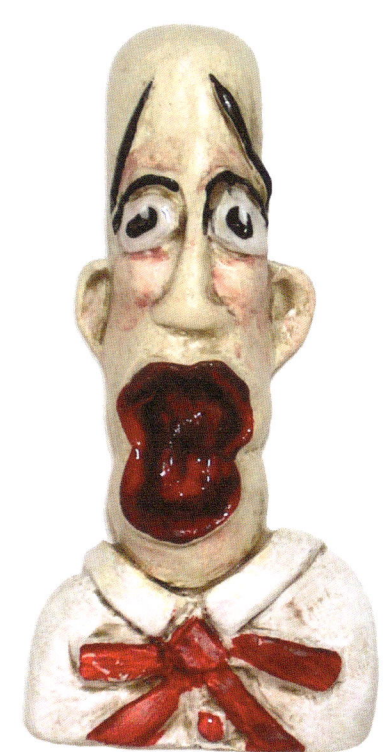

PolyMarket Press

Jeanne Rhea

Patty Barnes

Sherry Bailey

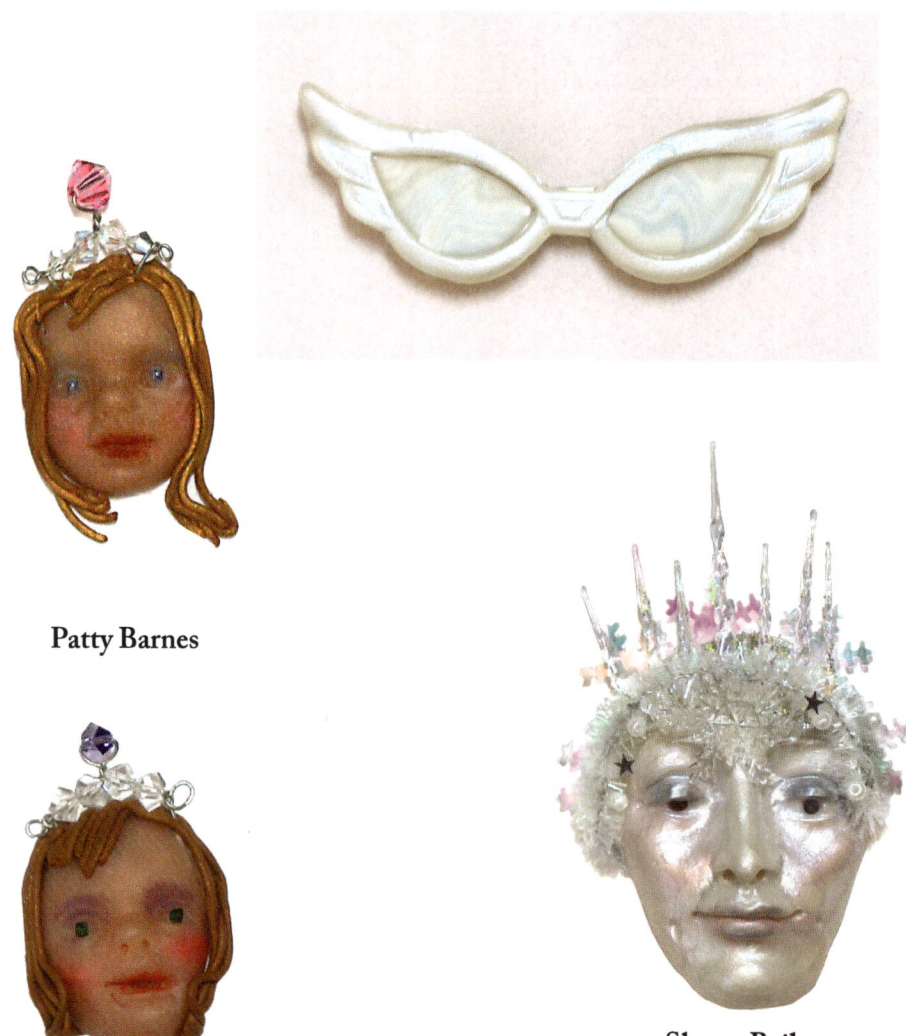

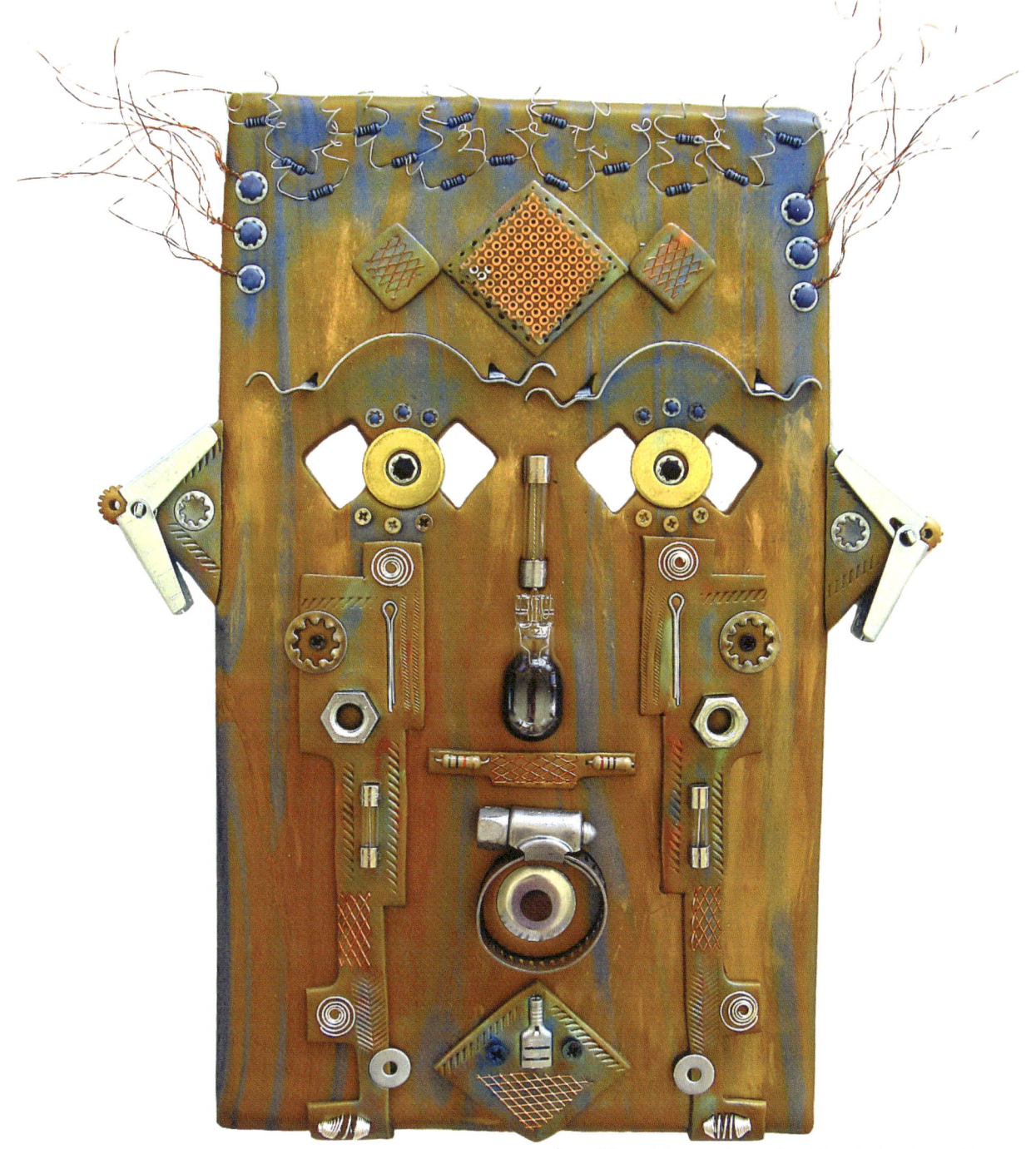

Ann Kruglak *photo Ann Kruglak* 13" x 8"

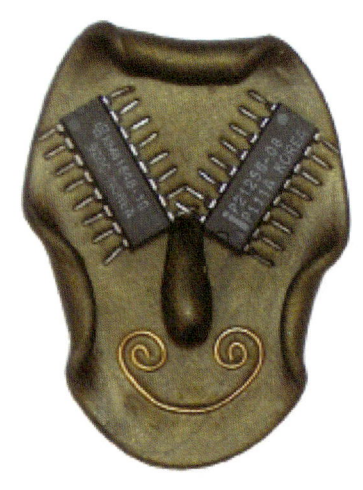

(artist not known)

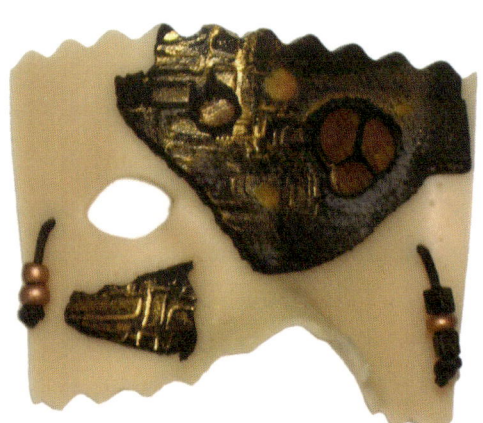

Cecelia Lehmann

Pörrö Sahlberg

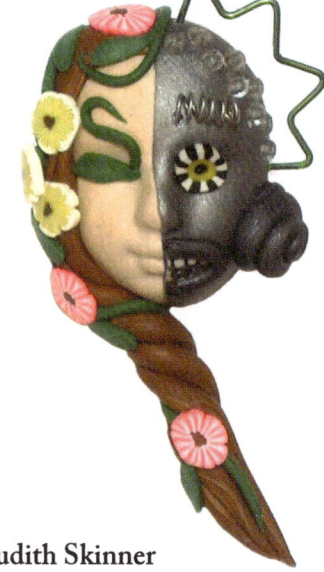

Judith Skinner

Deborah Coller

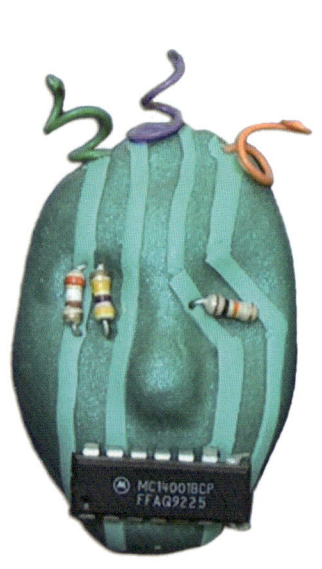

Ian Helm

A Collection Of Polymer Clay Masks

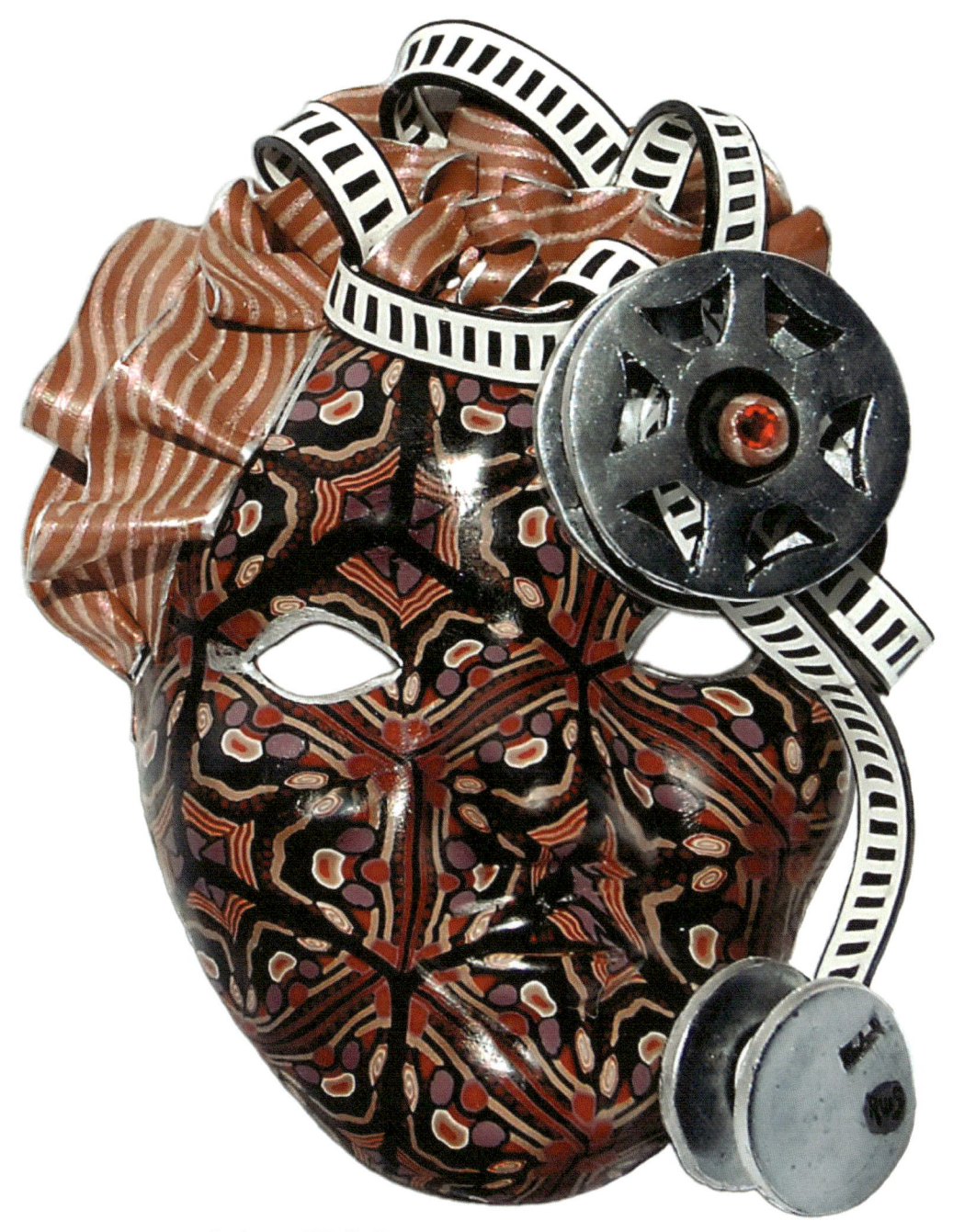

Rebecca Wells Stout *photo Gary Miller* 6" x 6"

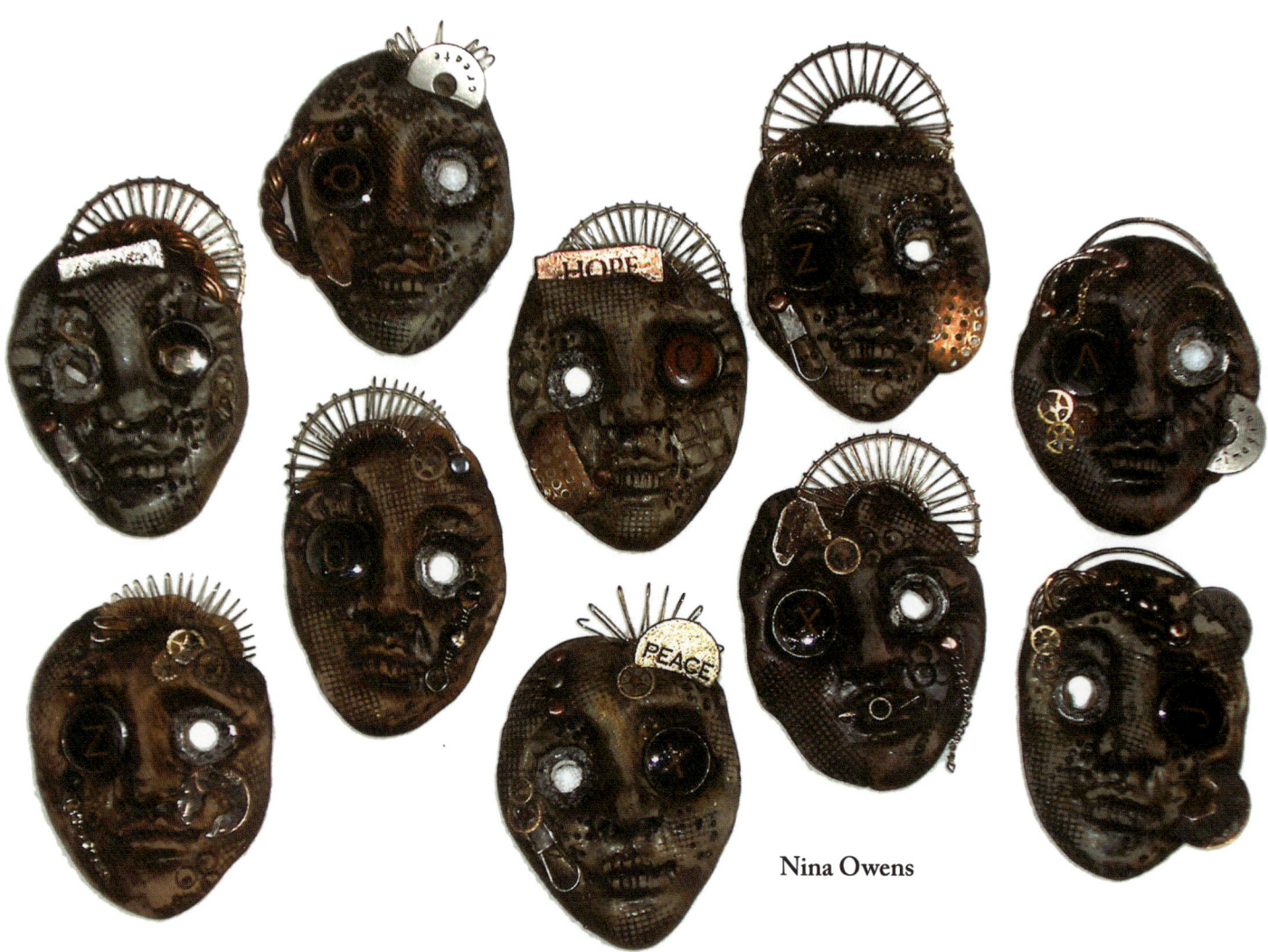

Nina Owens

A Collection Of Polymer Clay Masks

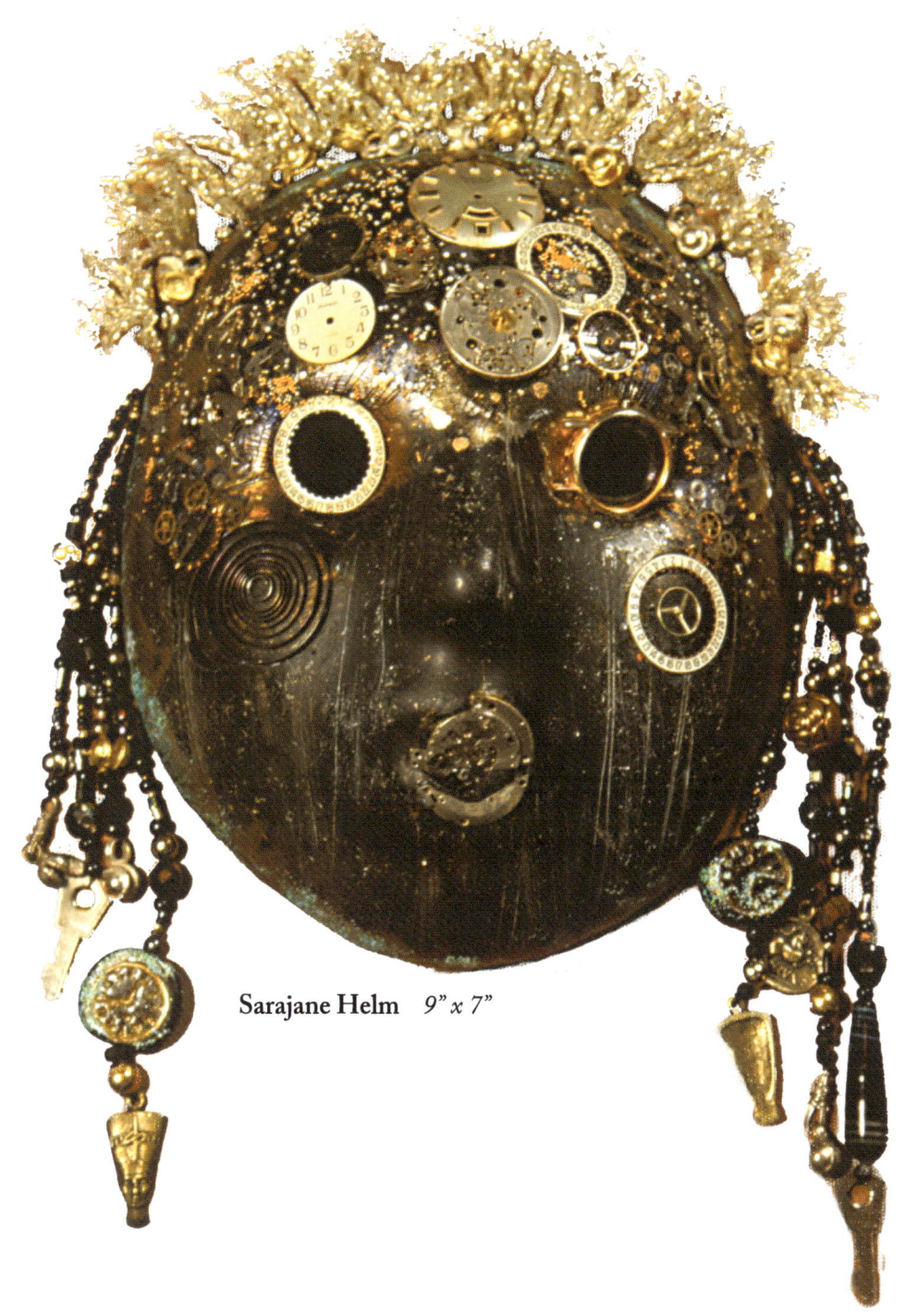

Sarajane Helm   9" x 7"

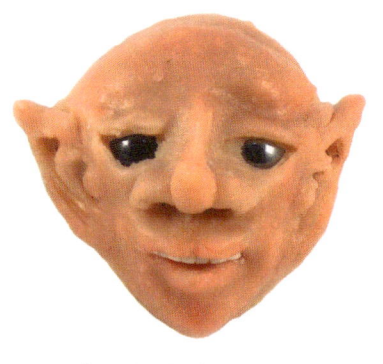

Ian Helm

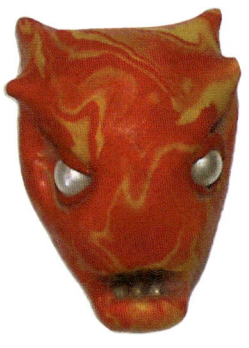

Cecelia Lehmann

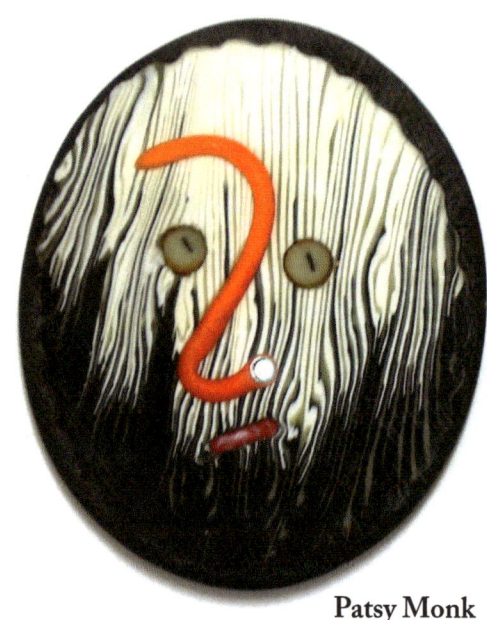

Patsy Monk

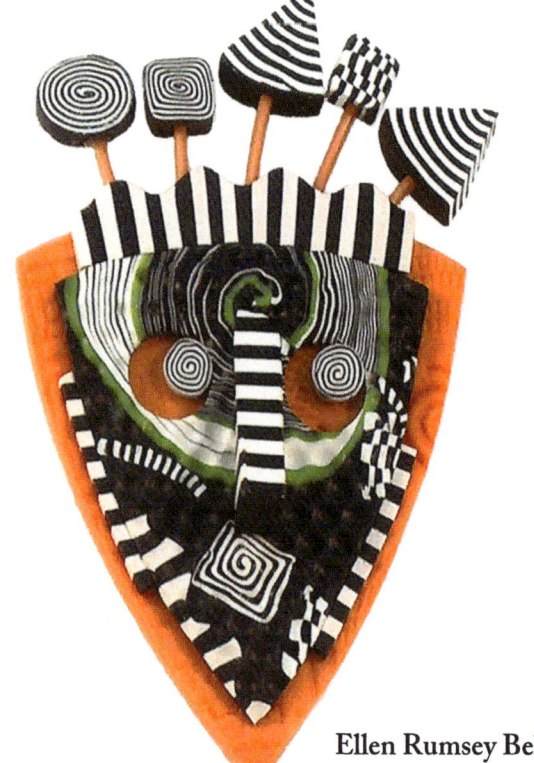

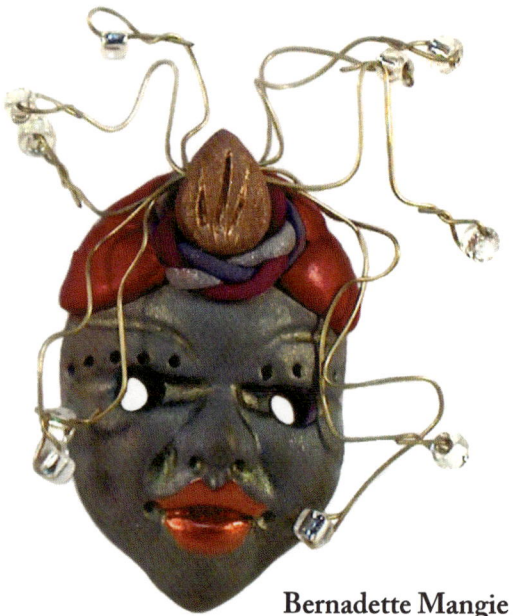

Ellen Rumsey Bellenot

Bernadette Mangie

74

A Collection Of Polymer Clay Masks

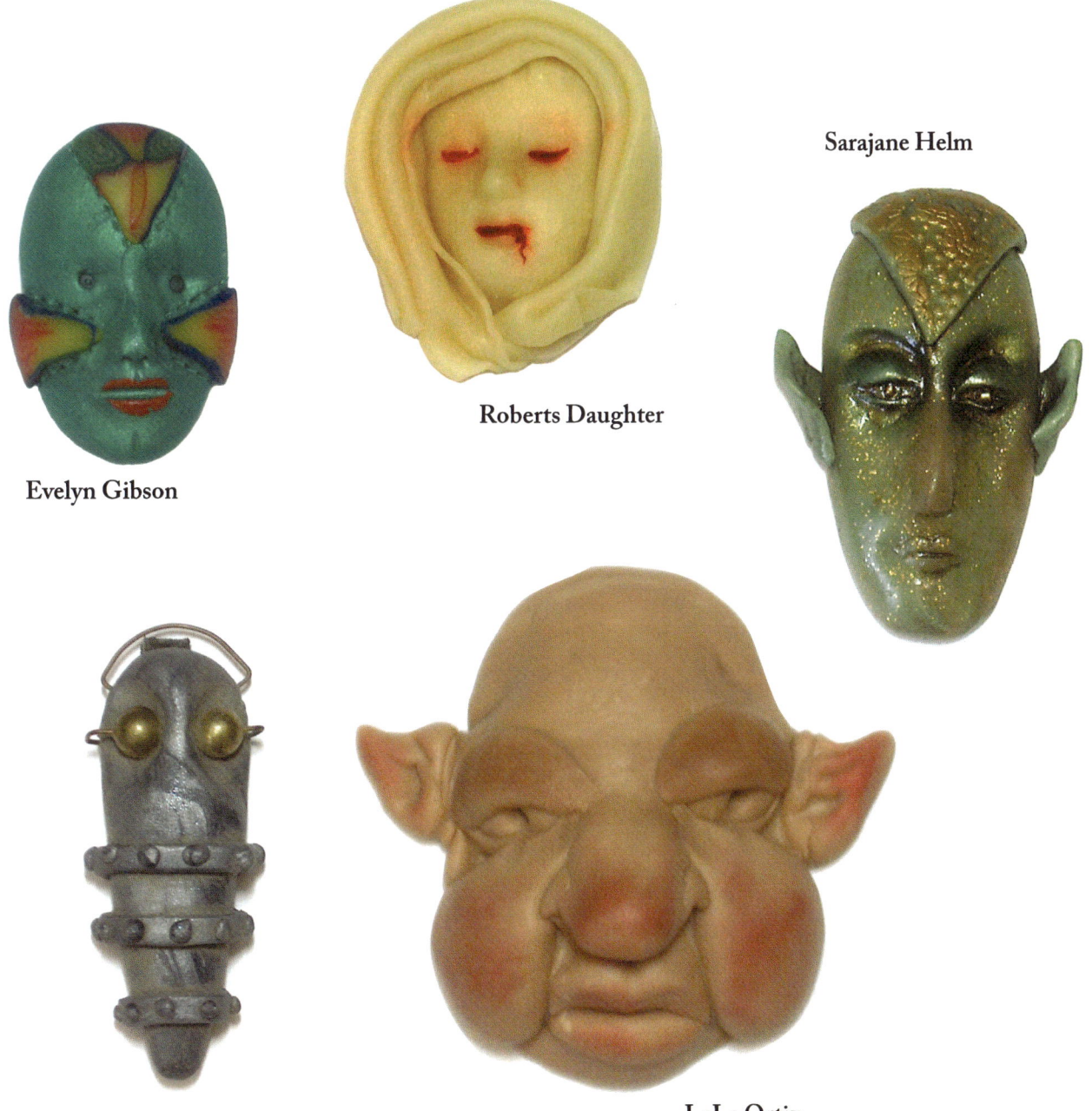

Evelyn Gibson

Roberts Daughter

Sarajane Helm

Ian Helm

LaLa Ortiz

PolyMarket Press

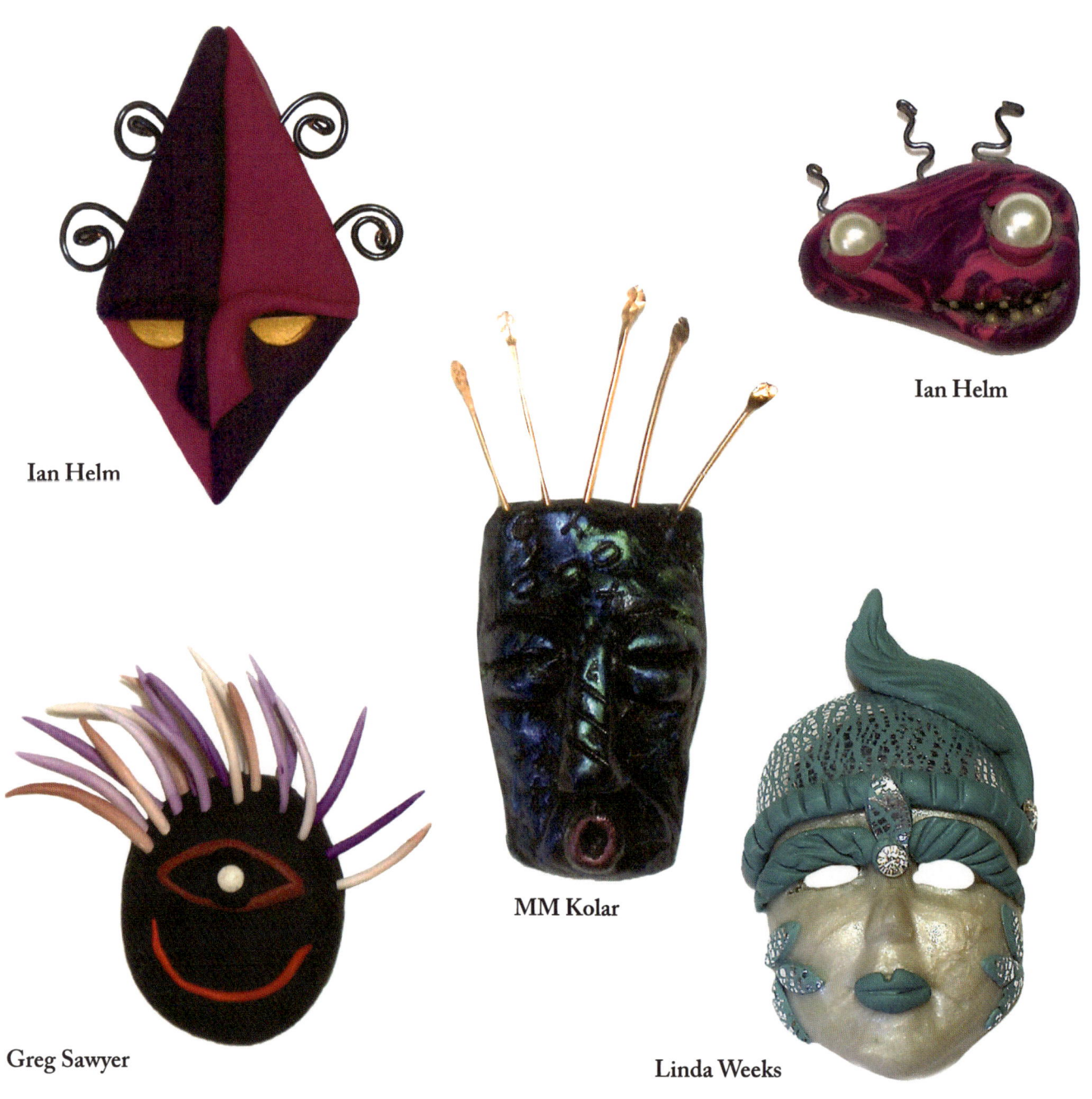

Ian Helm

Ian Helm

MM Kolar

Greg Sawyer

Linda Weeks

A Collection Of Polymer Clay Masks

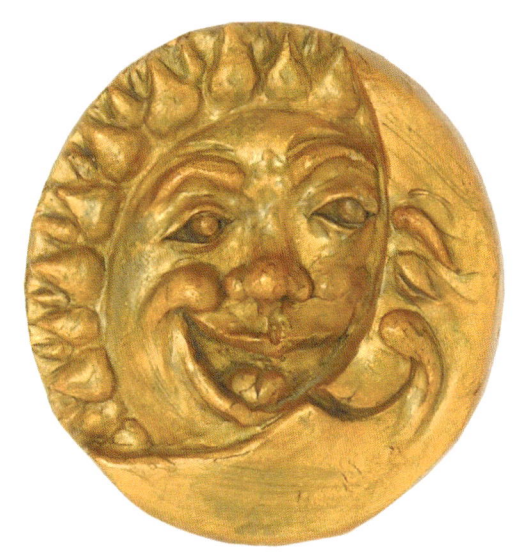

Robert Houghtaling

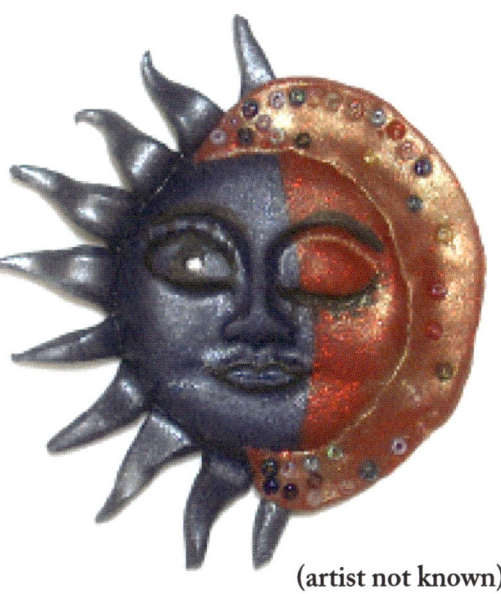

(artist not known)

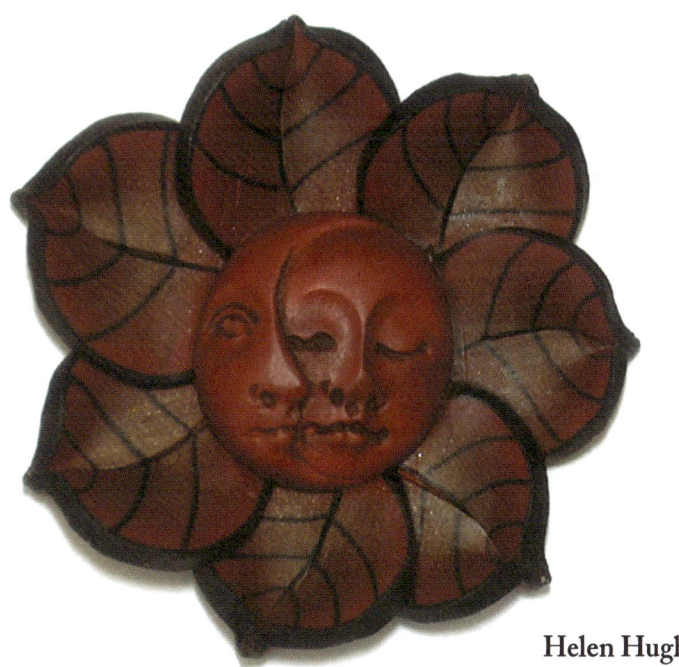

Helen Hughes

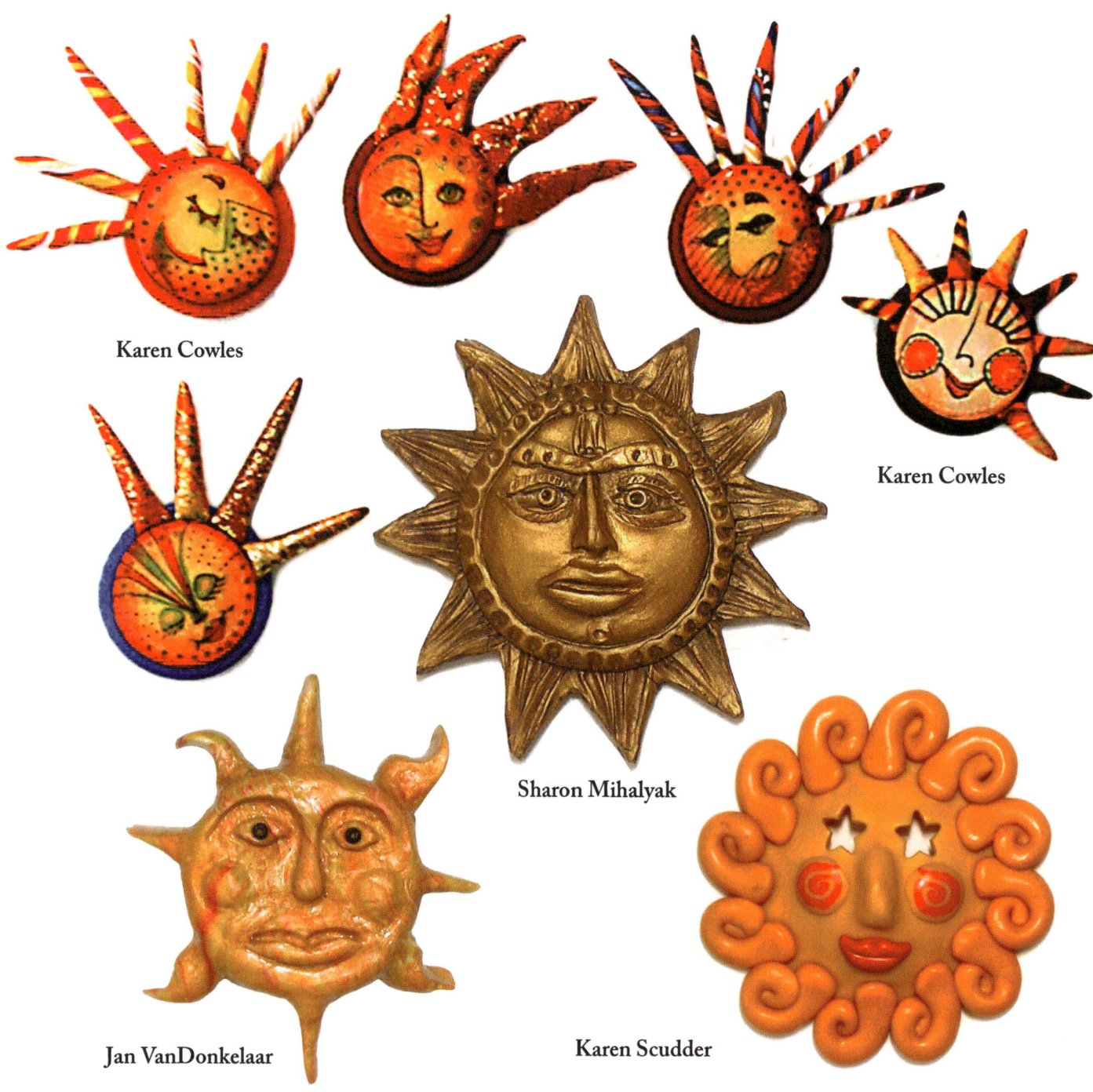

Karen Cowles

Karen Cowles

Sharon Mihalyak

Jan VanDonkelaar

Karen Scudder

A Collection Of Polymer Clay Masks

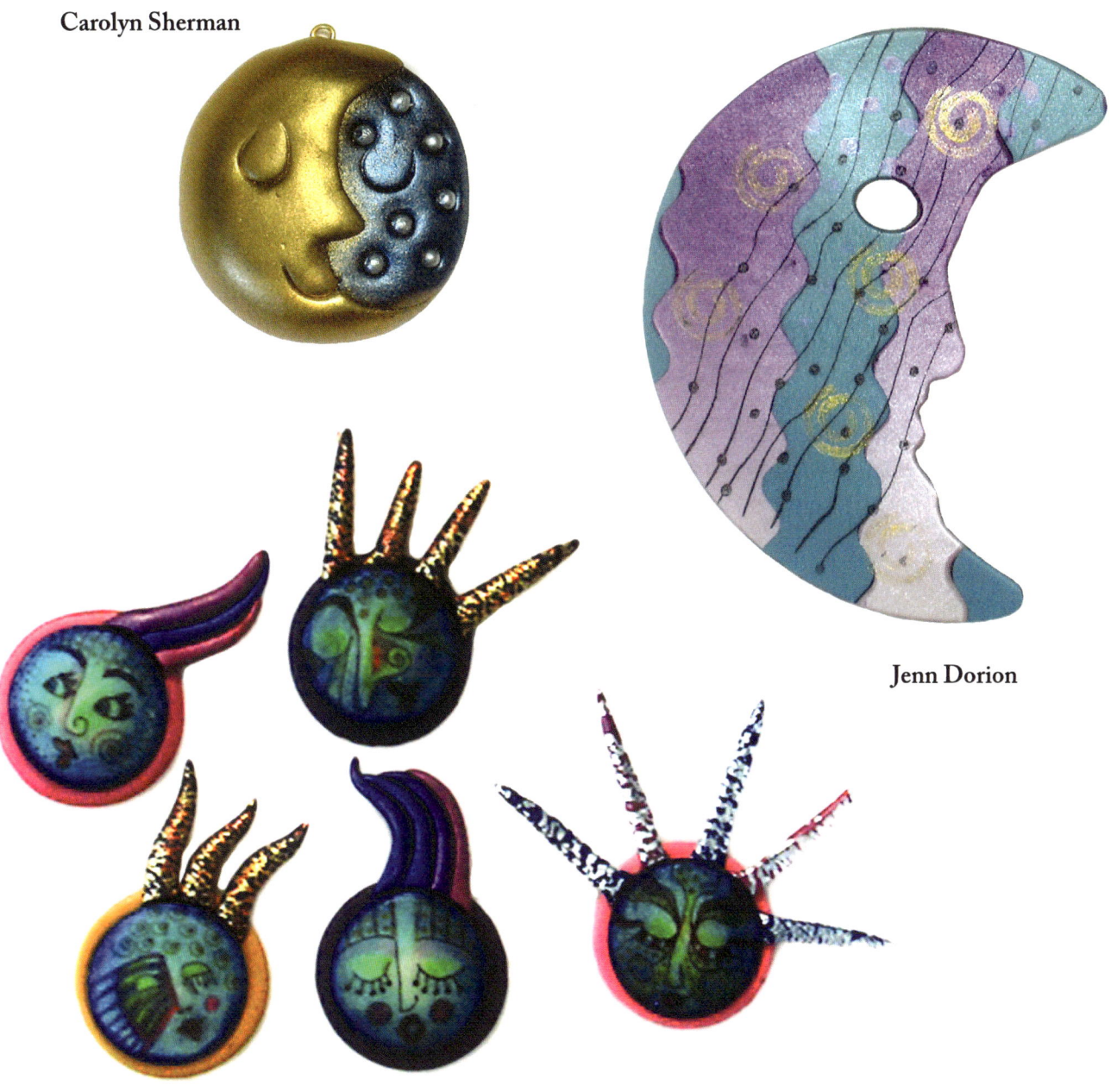

Carolyn Sherman

Jenn Dorion

Karen Cowles

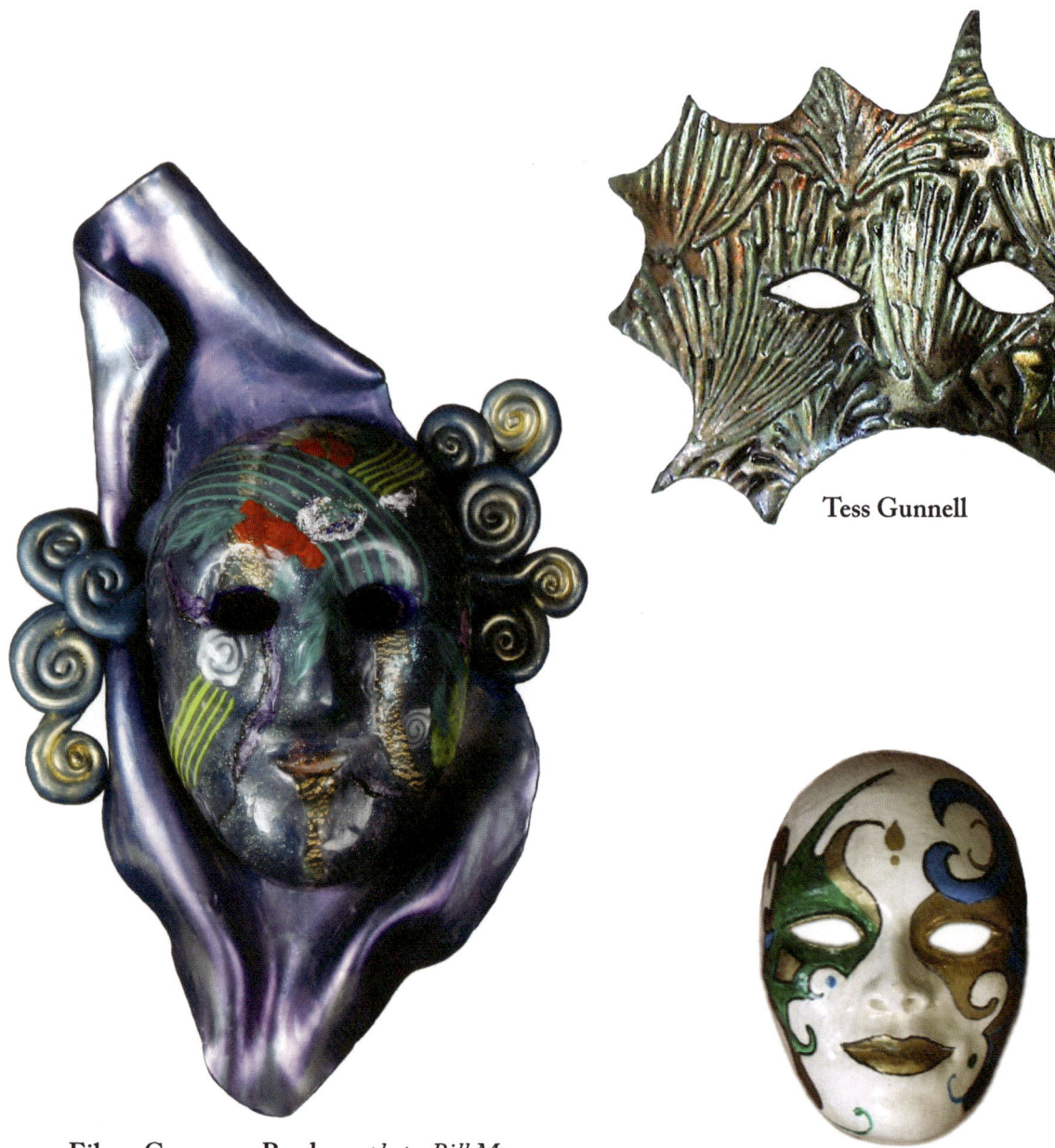

Tess Gunnell

Eileen Cressman-Reeder *photo Bill Mason*
10.5" x 6.5" x 4"

Bill Girard

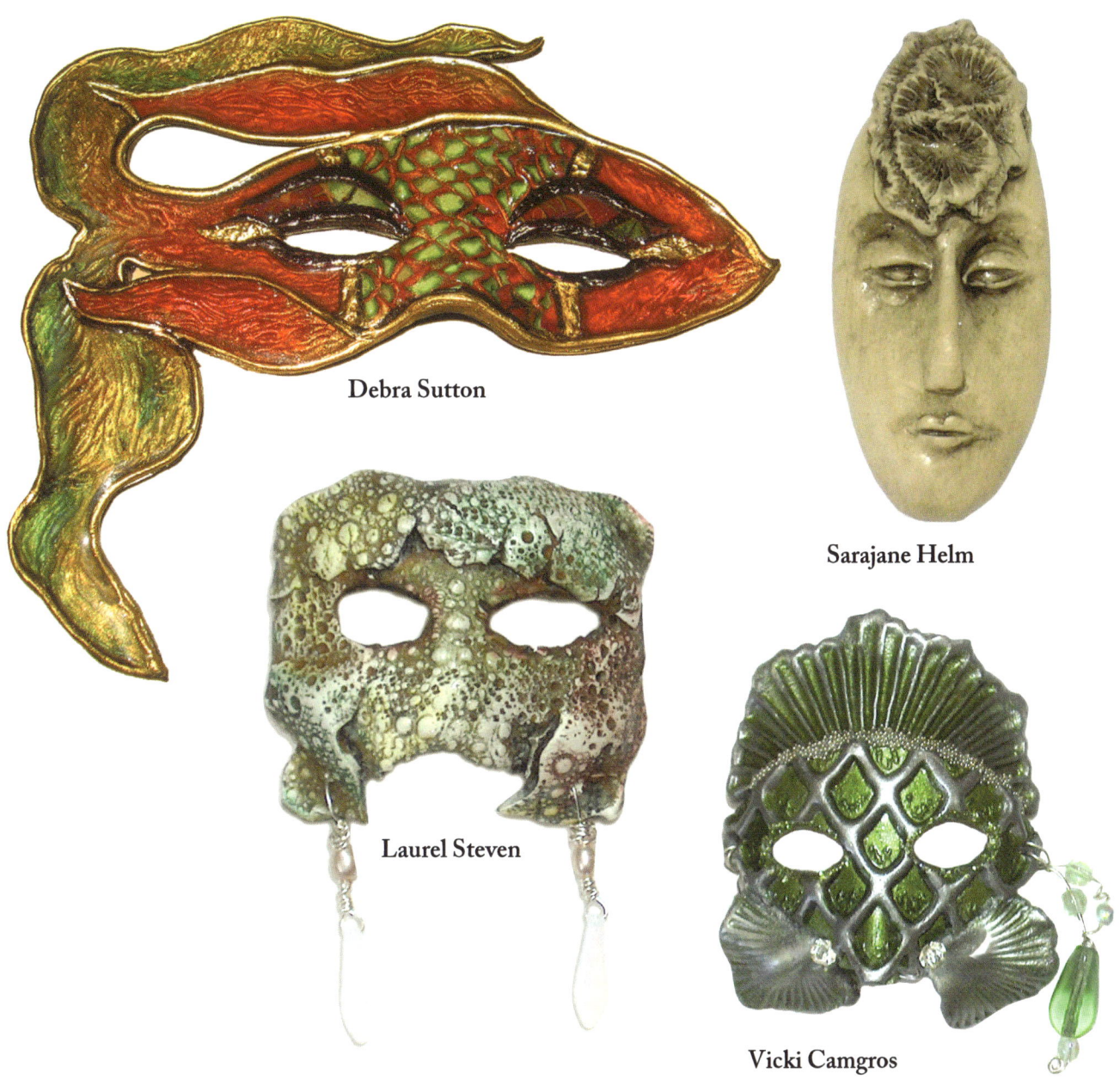

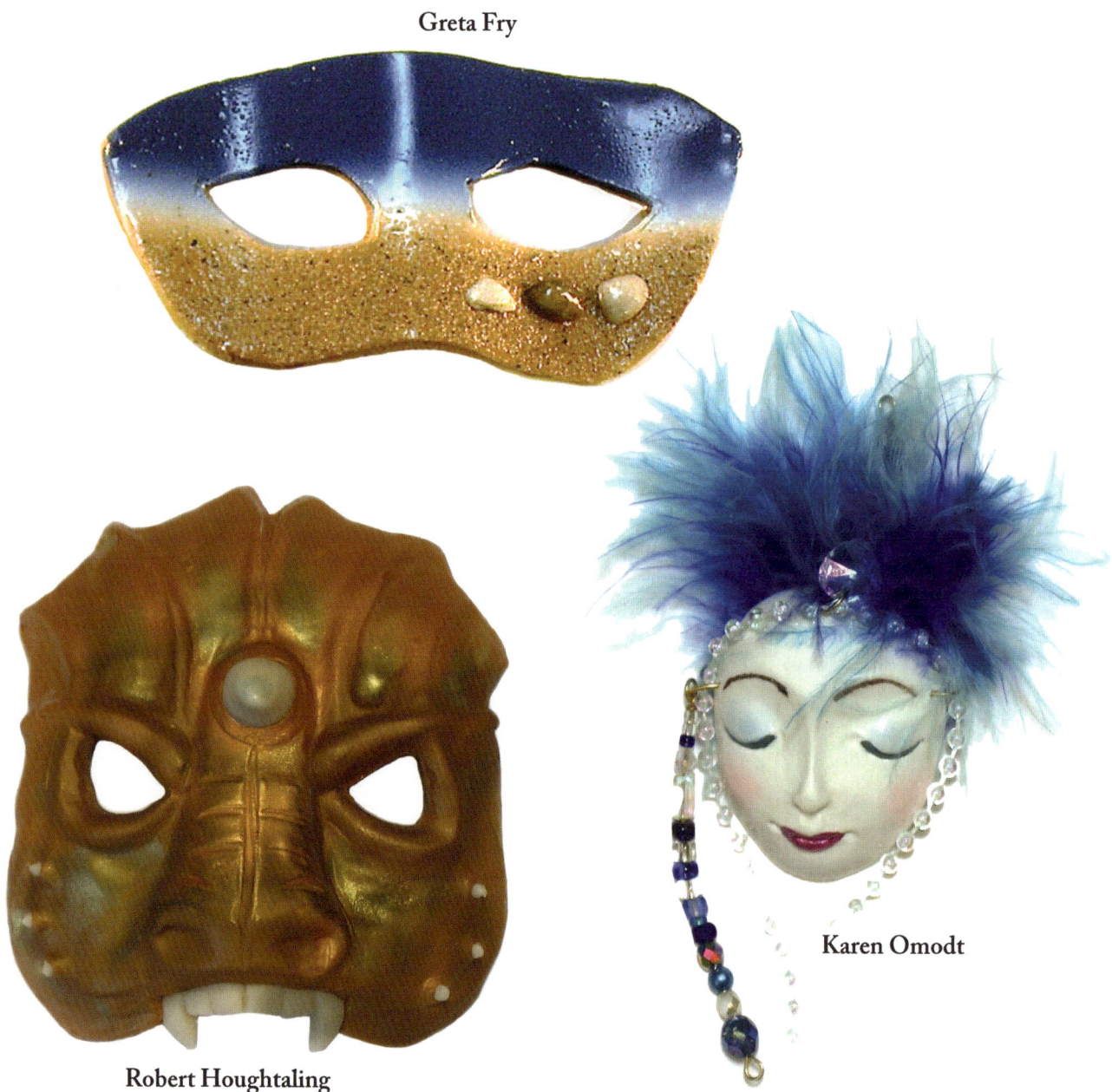

Greta Fry

Robert Houghtaling

Karen Omodt

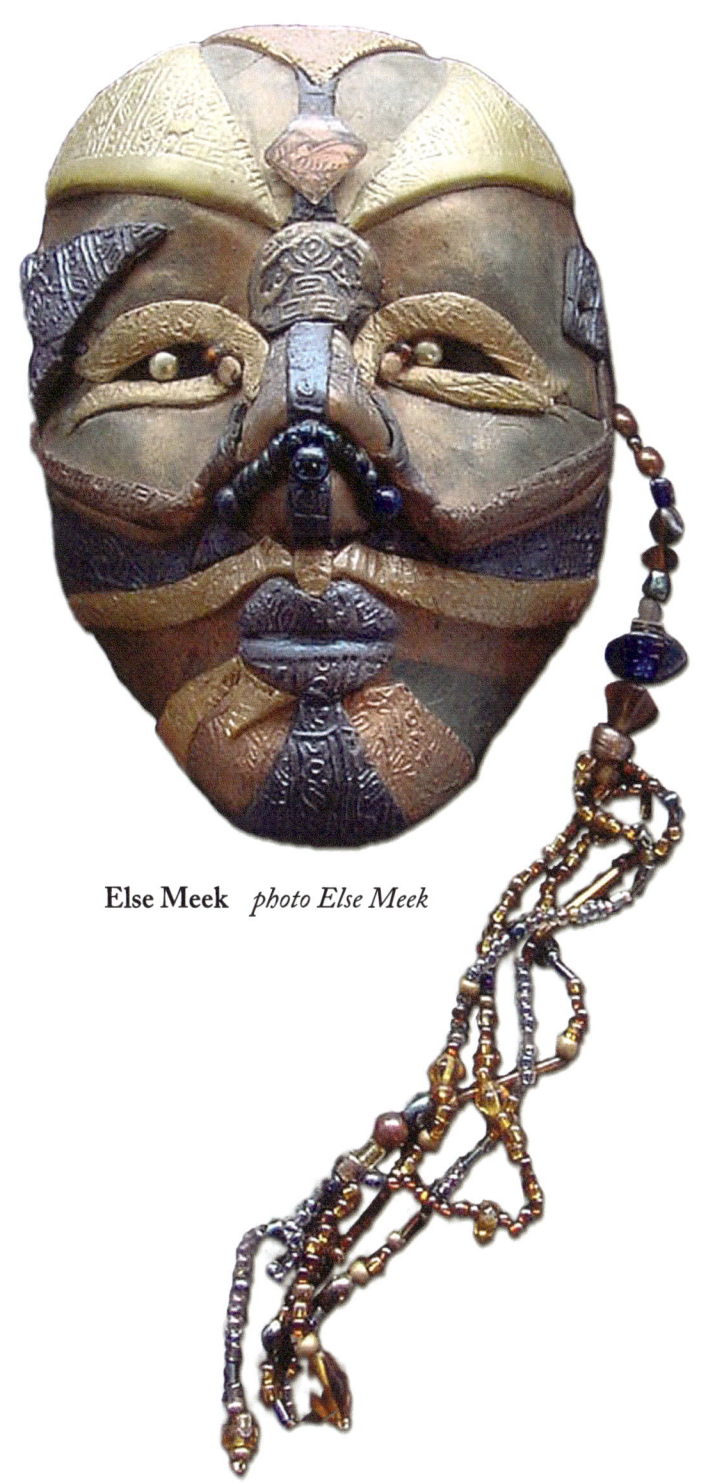

Else Meek *photo Else Meek*

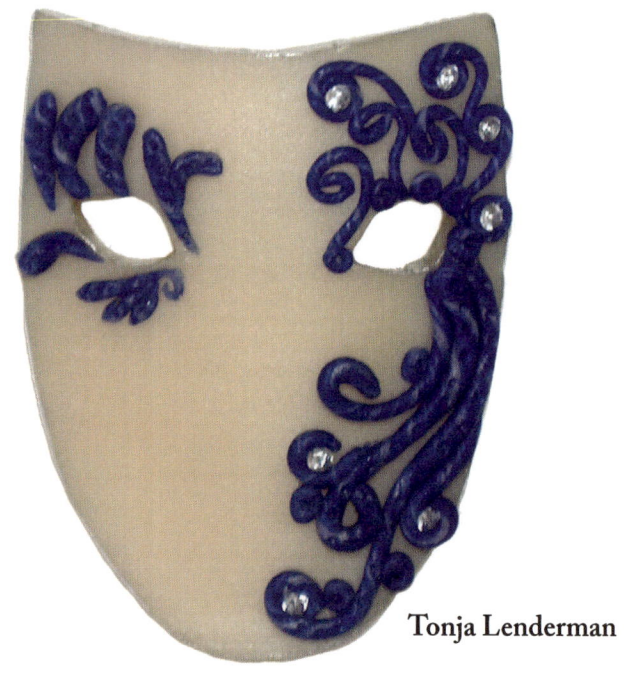

Tonja Lenderman

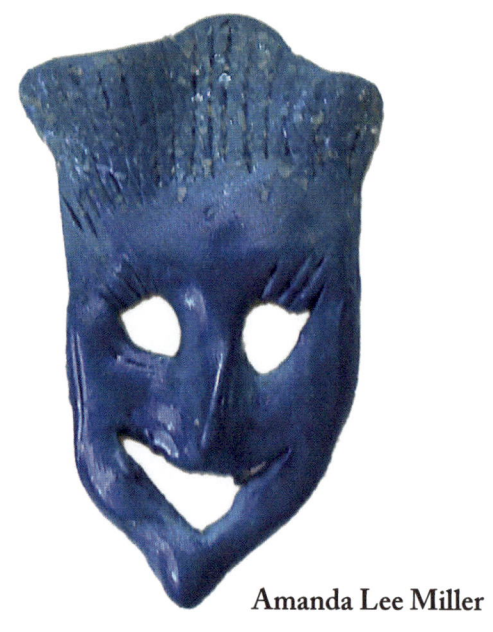

Amanda Lee Miller

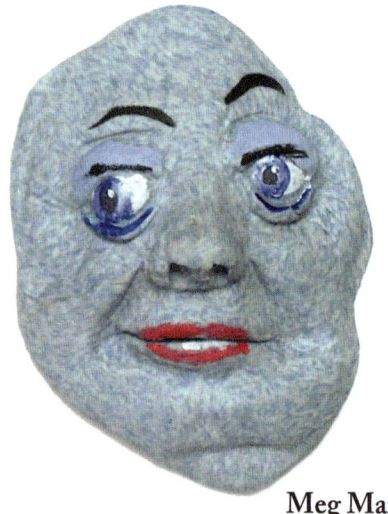

Meg Marchiando

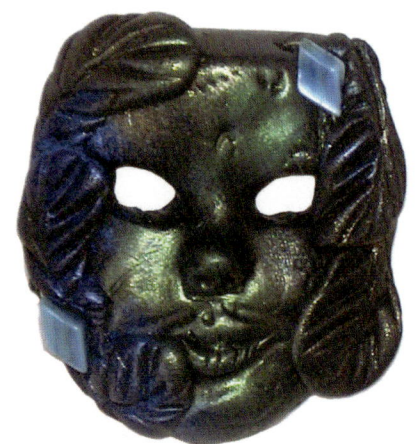

Nina Owens

A Collection Of Polymer Clay Masks

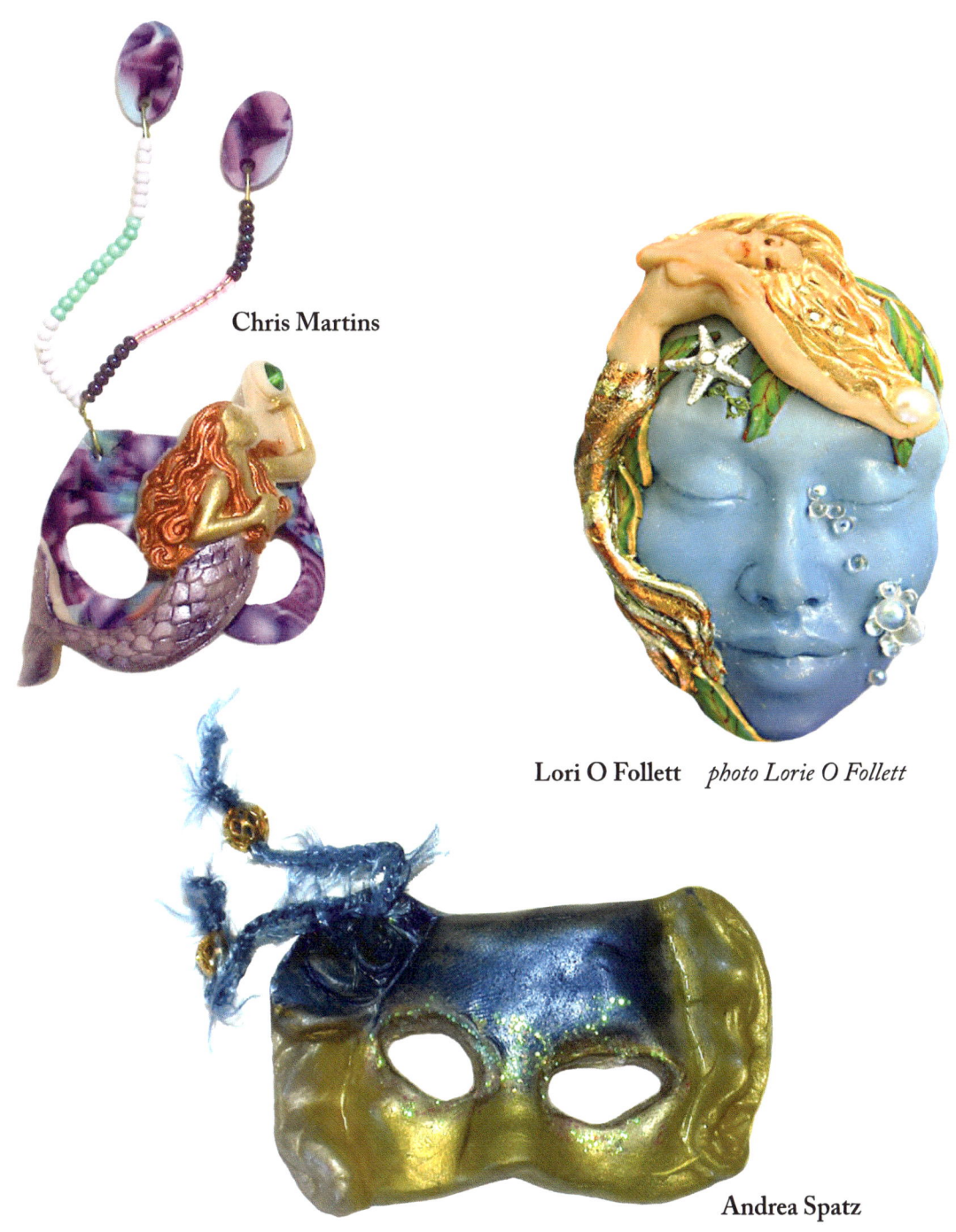

Chris Martins

Lori O Follett *photo Lorie O Follett*

Andrea Spatz

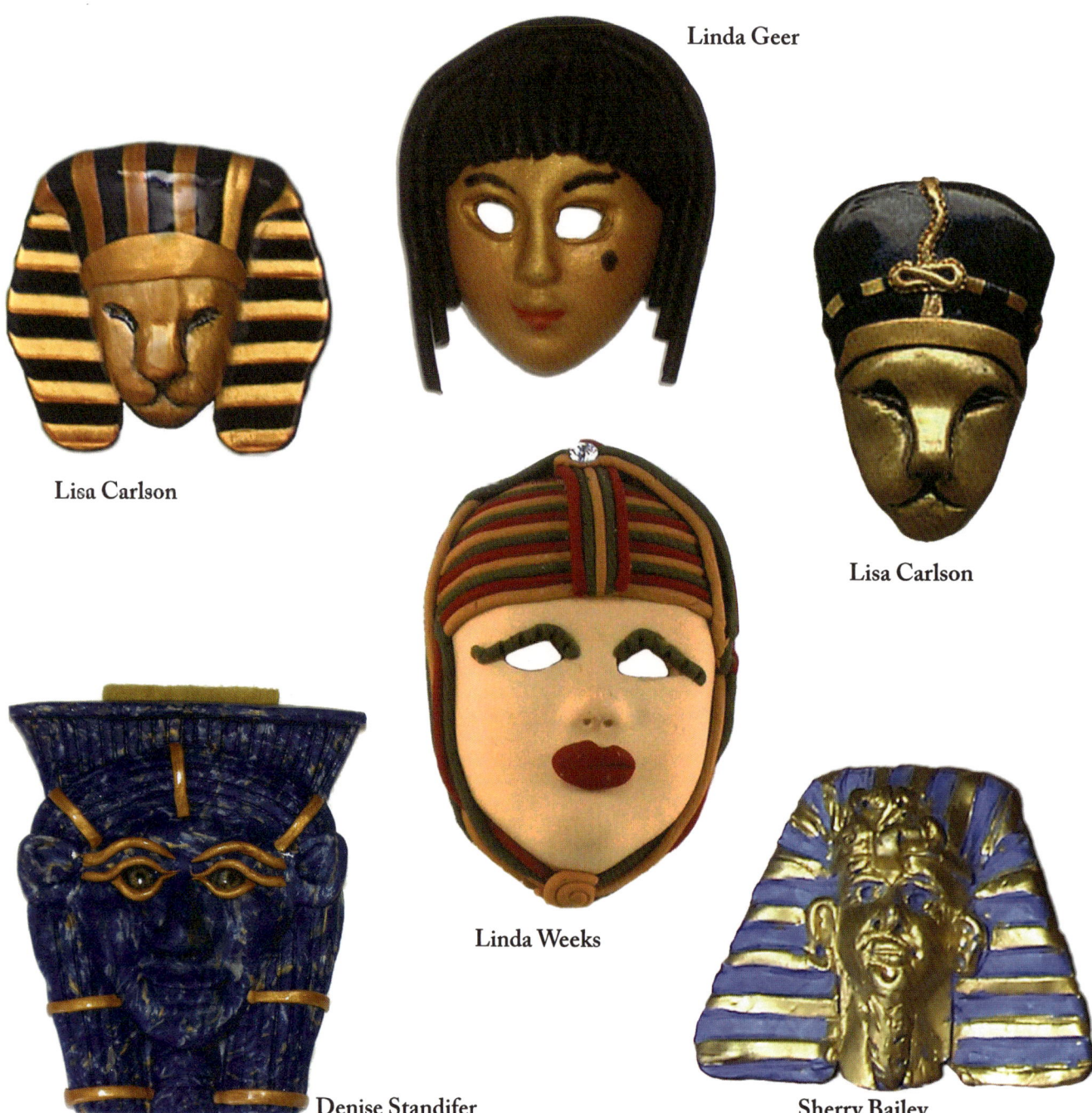

A Collection Of Polymer Clay Masks

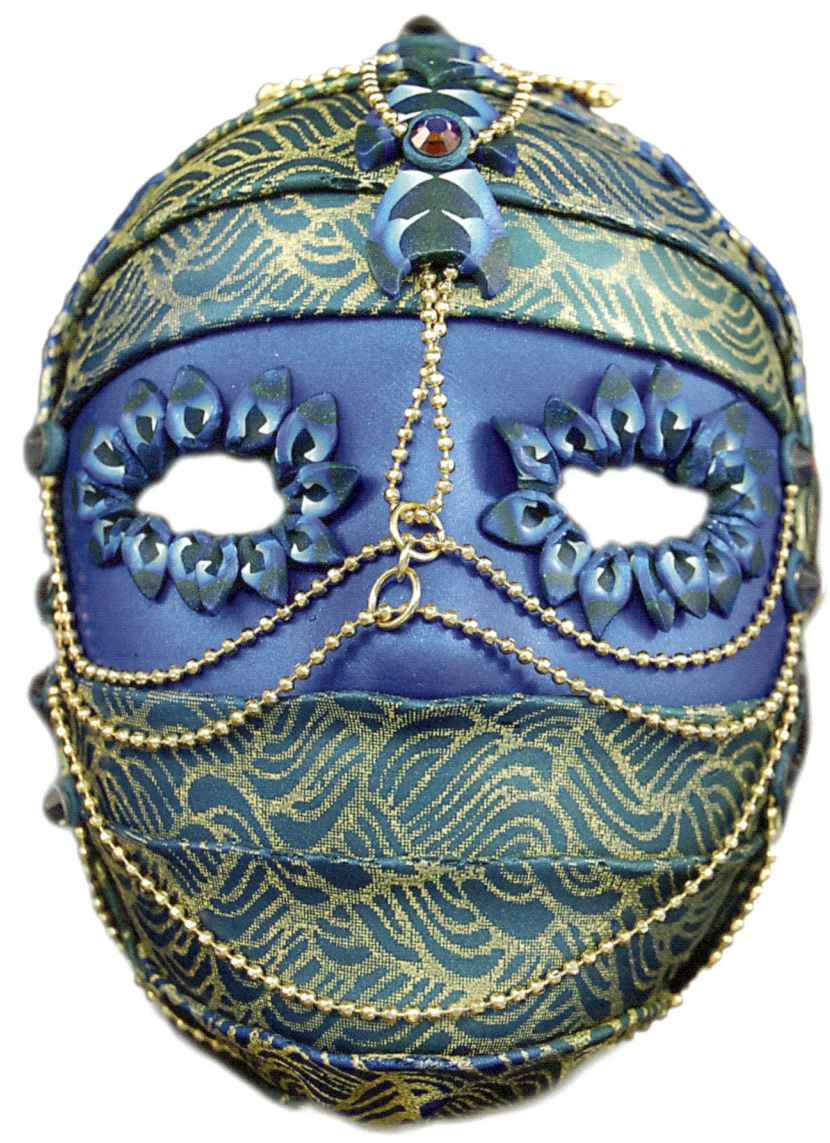

Rebecca Wells Stout *photo Mark Stout* 6" x 6"

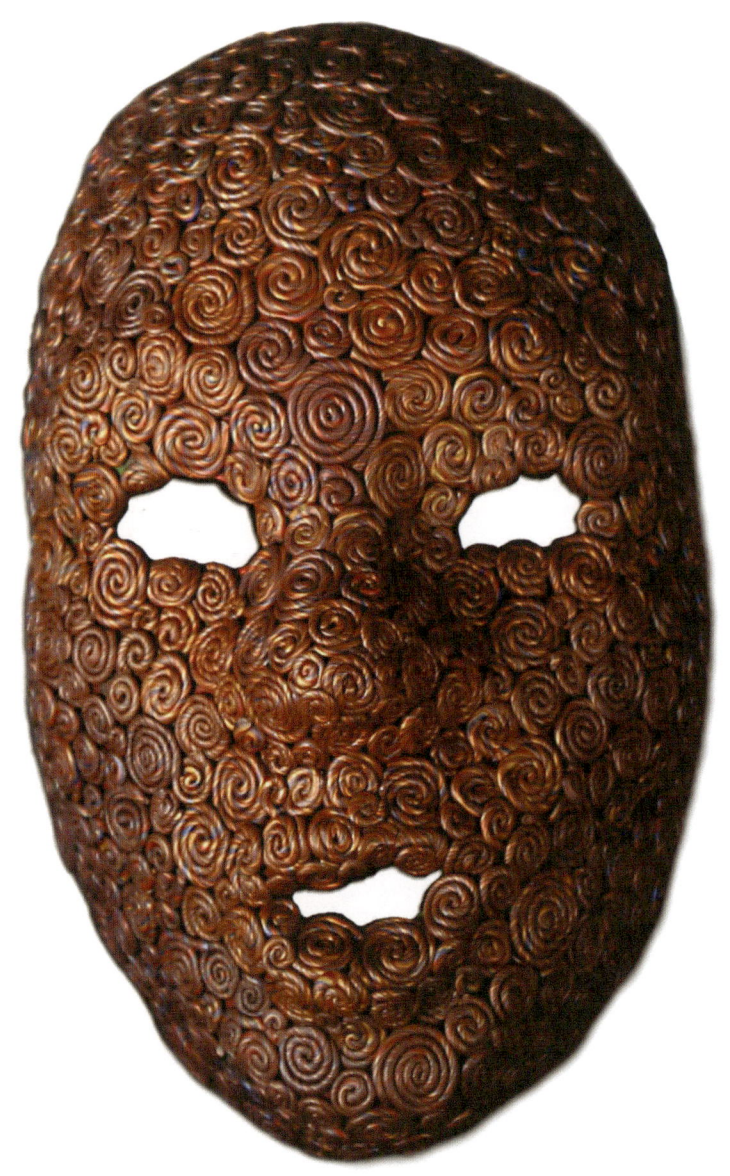

Eileen Cressman-Reeder *photo Bill Mason* 8" x 5.5" x 4"

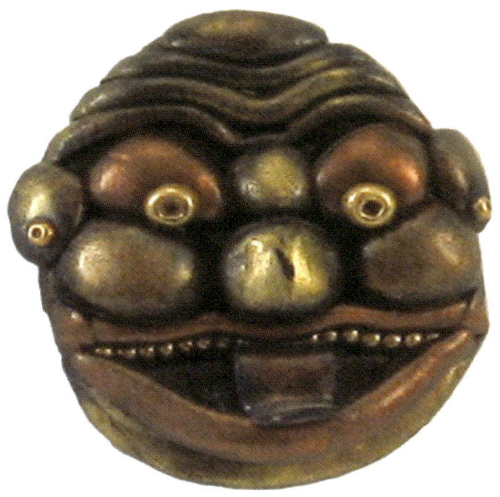

Sylvia Luppert

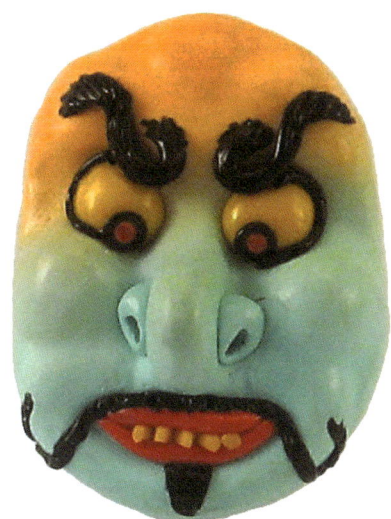

Sylvia Luppert

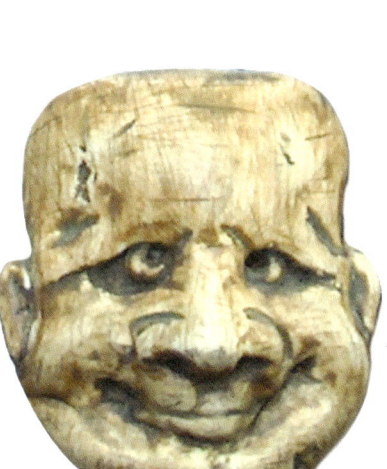

Sarajane Helm

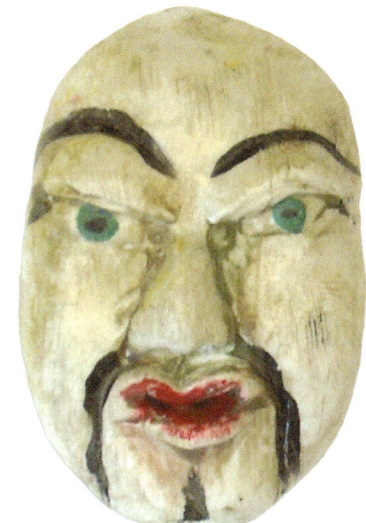

Rebecca Wells Stout

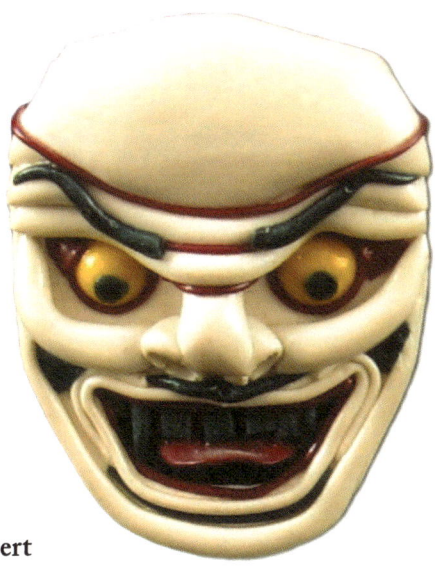

Sylvia Luppert

PolyMarket Press

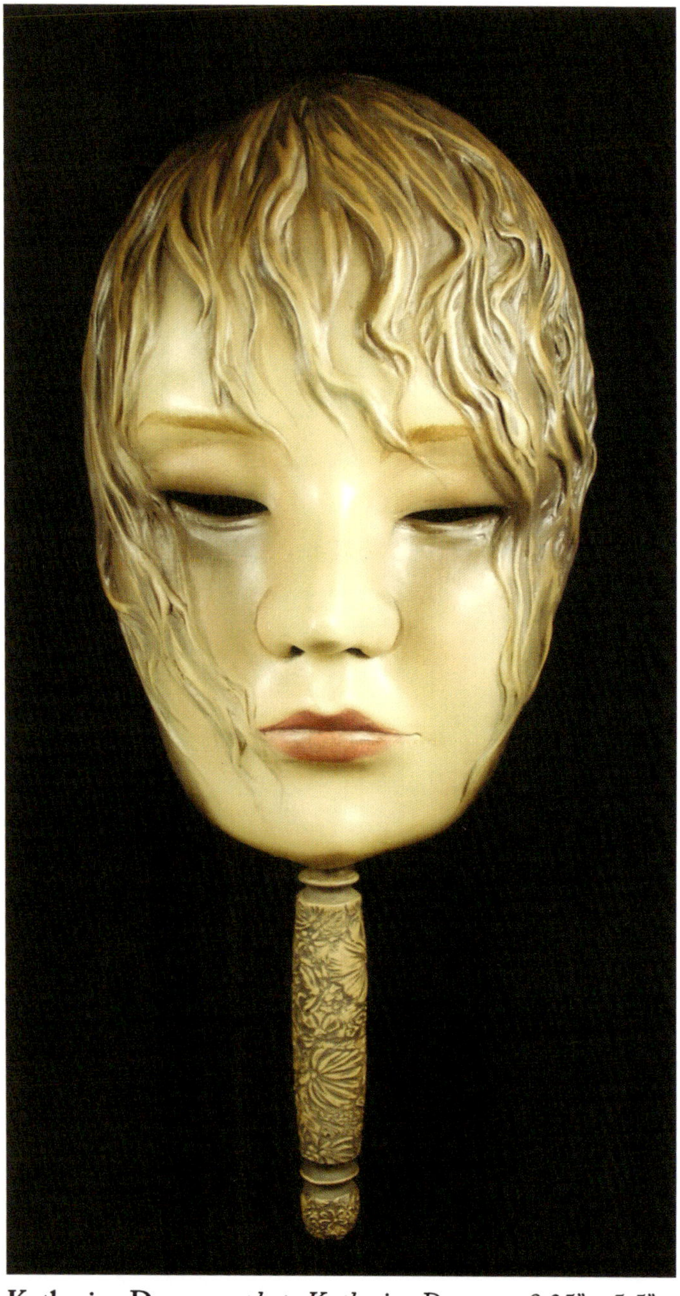

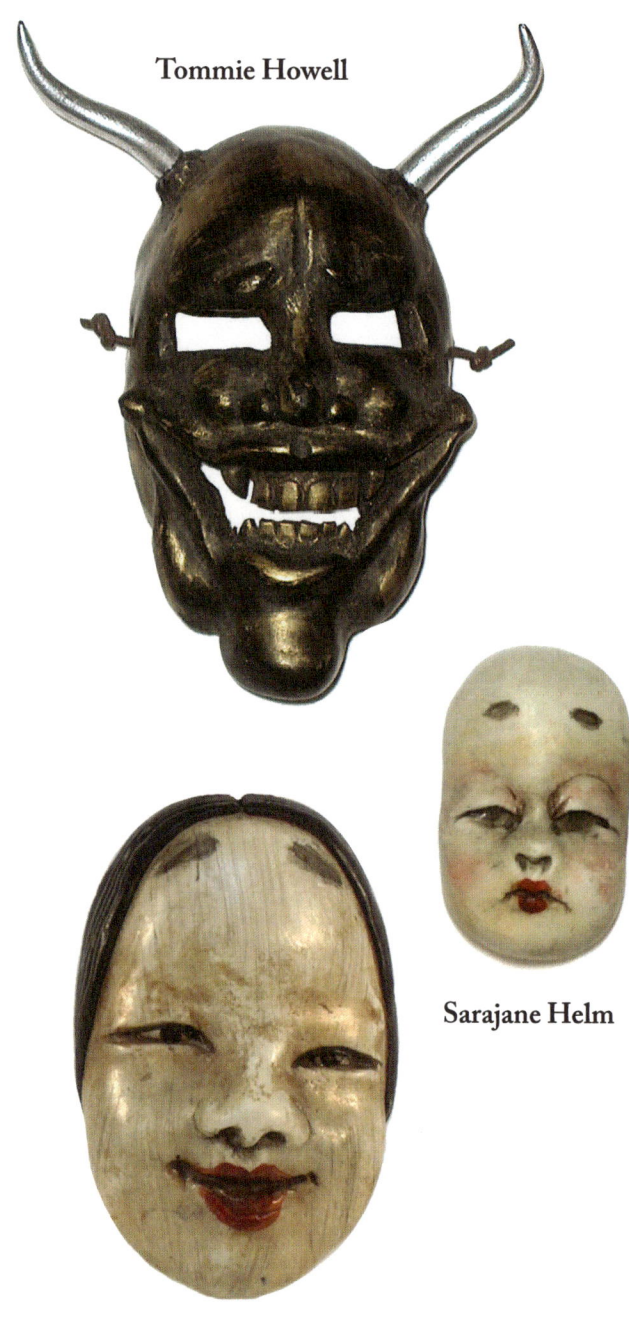

Katherine Dewey *photo Katherine Dewey* 8.25" x 5.5"
handle 4.25"

Tommie Howell

Sarajane Helm

90

A Collection Of Polymer Clay Masks

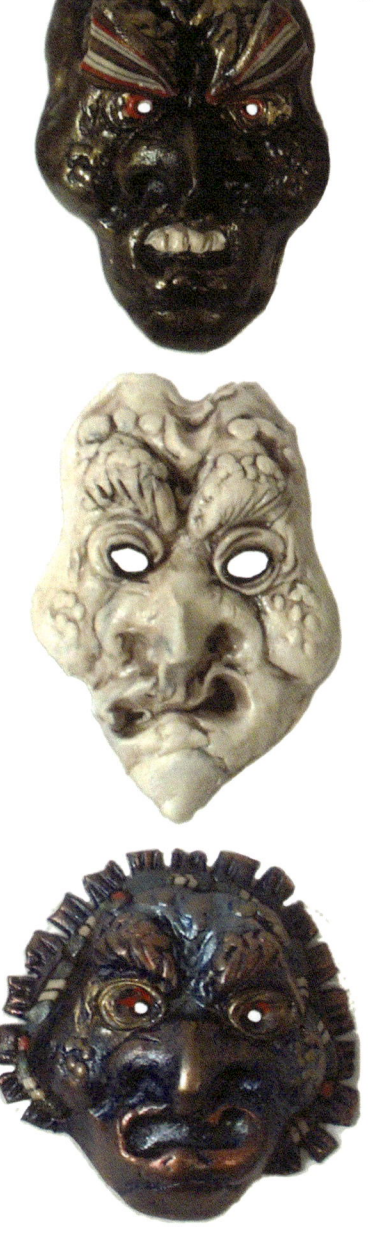

Sarajane Helm

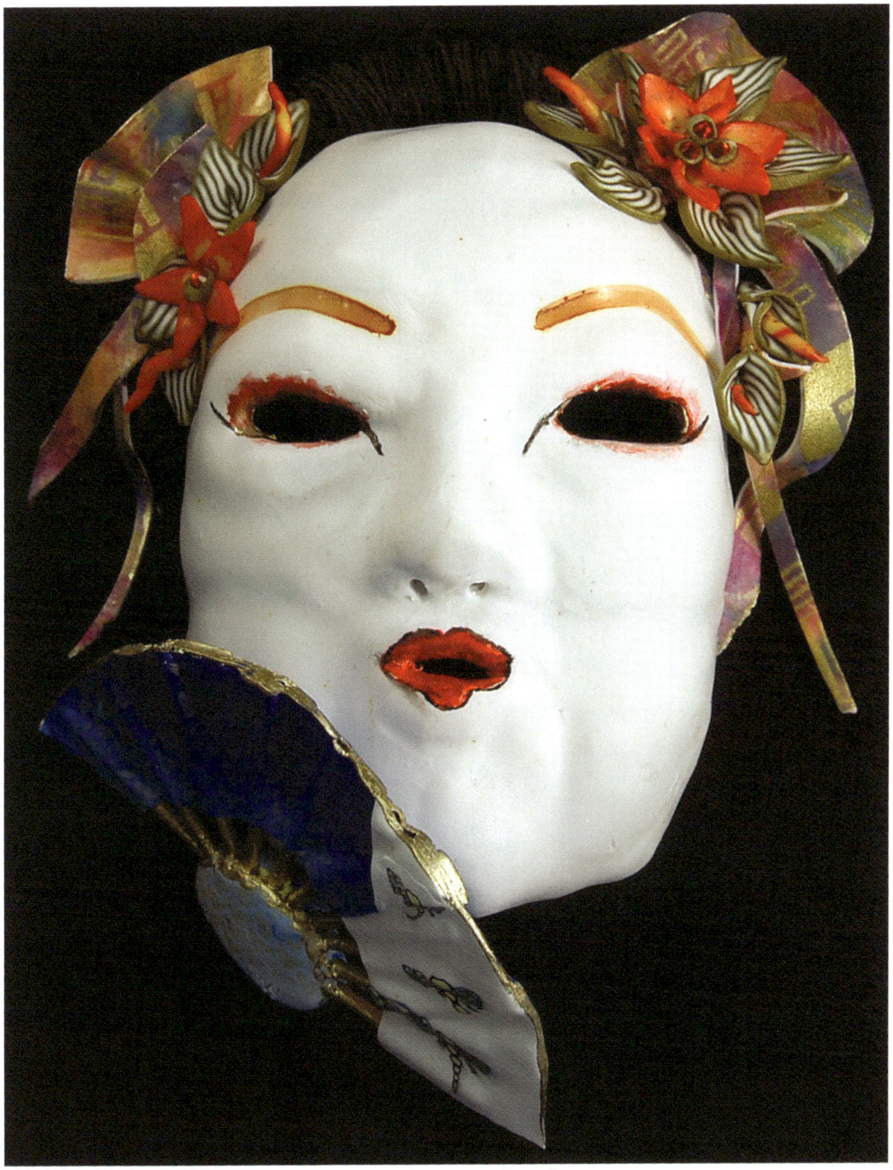

Rebecca Wells Stout *photo Mark Stout* 6" x 6"

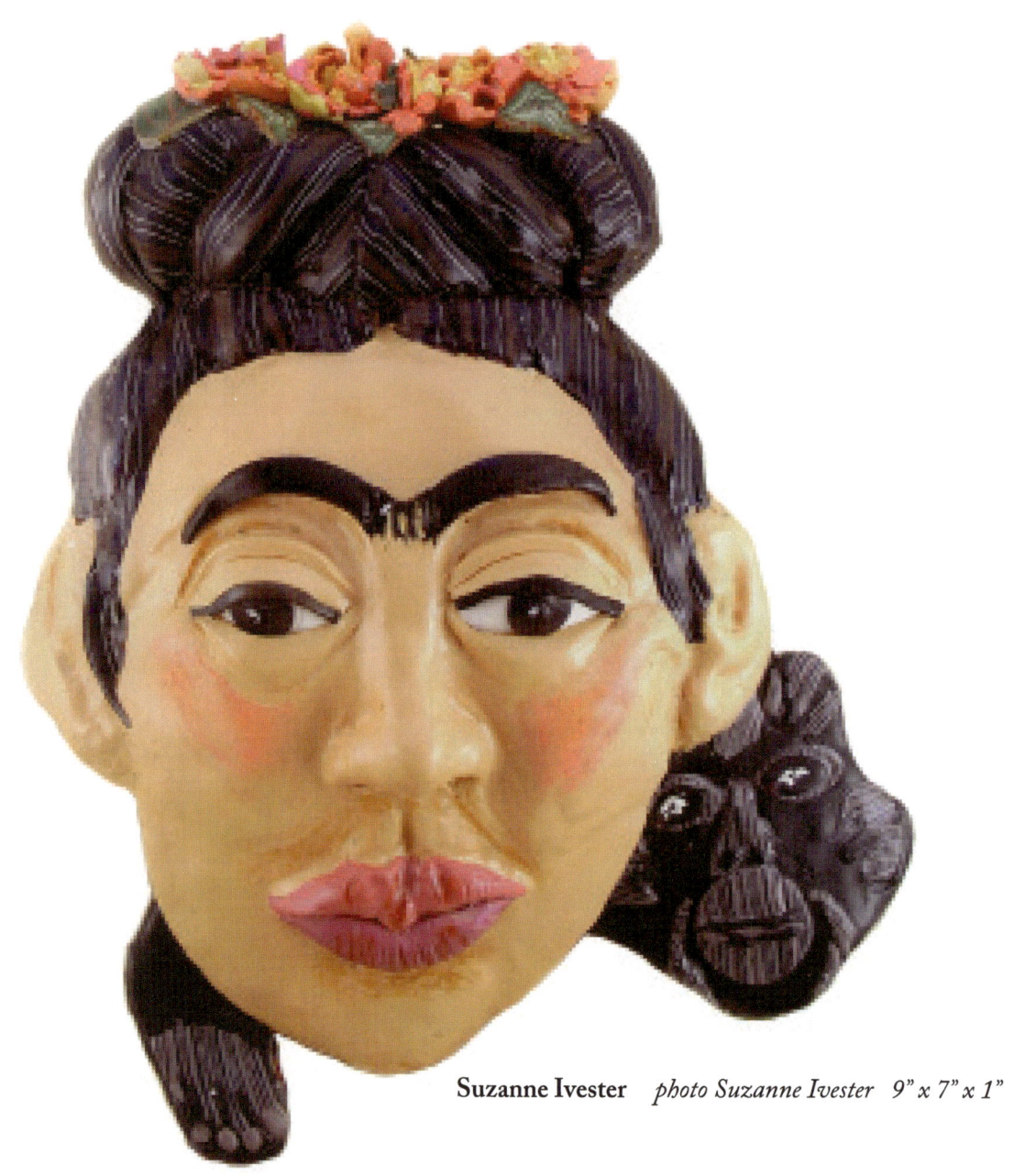

Suzanne Ivester   *photo Suzanne Ivester   9" x 7" x 1"*

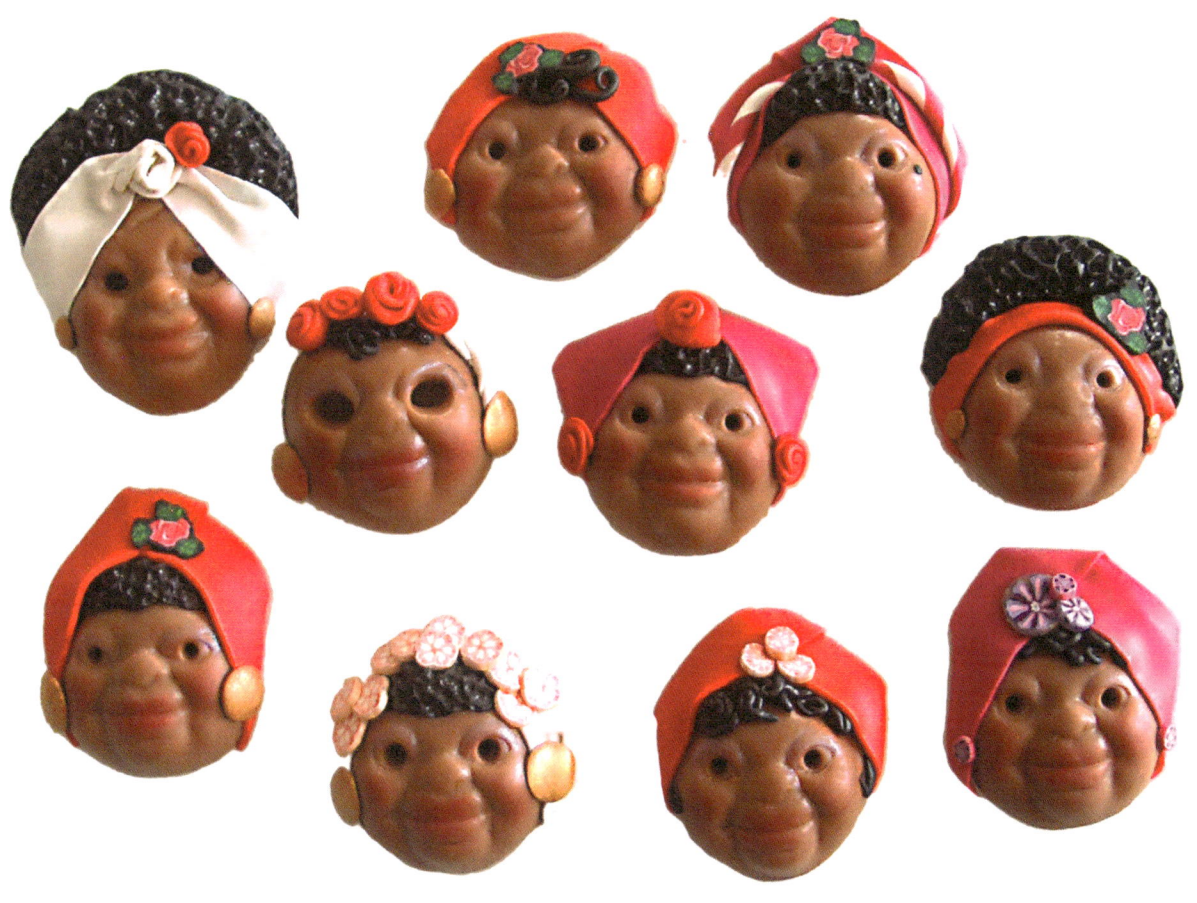

Lala Ortiz

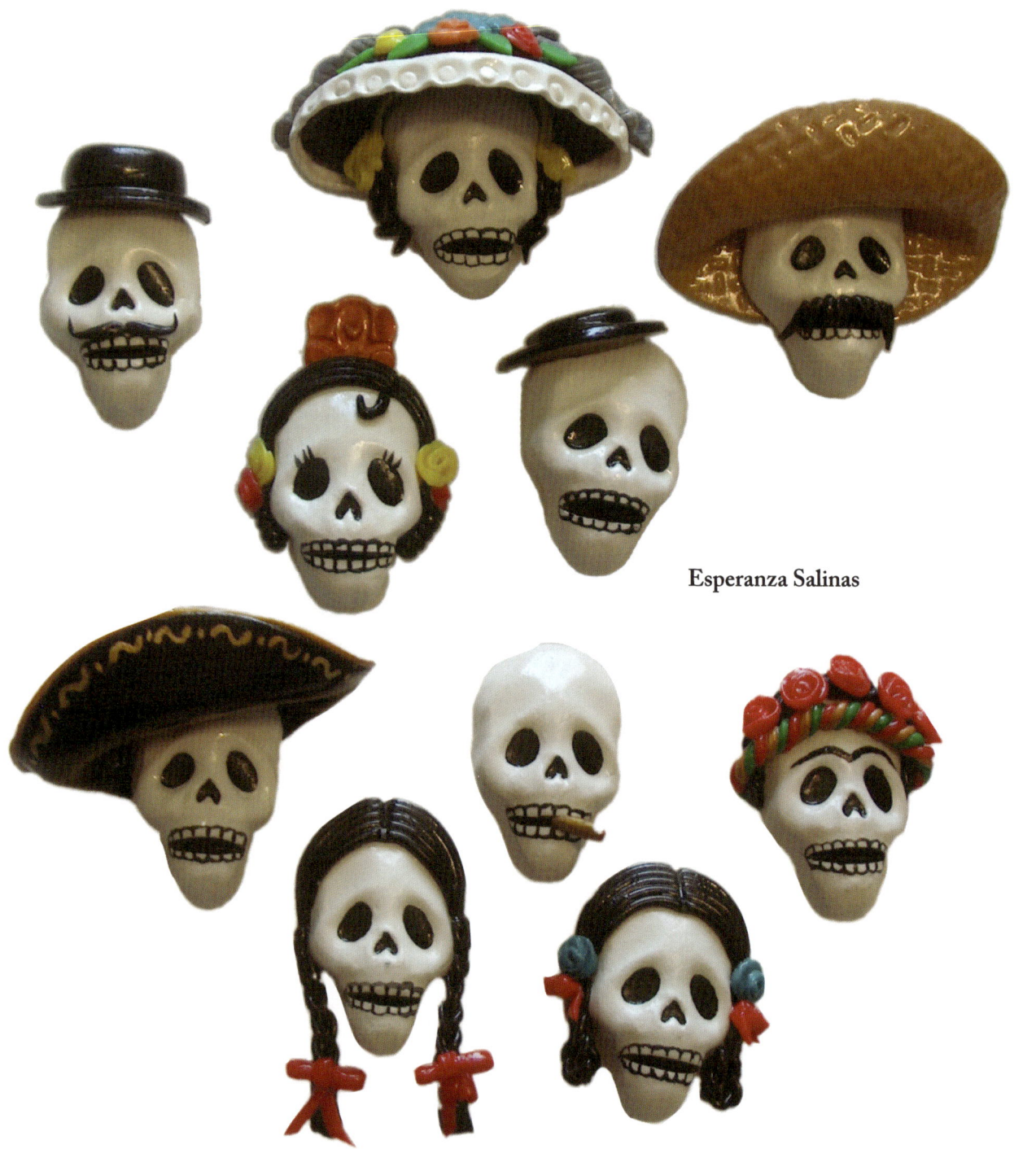

Esperanza Salinas

A Collection Of Polymer Clay Masks

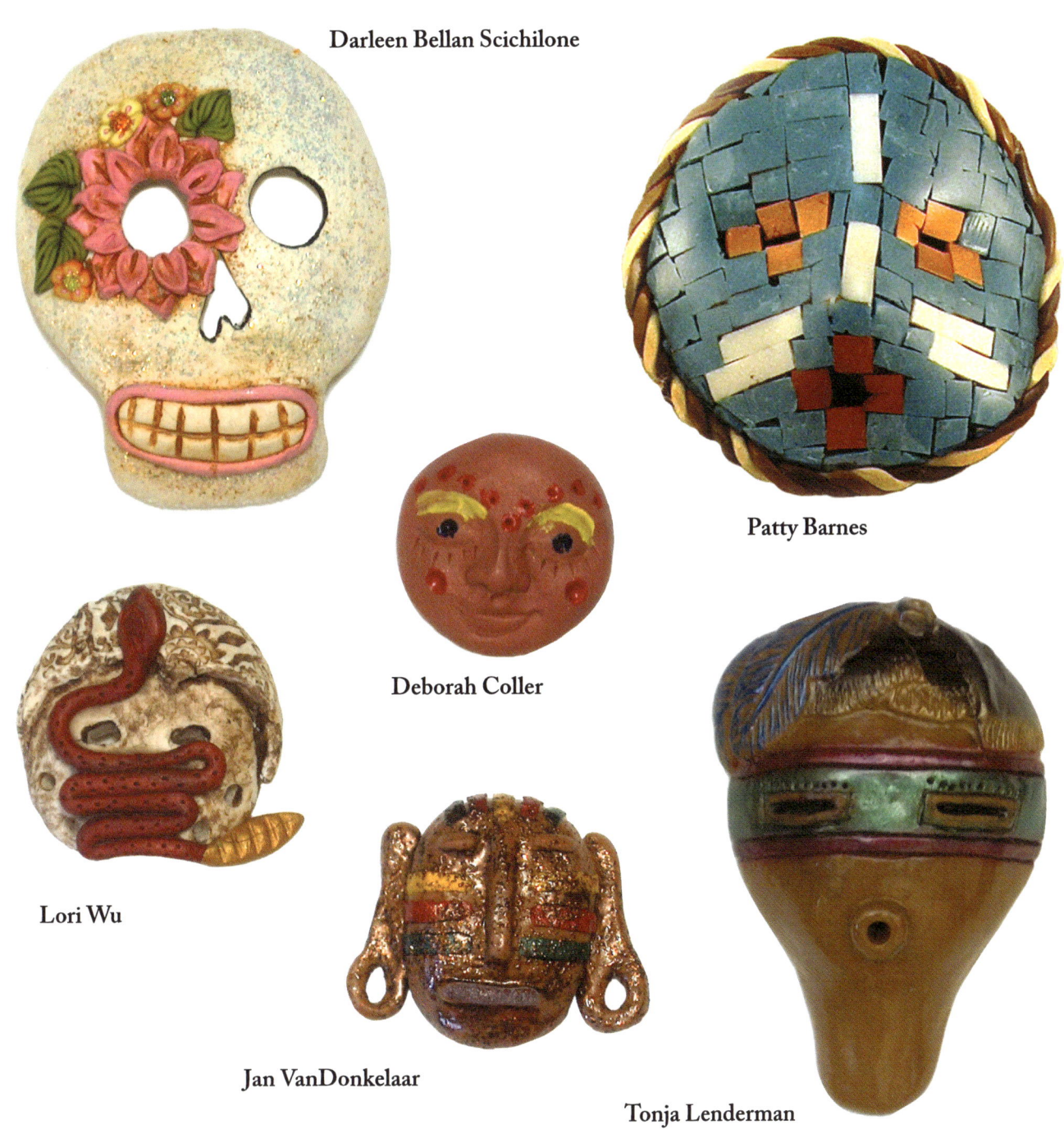

Darleen Bellan Scichilone

Patty Barnes

Deborah Coller

Lori Wu

Jan VanDonkelaar

Tonja Lenderman

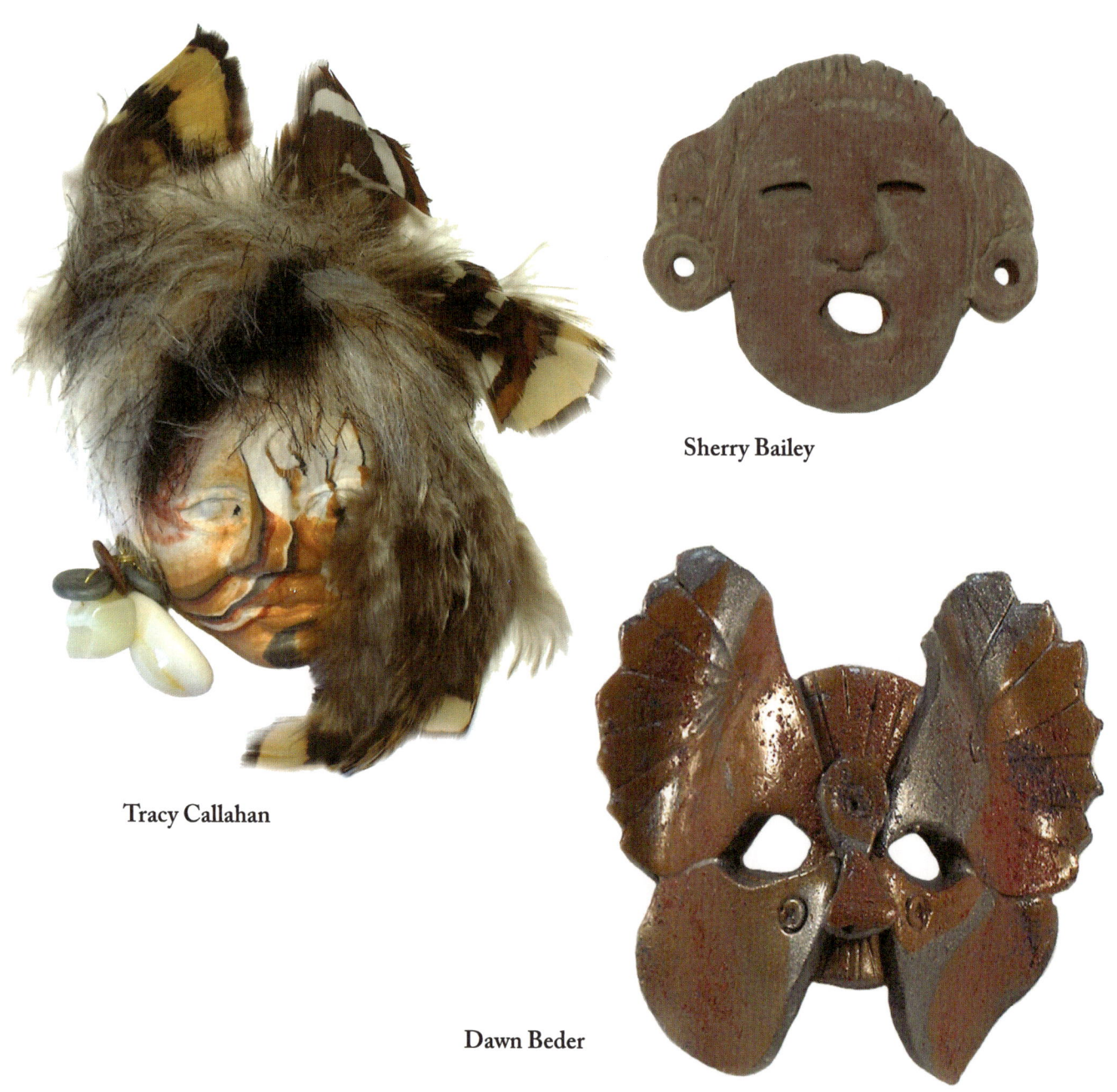

Sherry Bailey

Tracy Callahan

Dawn Beder

A Collection Of Polymer Clay Masks

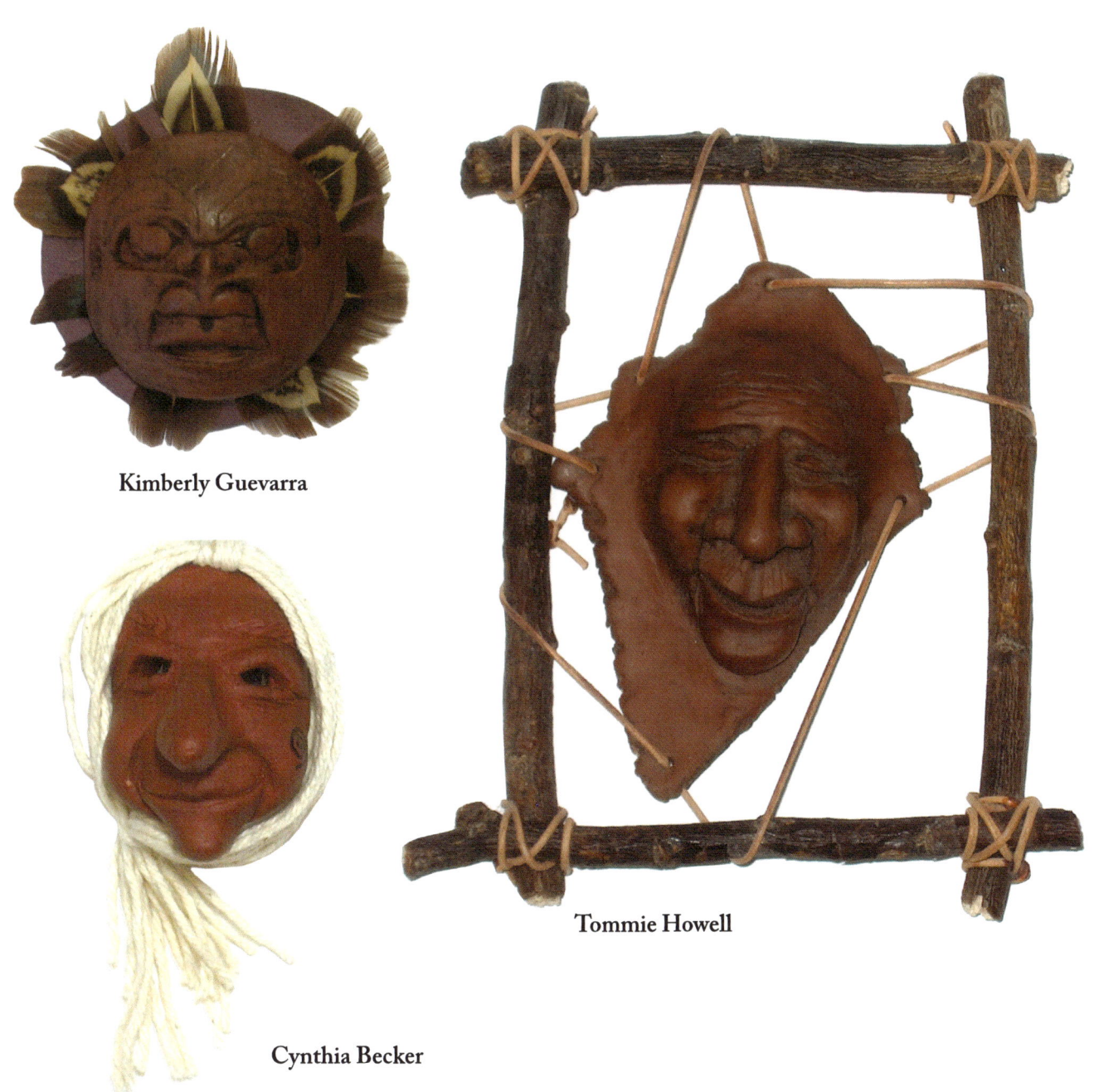

Kimberly Guevarra

Cynthia Becker

Tommie Howell

PolyMarket Press

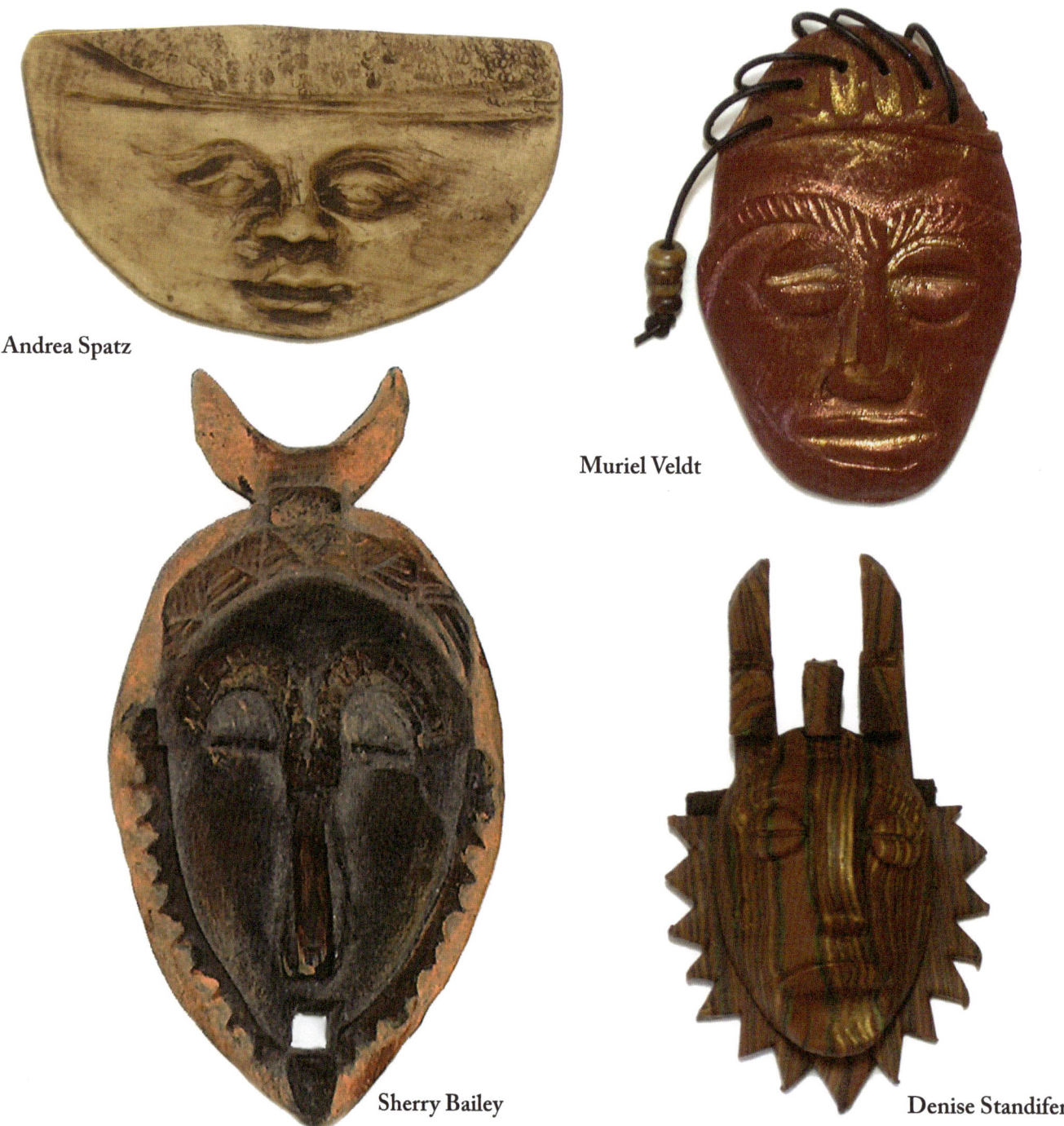

Andrea Spatz

Muriel Veldt

Sherry Bailey

Denise Standifer

A Collection Of Polymer Clay Masks

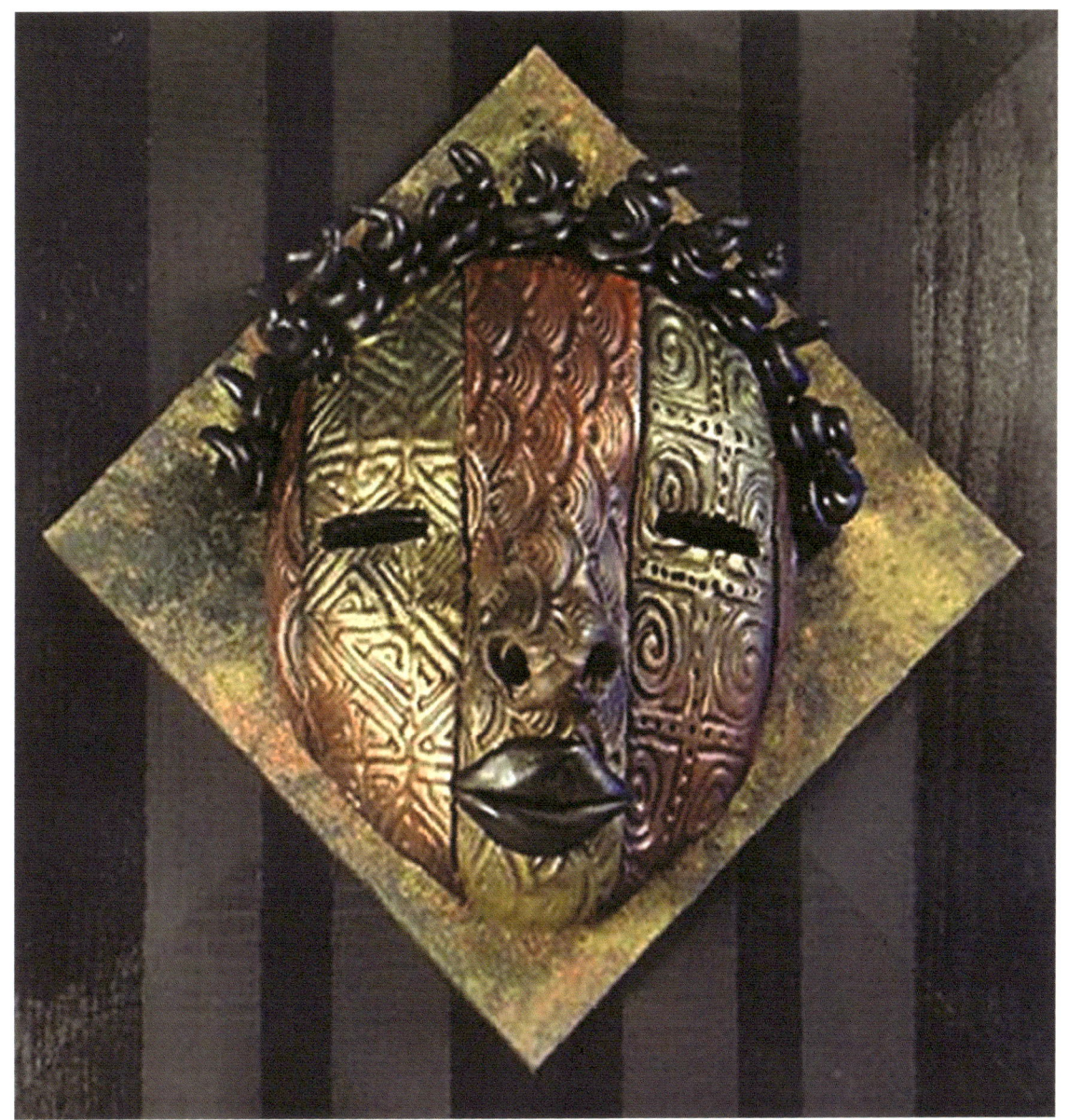

Michelle Petelinz   *photo Stan Petelinz*   10" x 10"

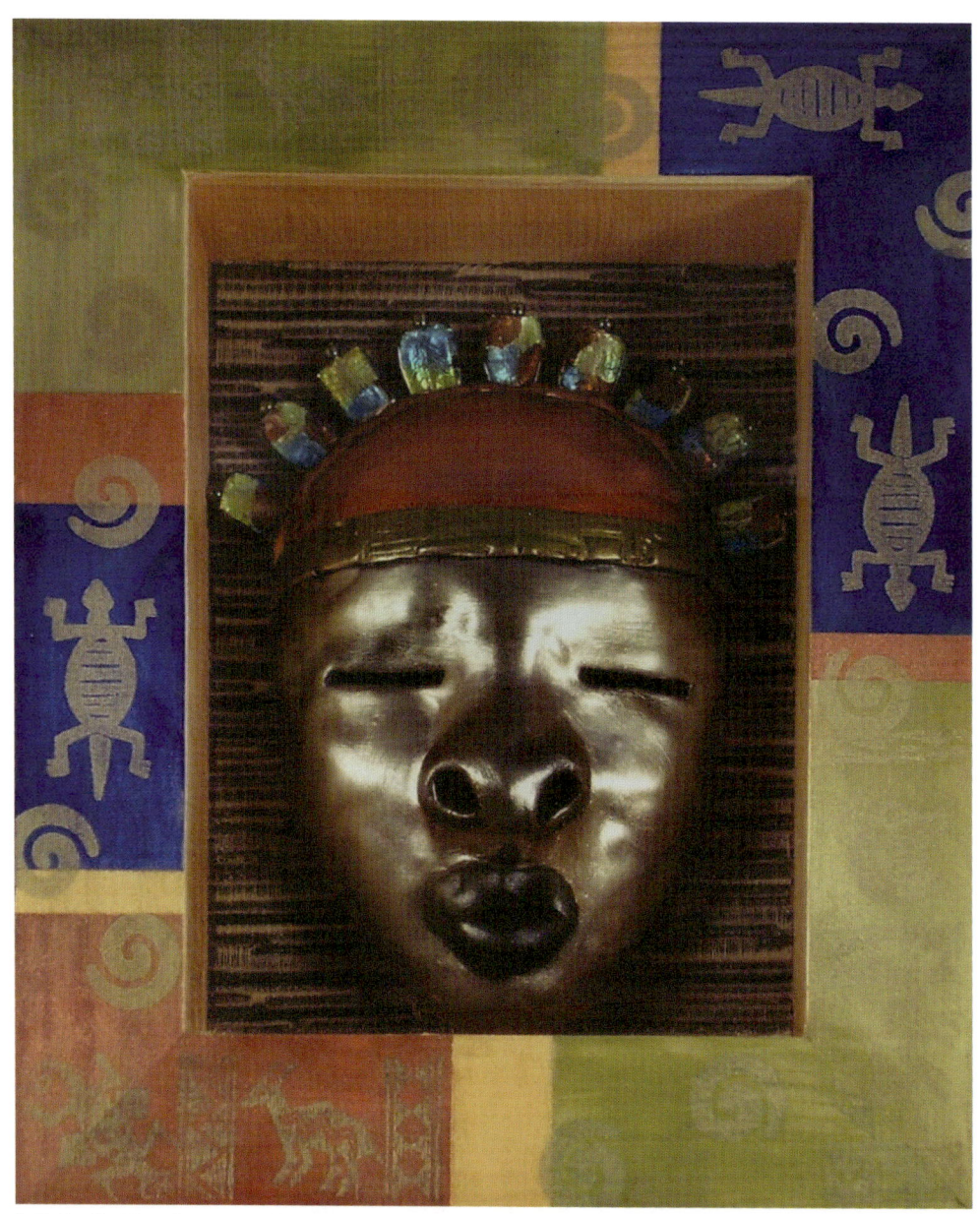

Michelle Petelinz   *photo Stan Petelinz*   10" x 8"

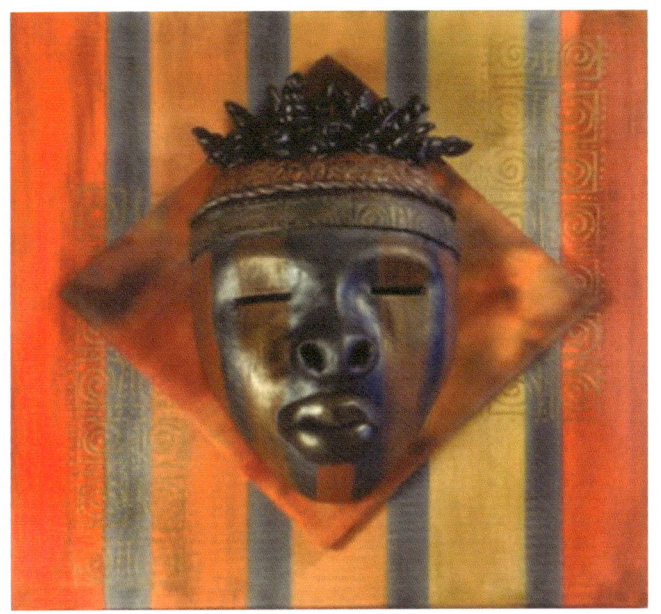

Michelle Petelinz   *photo Stan Petelinz*   10" x 10"

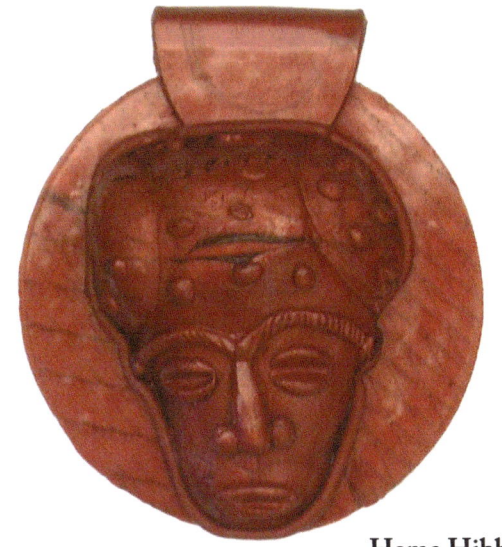

Hema Hibbert

Jackie Hollis

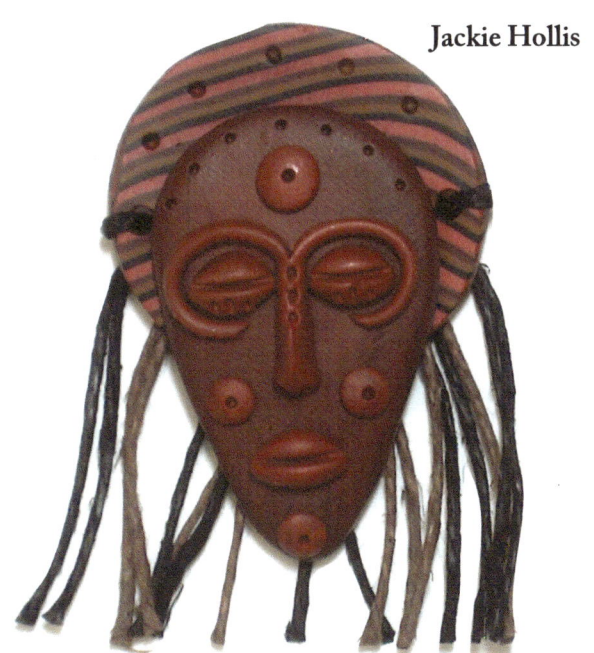

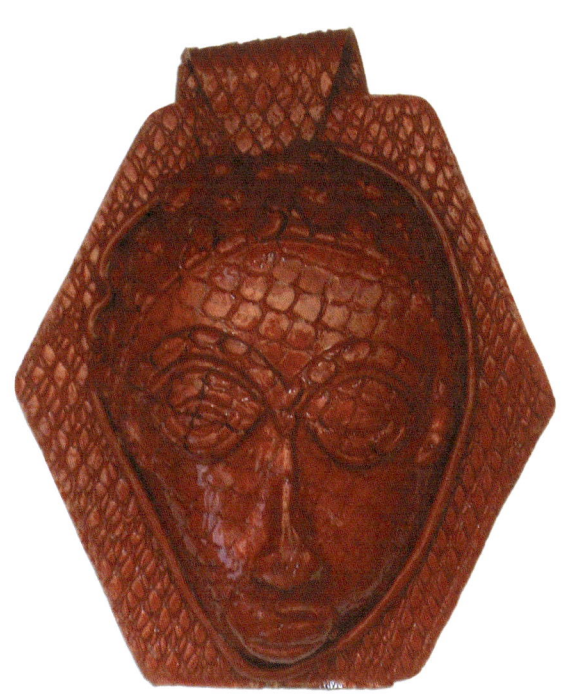

Hema Hibbert

PolyMarket Press

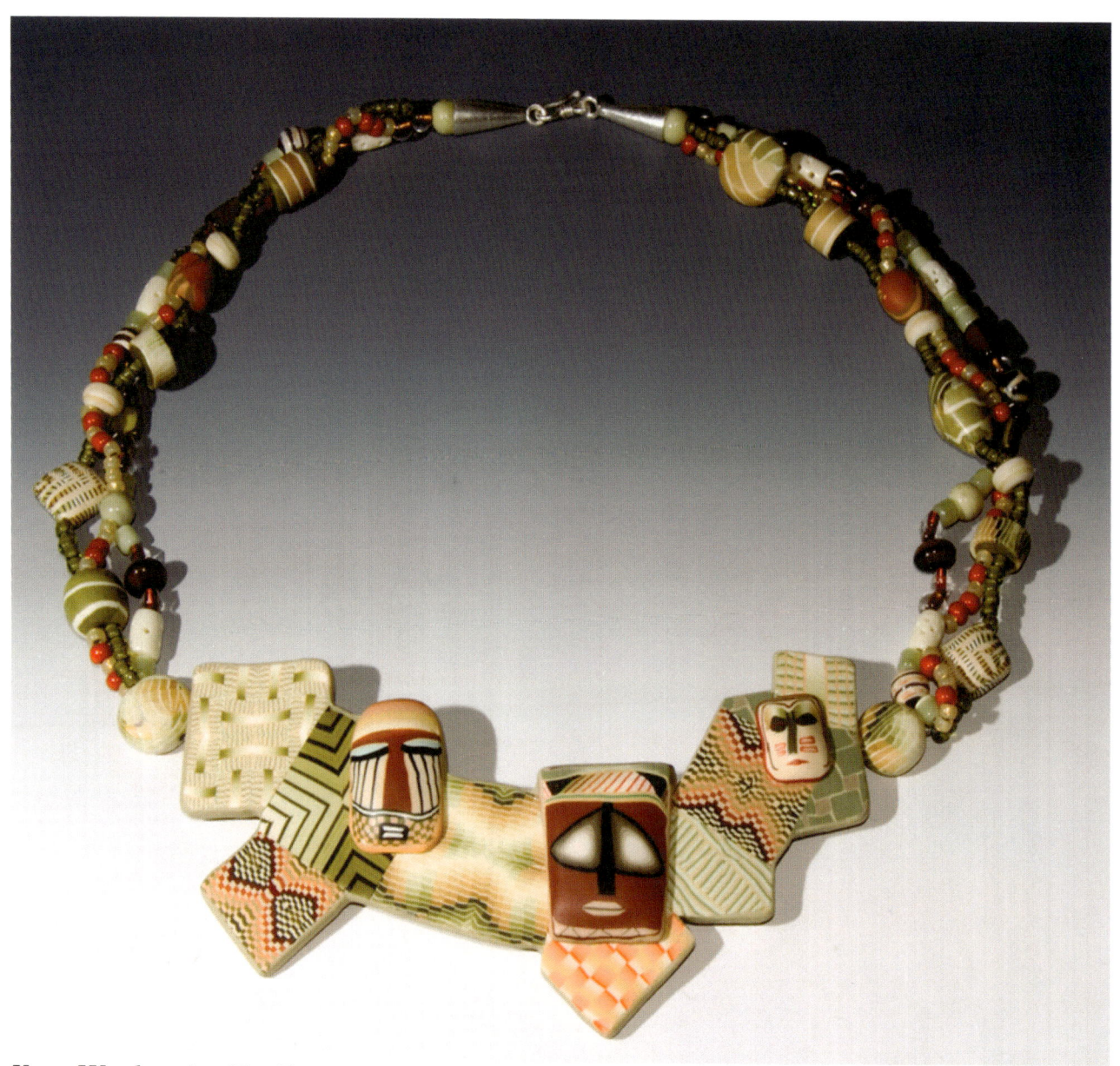

Karen Woods *photo Tom Frazier*

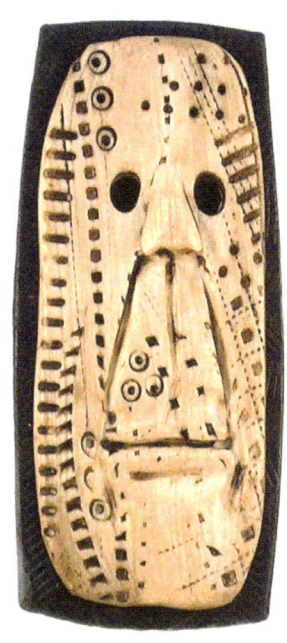

Ellen Rumsey Bellenot

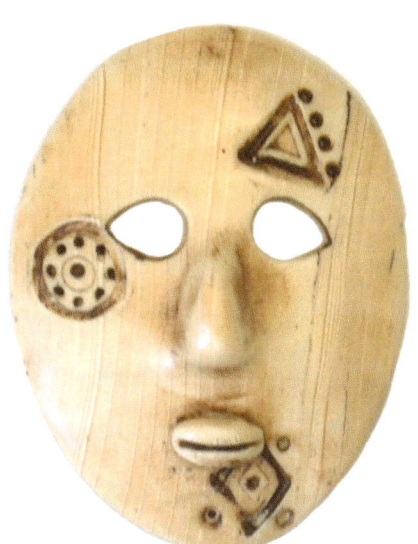

Karen Scudder

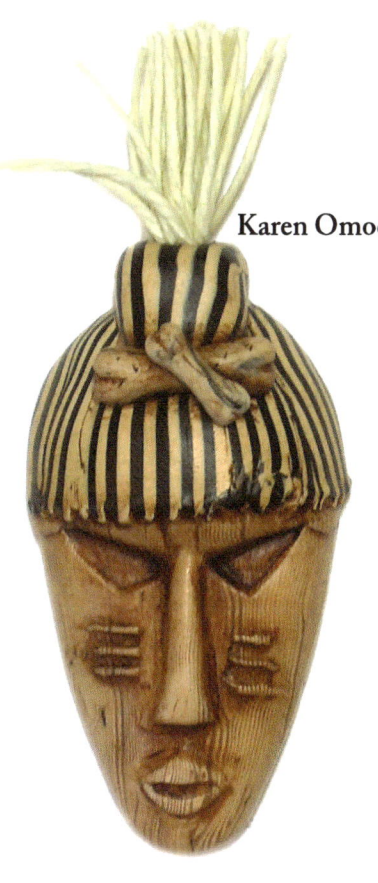

Karen Omodt

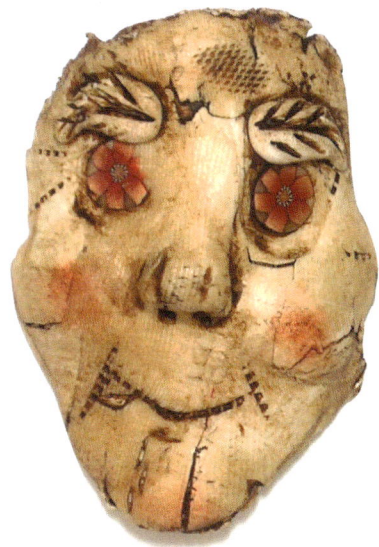

Diane MacCallum

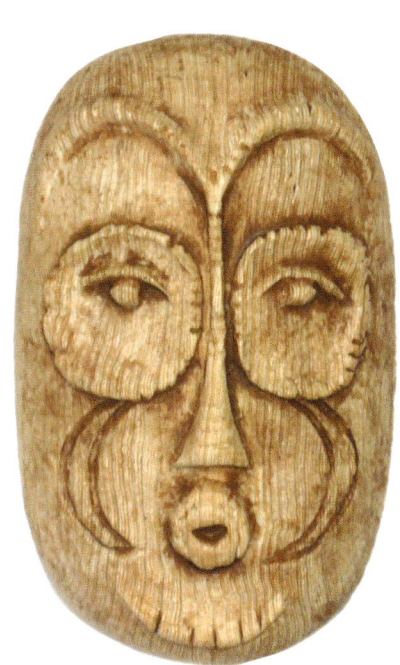

Tonja Lenderman

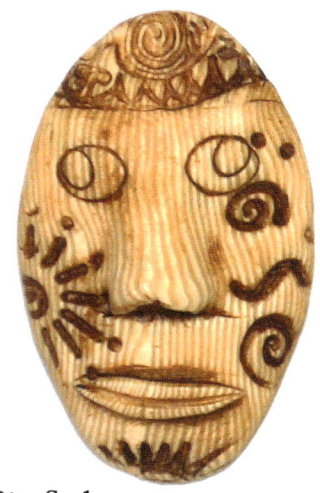

Rita Seale

PolyMarket Press

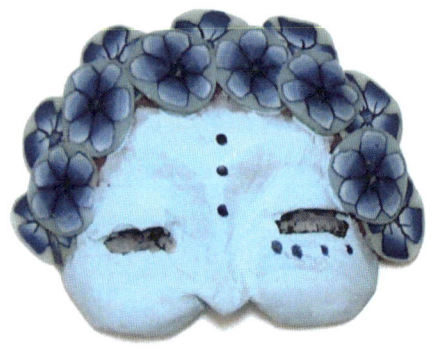

Elaine Robitaille

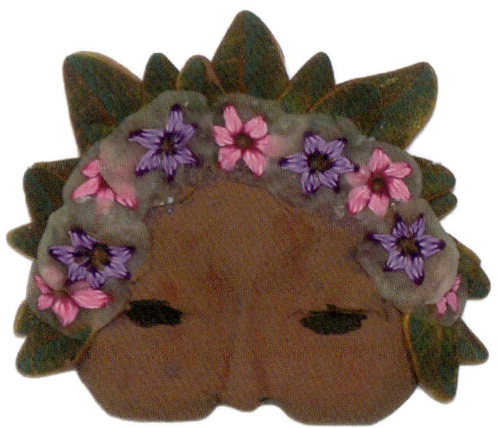

Elaine Robitaille

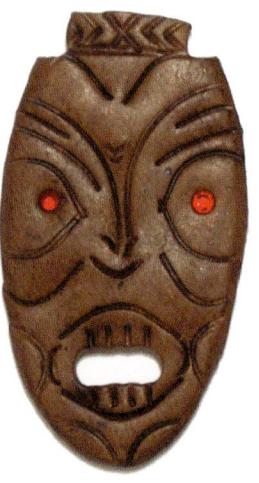

Kathi Briefer-Gose

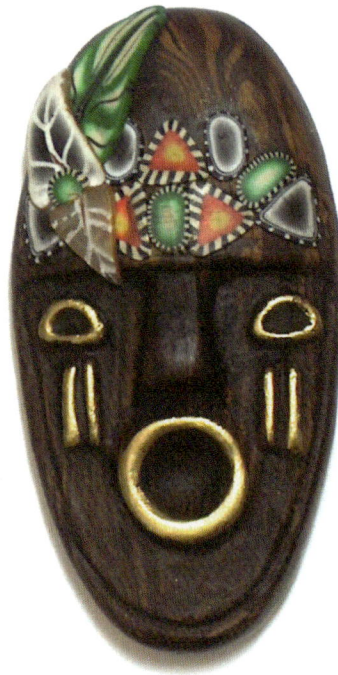

Karen Omodt

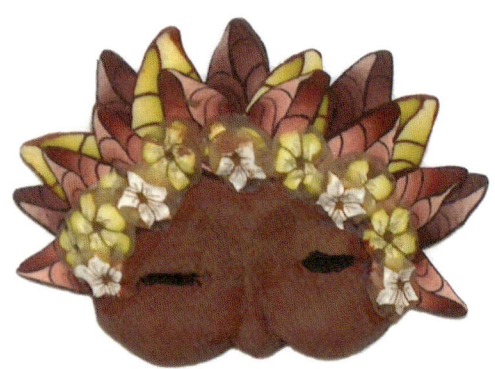

Elaine Robitaille

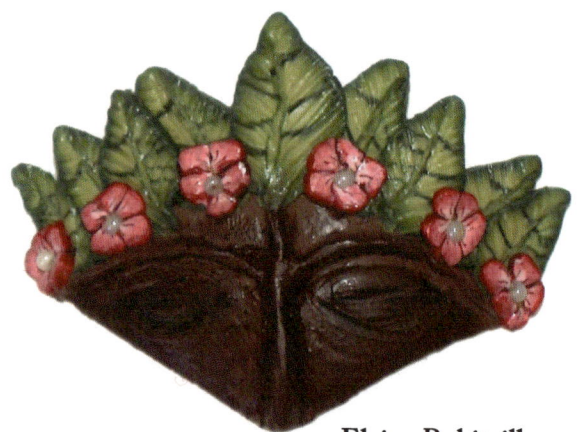

Elaine Robitaille

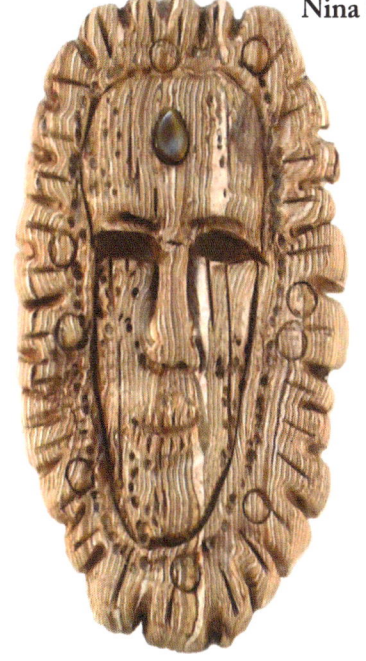
Nina Owens

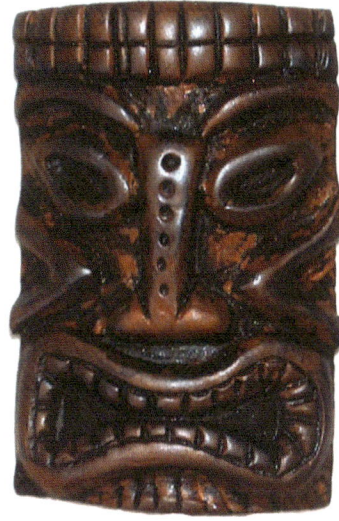
Jainnie Cox Jenkins

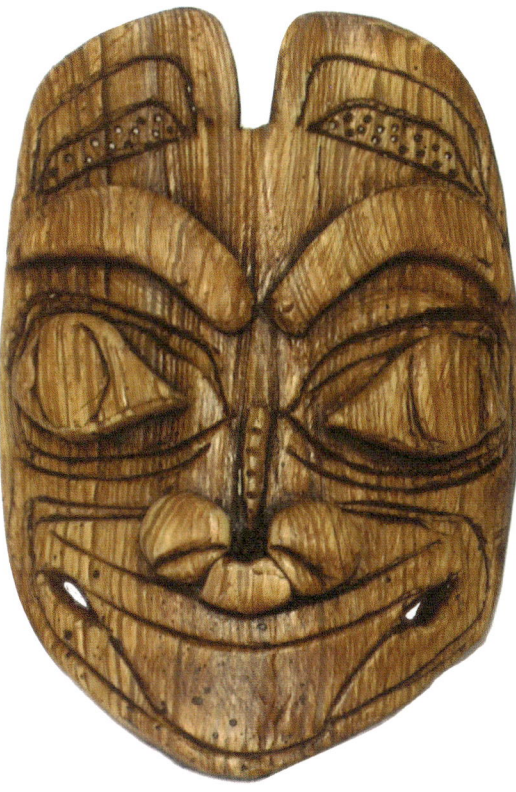
Tracy Callahan

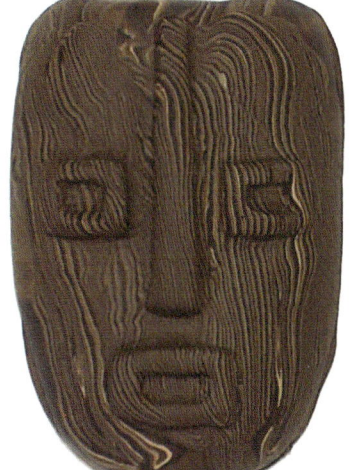
Sharon Mihalyak

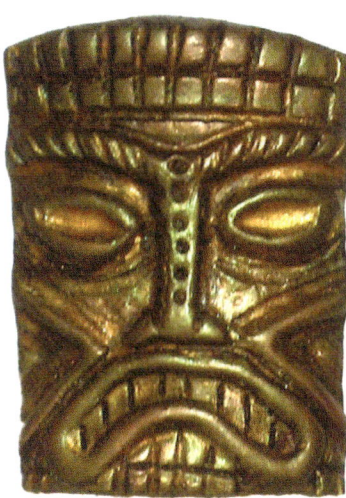
Jainnie Cox Jenkins

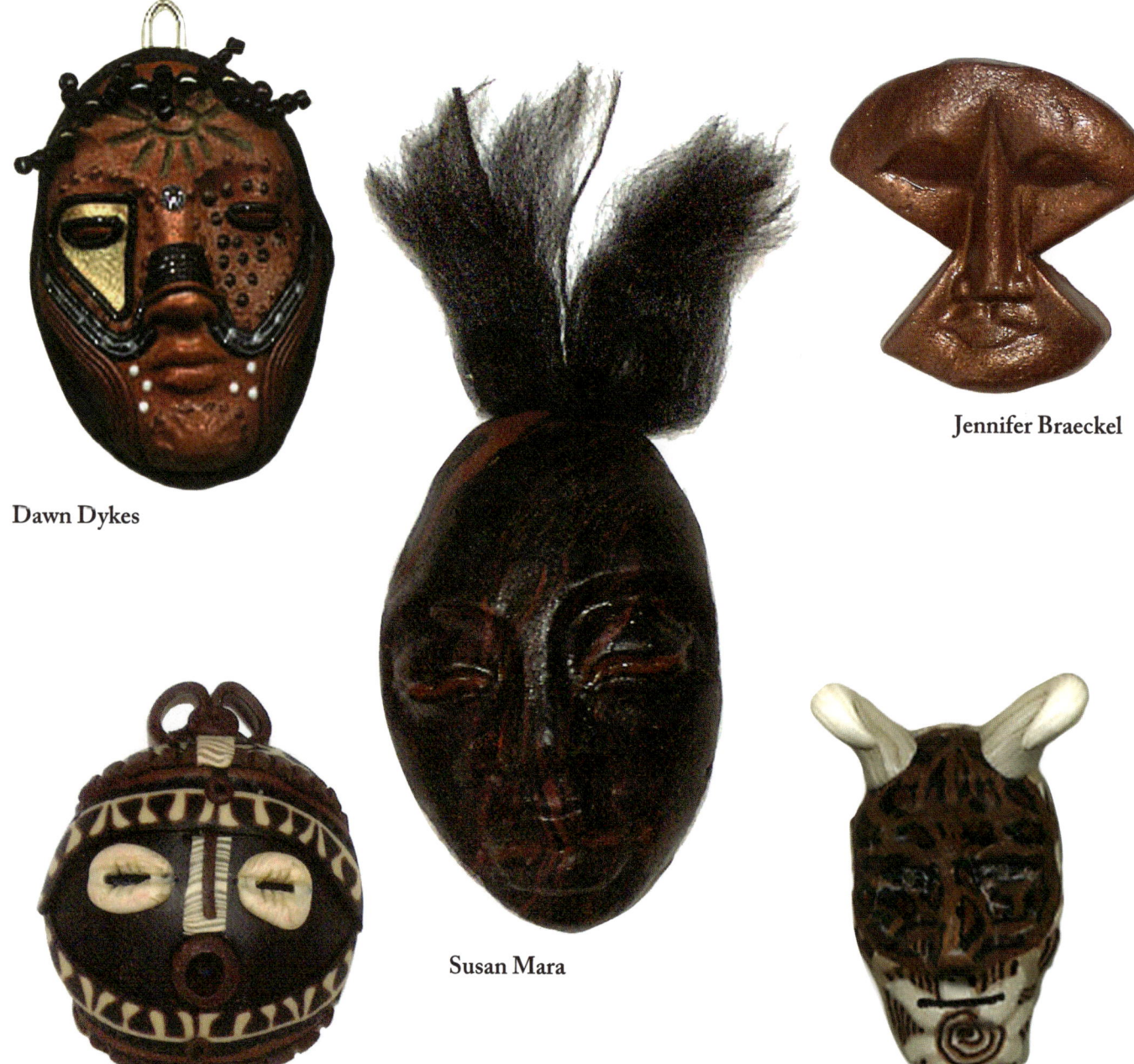

Dawn Dykes

Jennifer Braeckel

Susan Mara

Lynne DeNio

Denise Standifer

A Collection Of Polymer Clay Masks

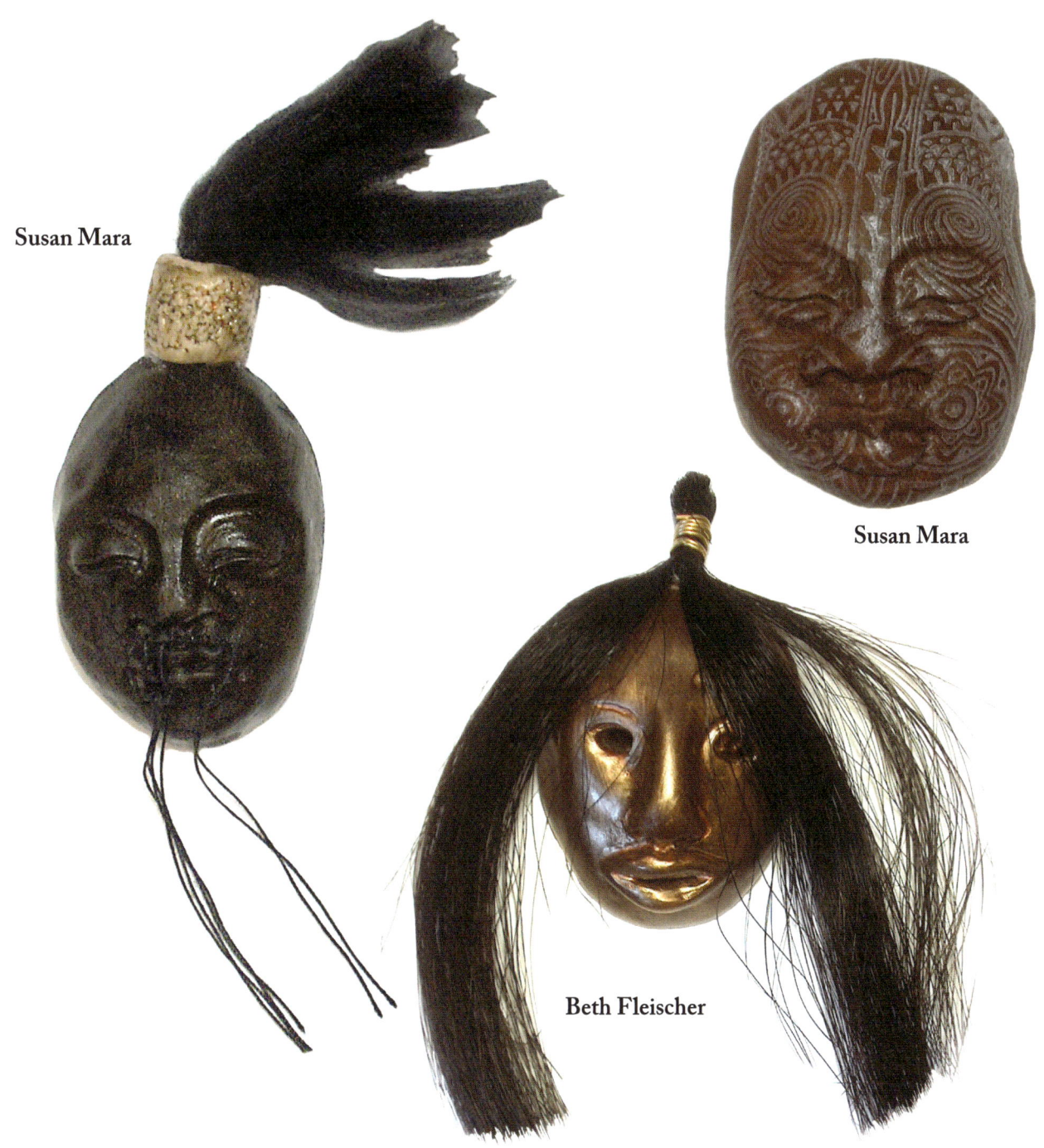

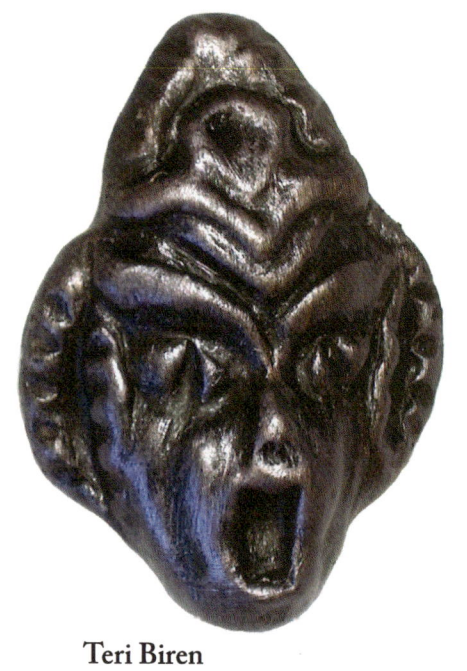

Jenn Dorion

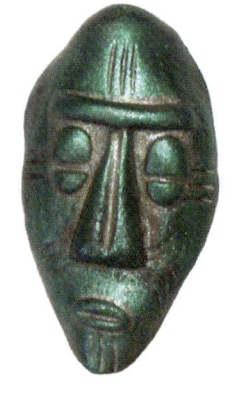

Karen Omodt

Teri Biren

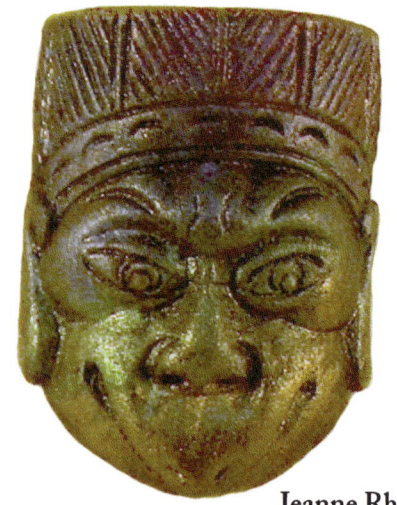

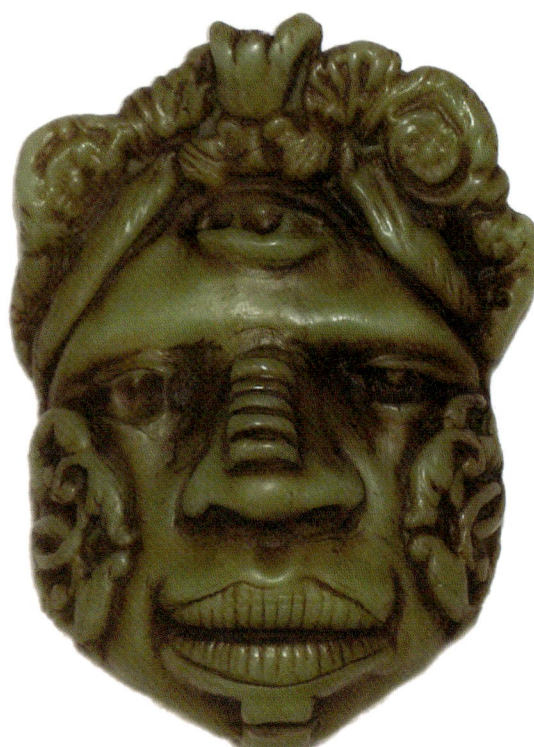

Rebecca Wells Stout

Jeanne Rhea

Michelle Zimmerman

A Collection Of Polymer Clay Masks

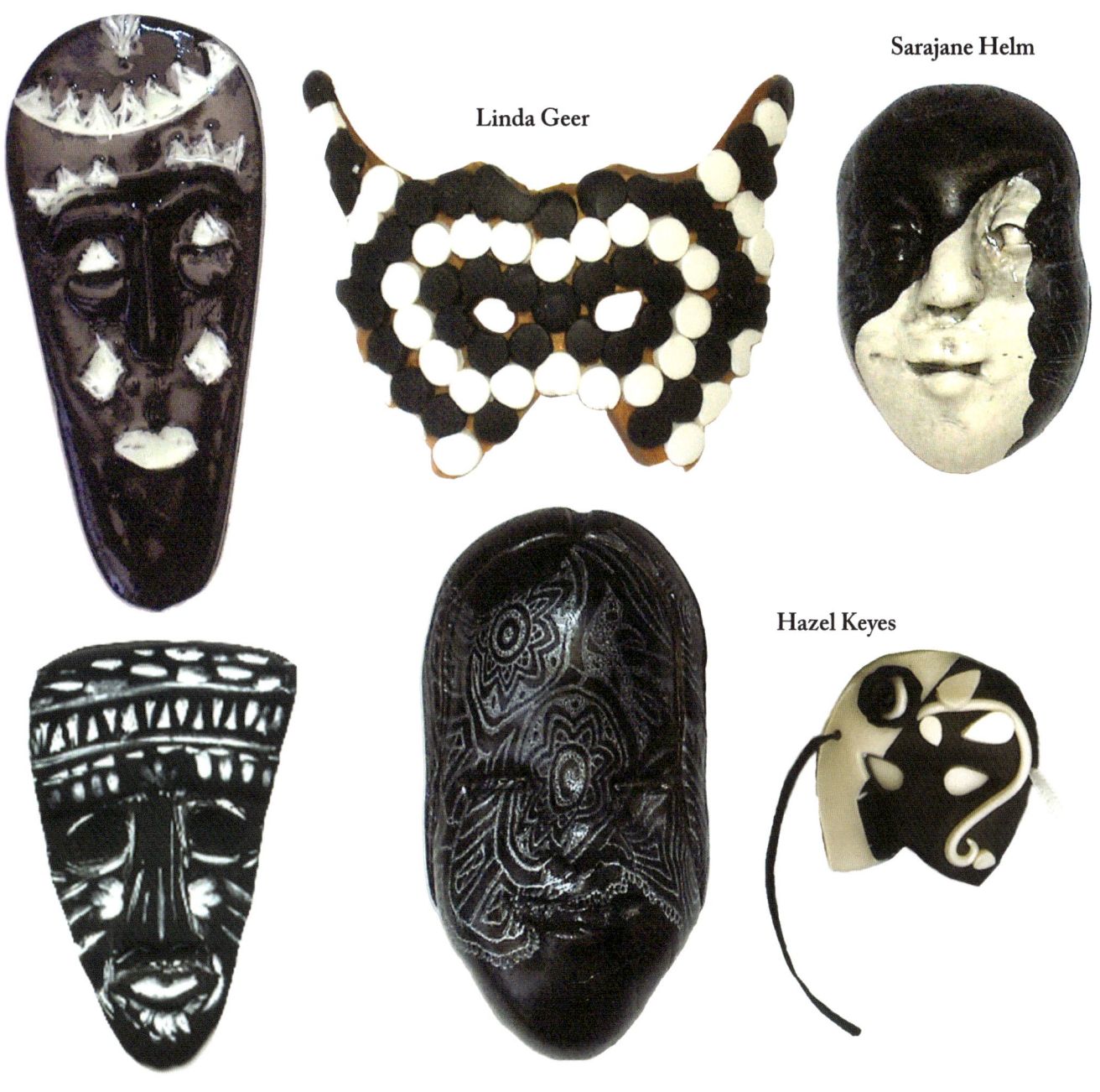

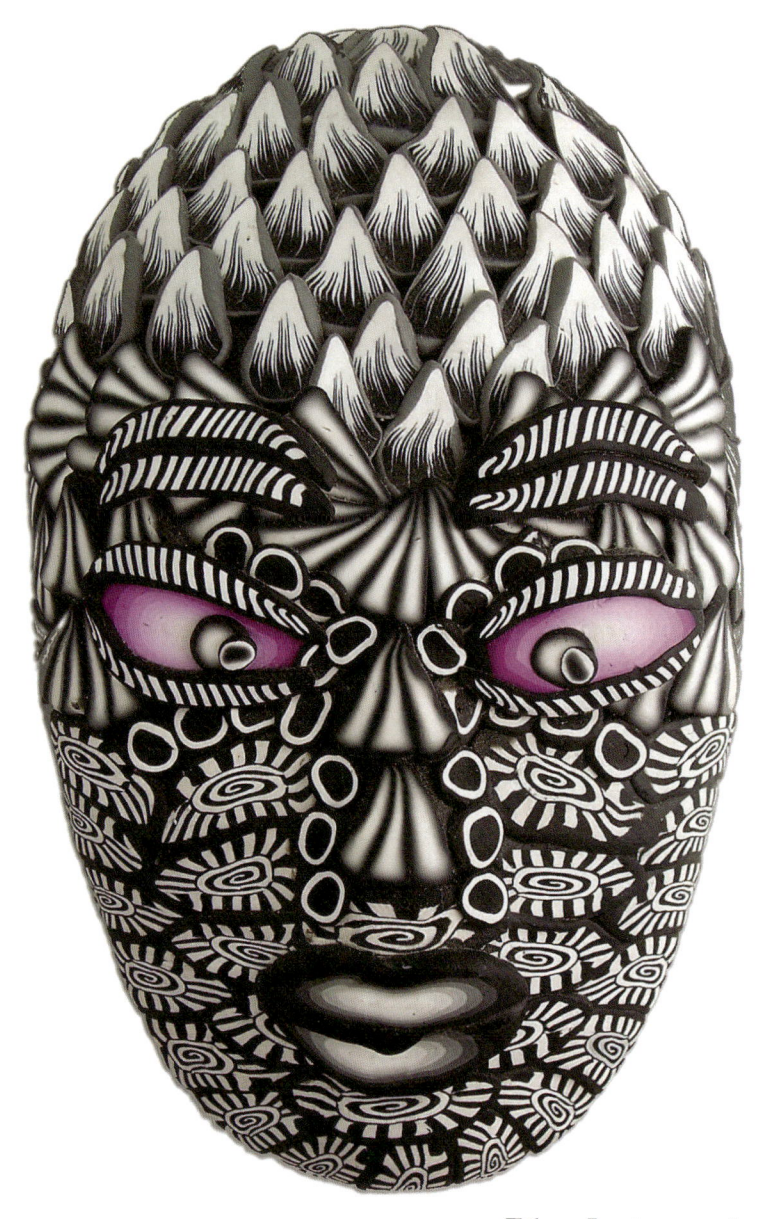

Eileen Loring   *photo Eileen Loring*

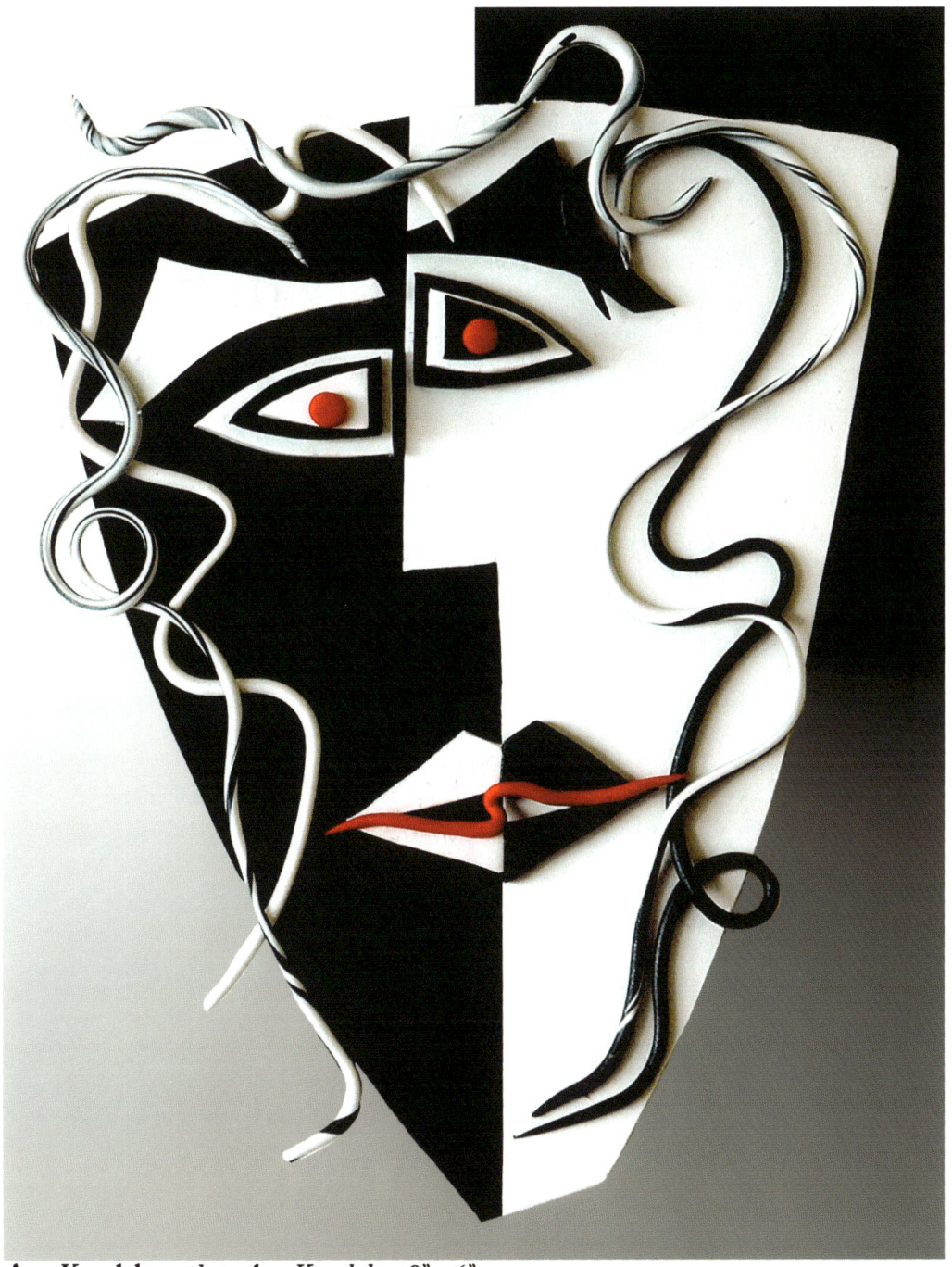

Ann Kruglak *photo Ann Kruglak 9" x 6"*

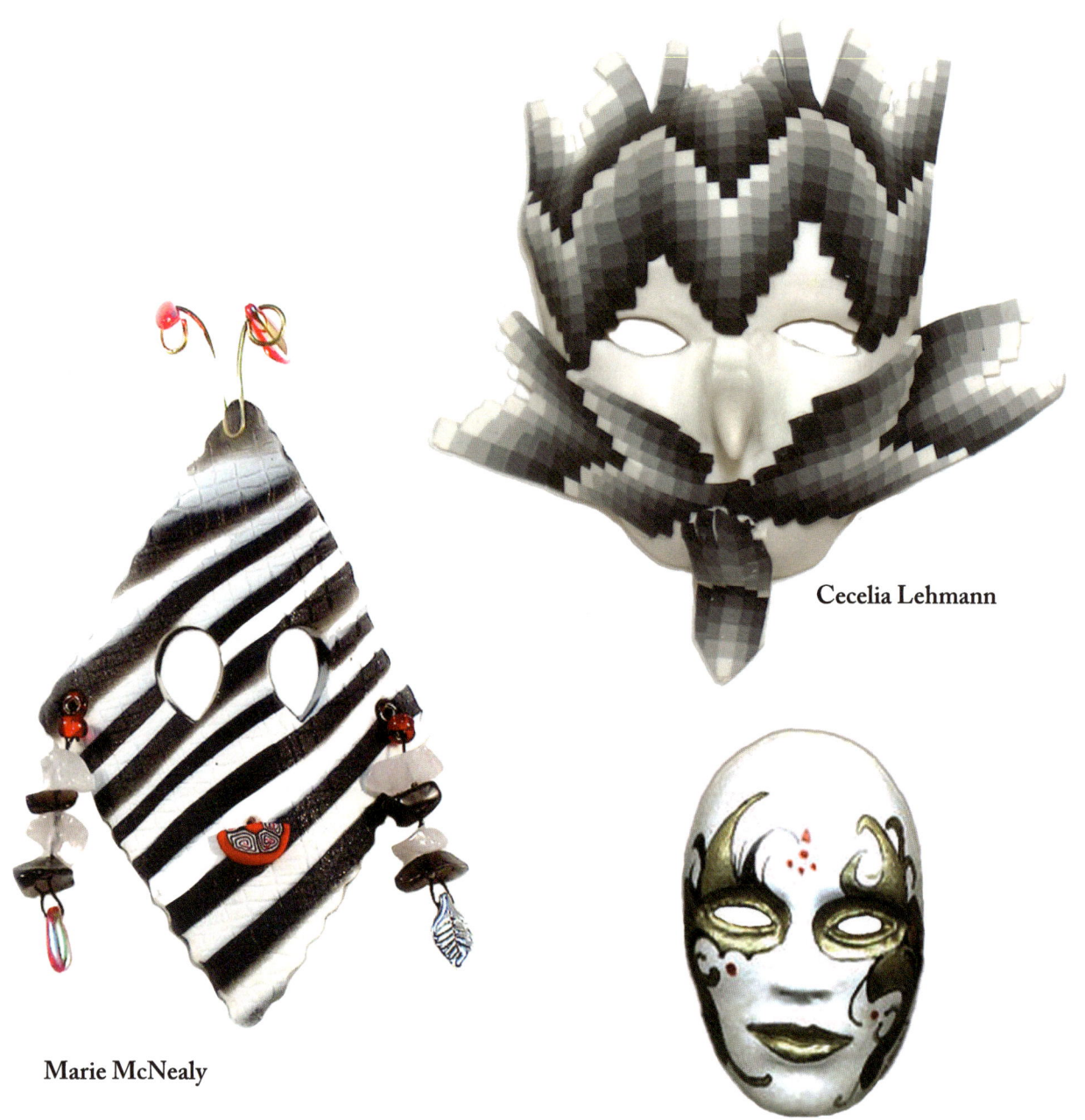

Cecelia Lehmann

Marie McNealy

Bill Girard

112

A Collection Of Polymer Clay Masks

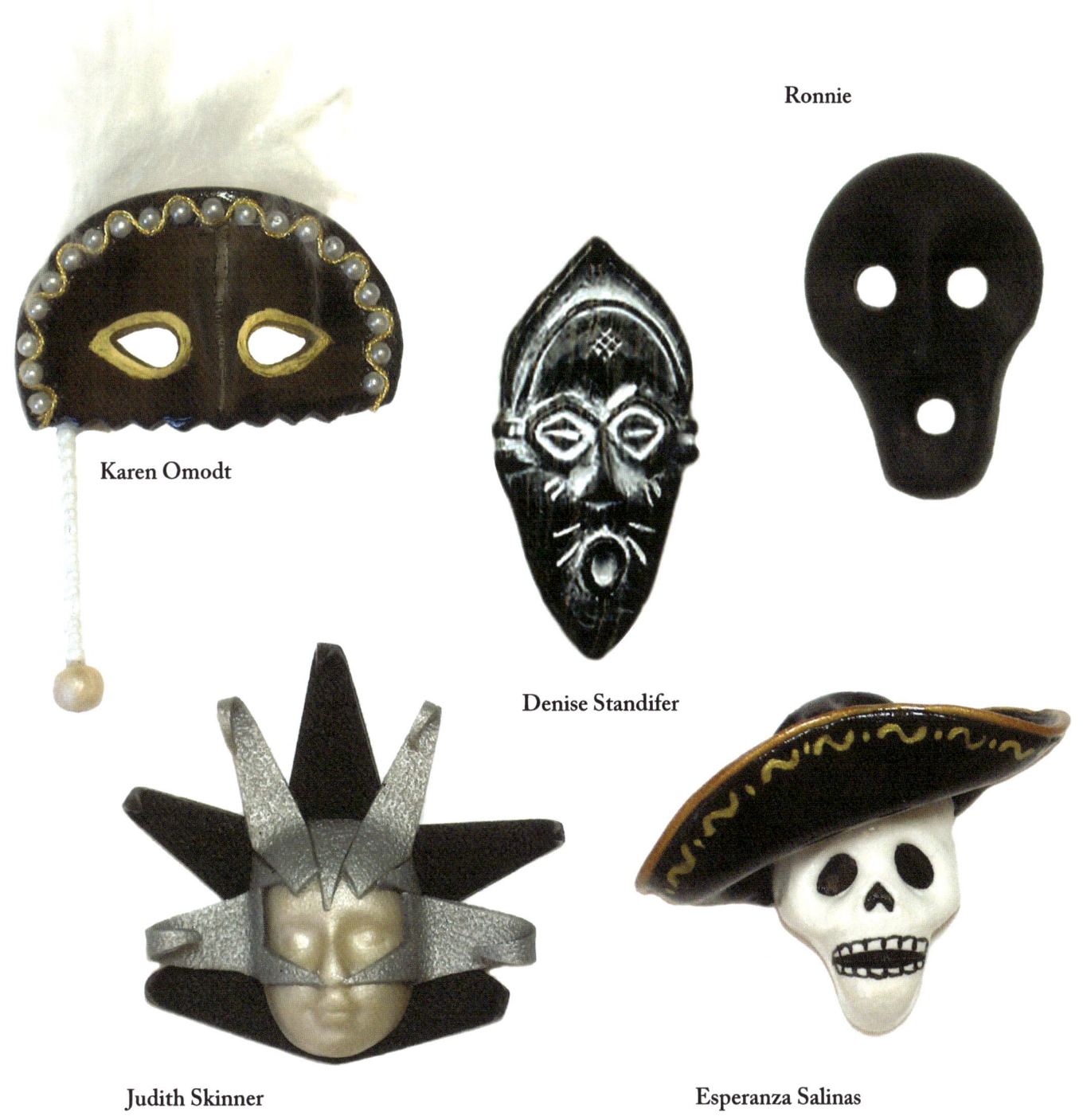

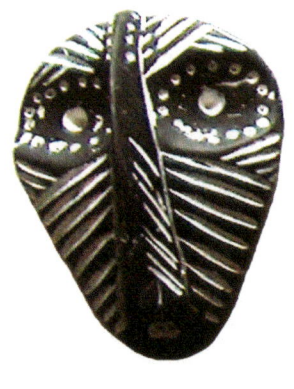 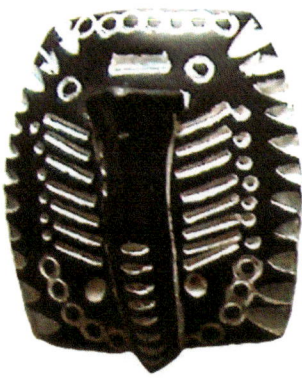 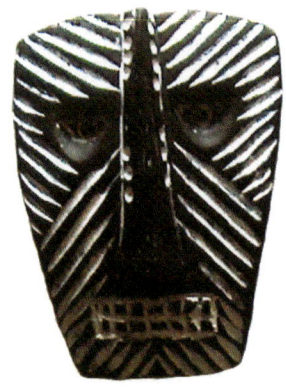 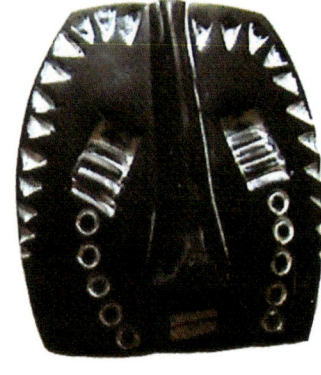

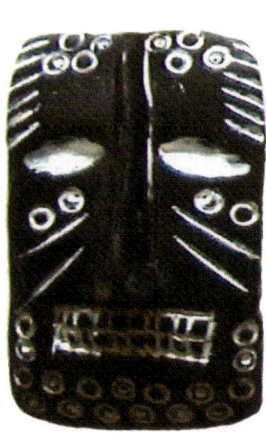 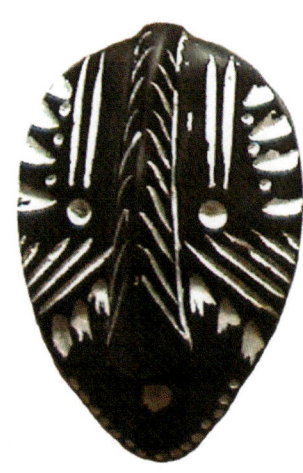 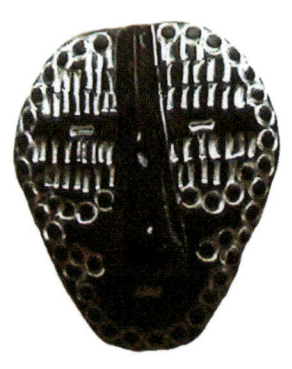 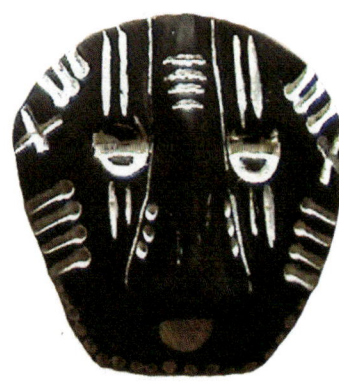

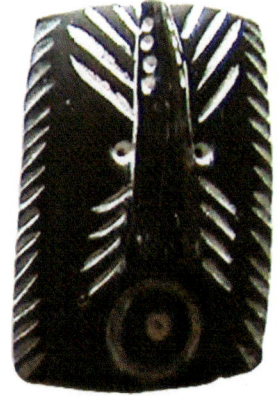 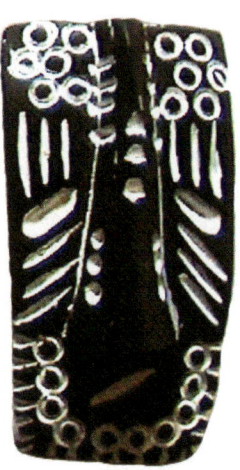

Melanie West

114 A Collection Of Polymer Clay Masks

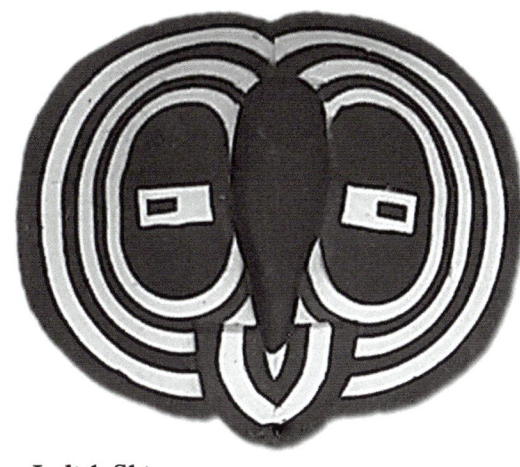

Judith Skinner

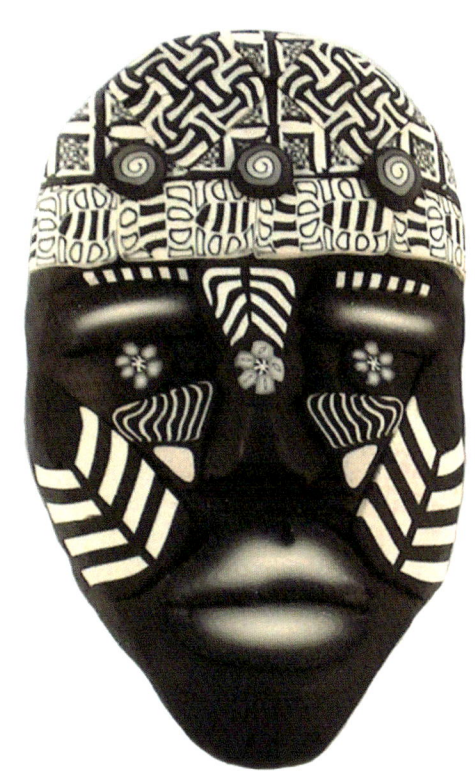

Diane MacCallum

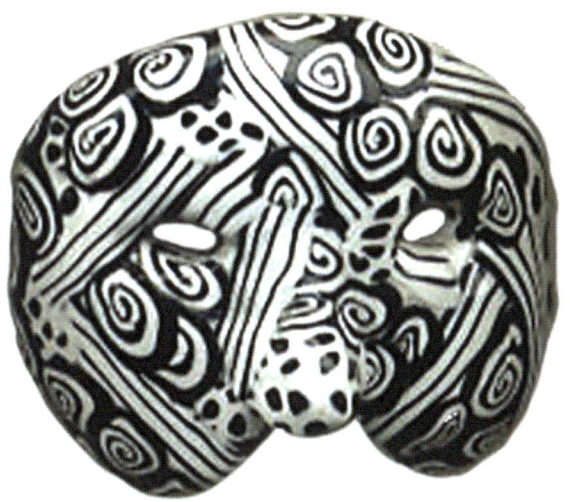

Gail Teunis

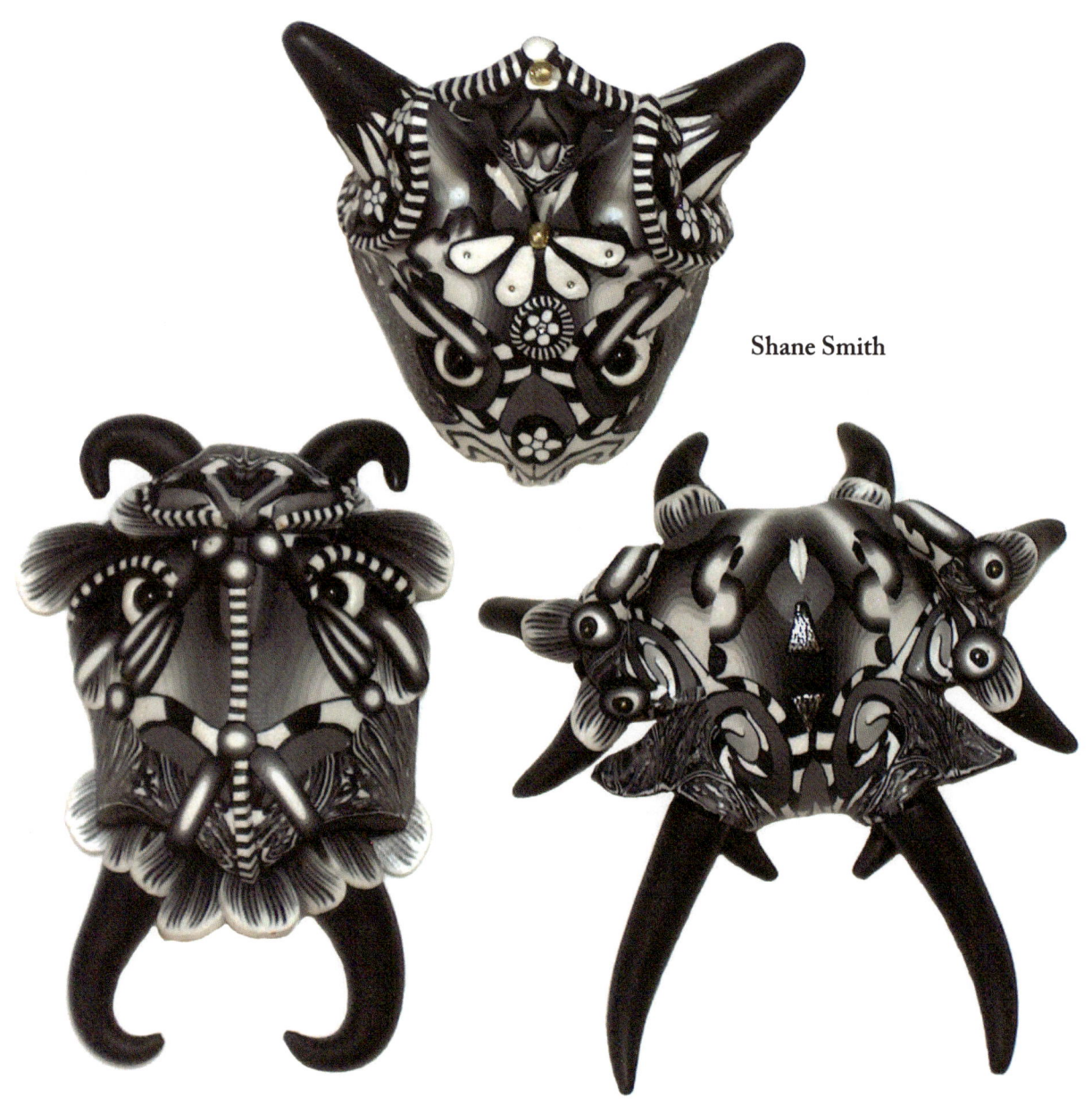

Shane Smith

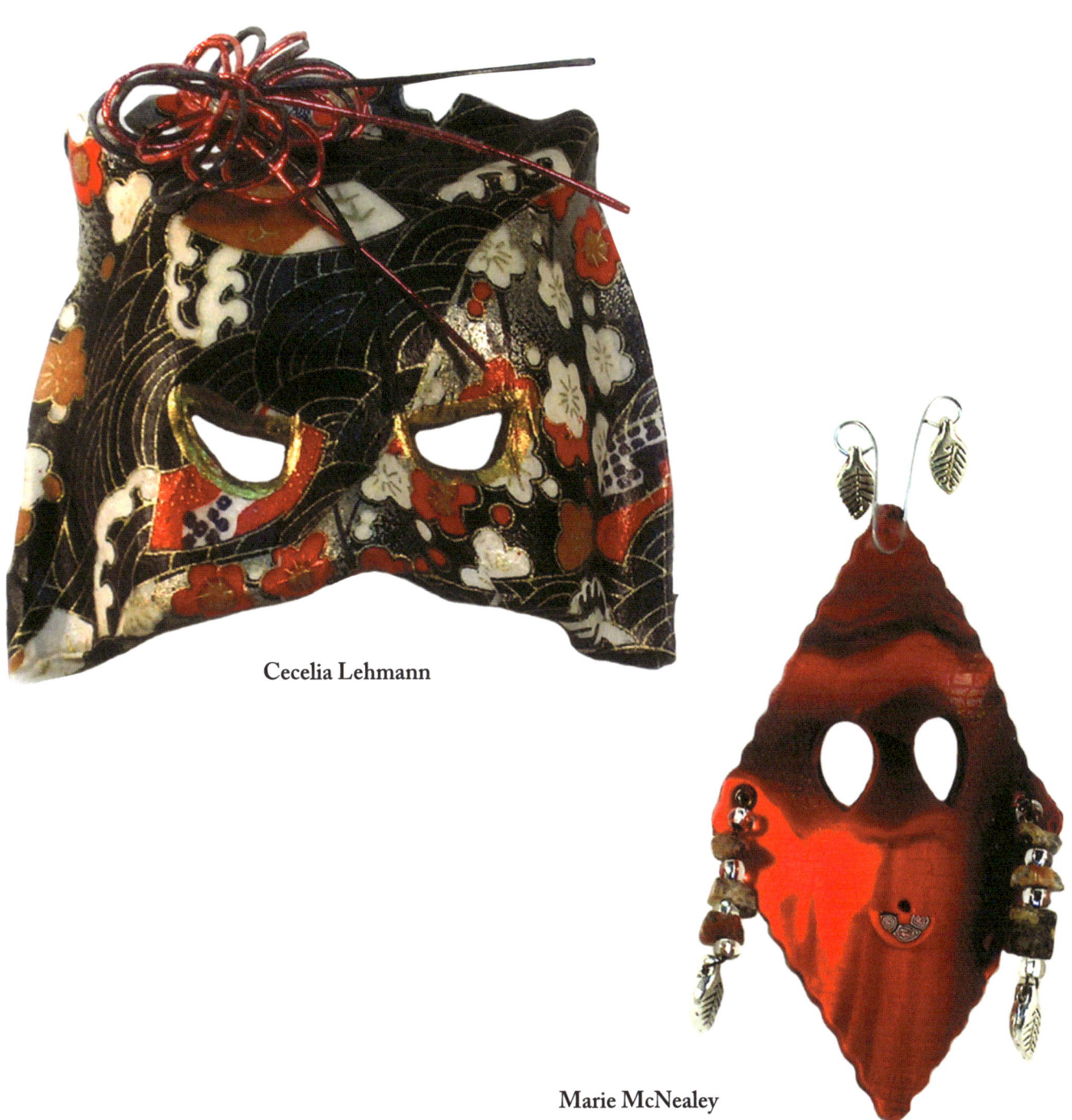

Cecelia Lehmann

Marie McNealey

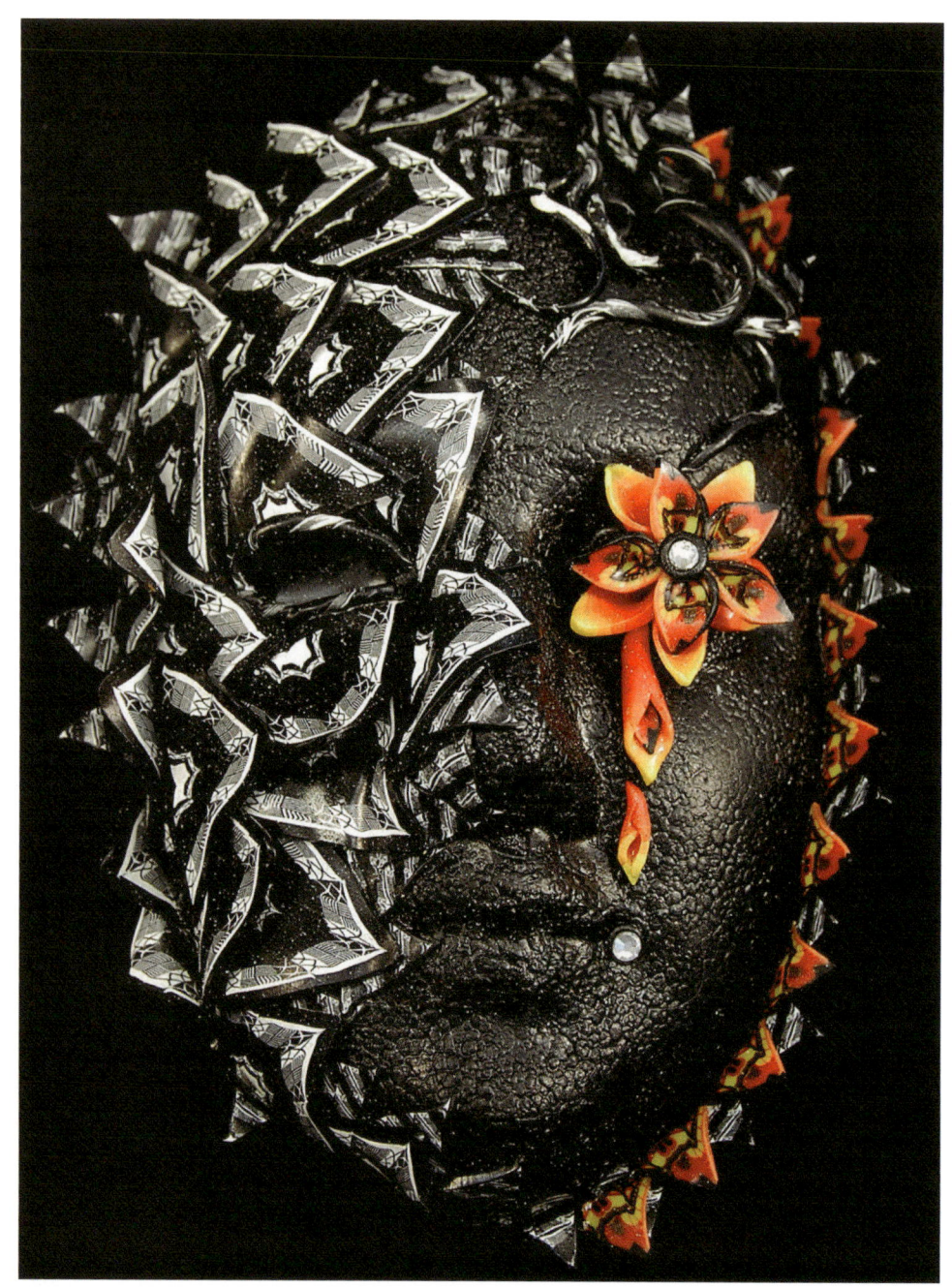

Rebecca Wells Stout   *photo Mark Stout*   5" x 6.5"

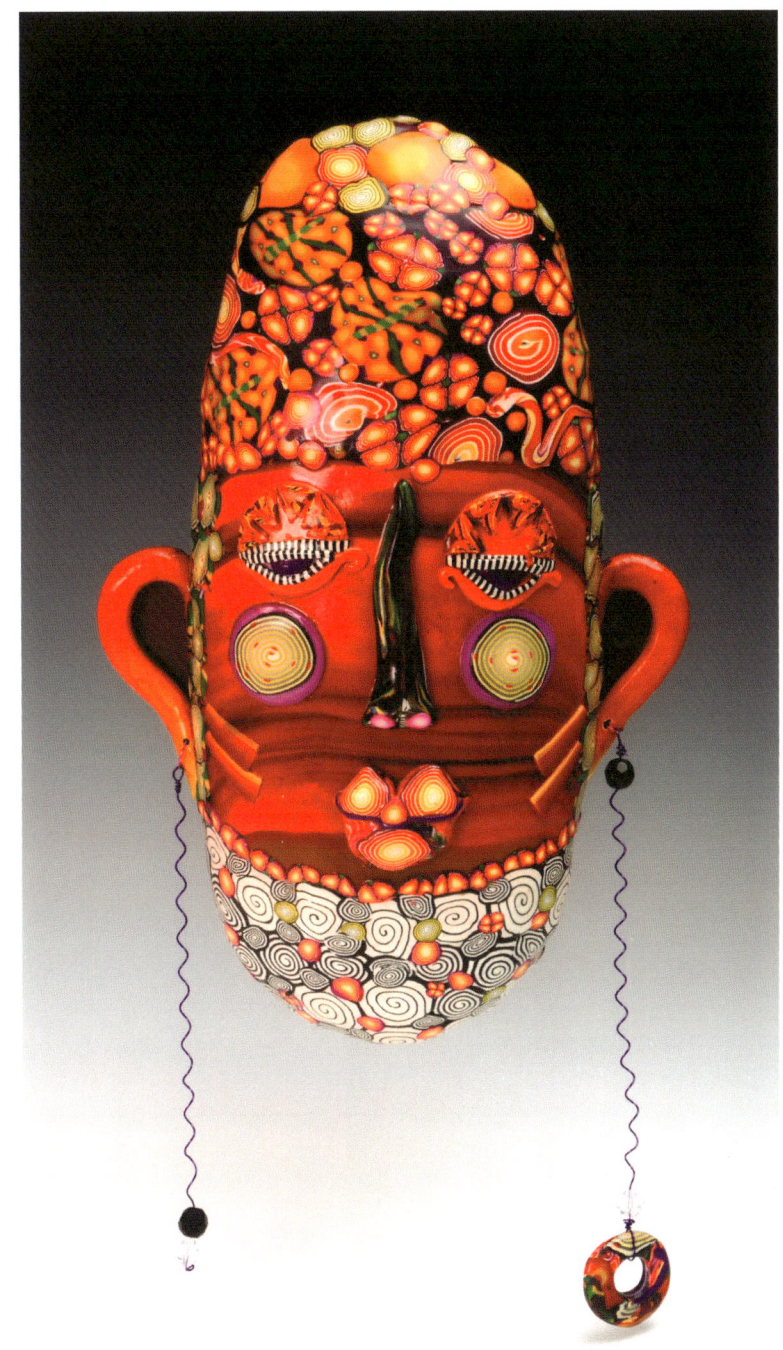

Judy Summer   *photo Michael Doogan   18" x 6" x 3"*

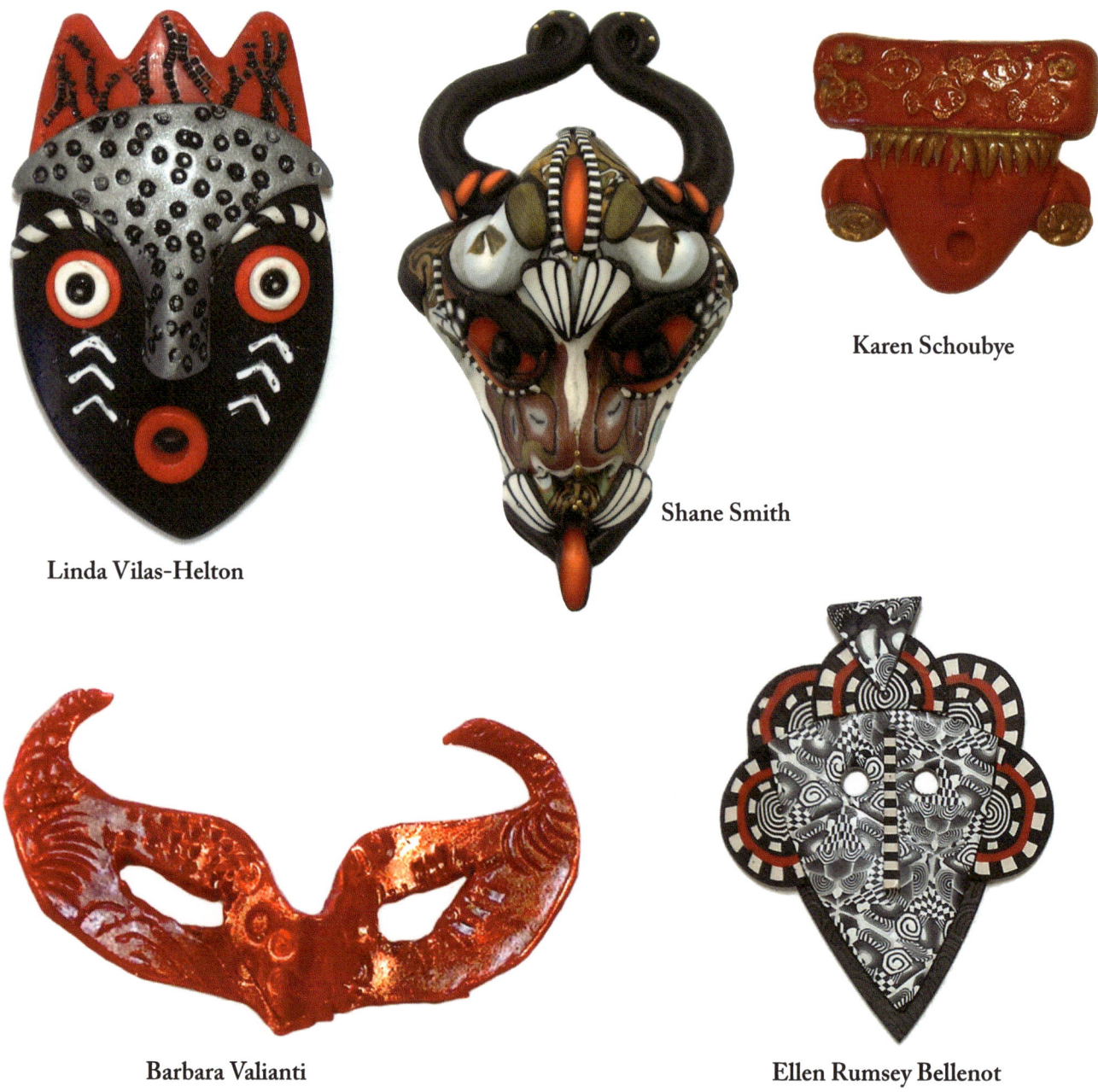

Linda Vilas-Helton

Shane Smith

Karen Schoubye

Barbara Valianti

Ellen Rumsey Bellenot

A Collection Of Polymer Clay Masks

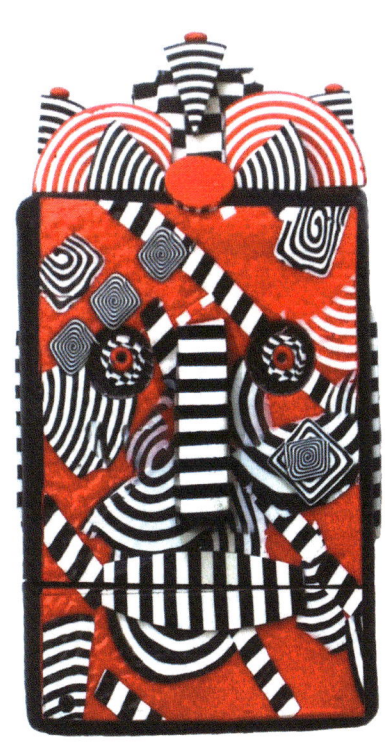

Ellen Rumsey Bellenot

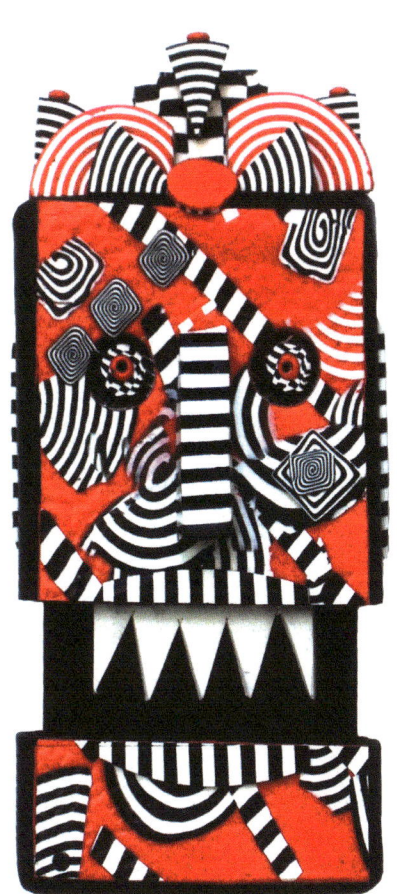

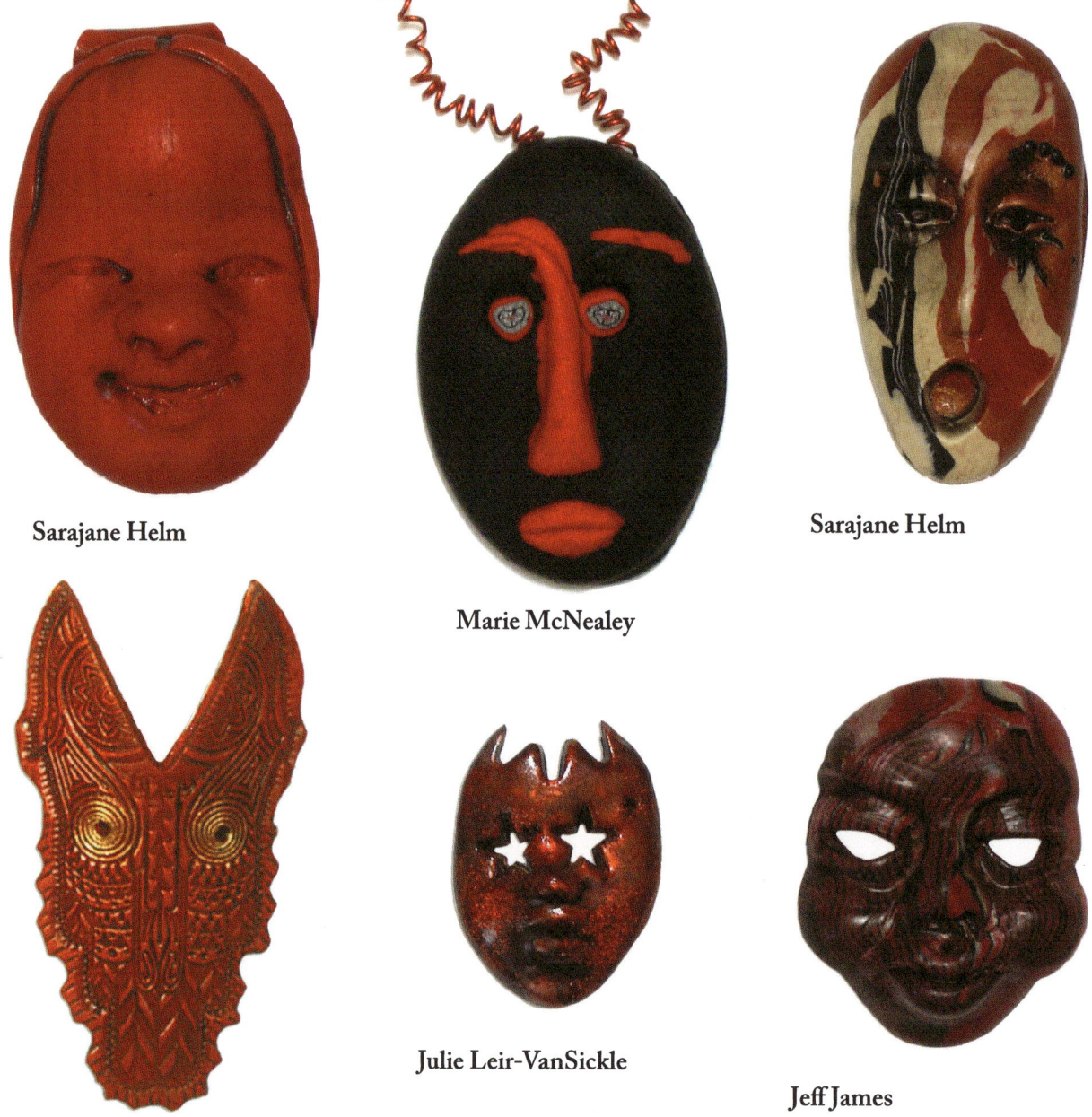

Sarajane Helm

Marie McNealey

Sarajane Helm

Sarajane Helm

Julie Leir-VanSickle

Jeff James

A Collection Of Polymer Clay Masks

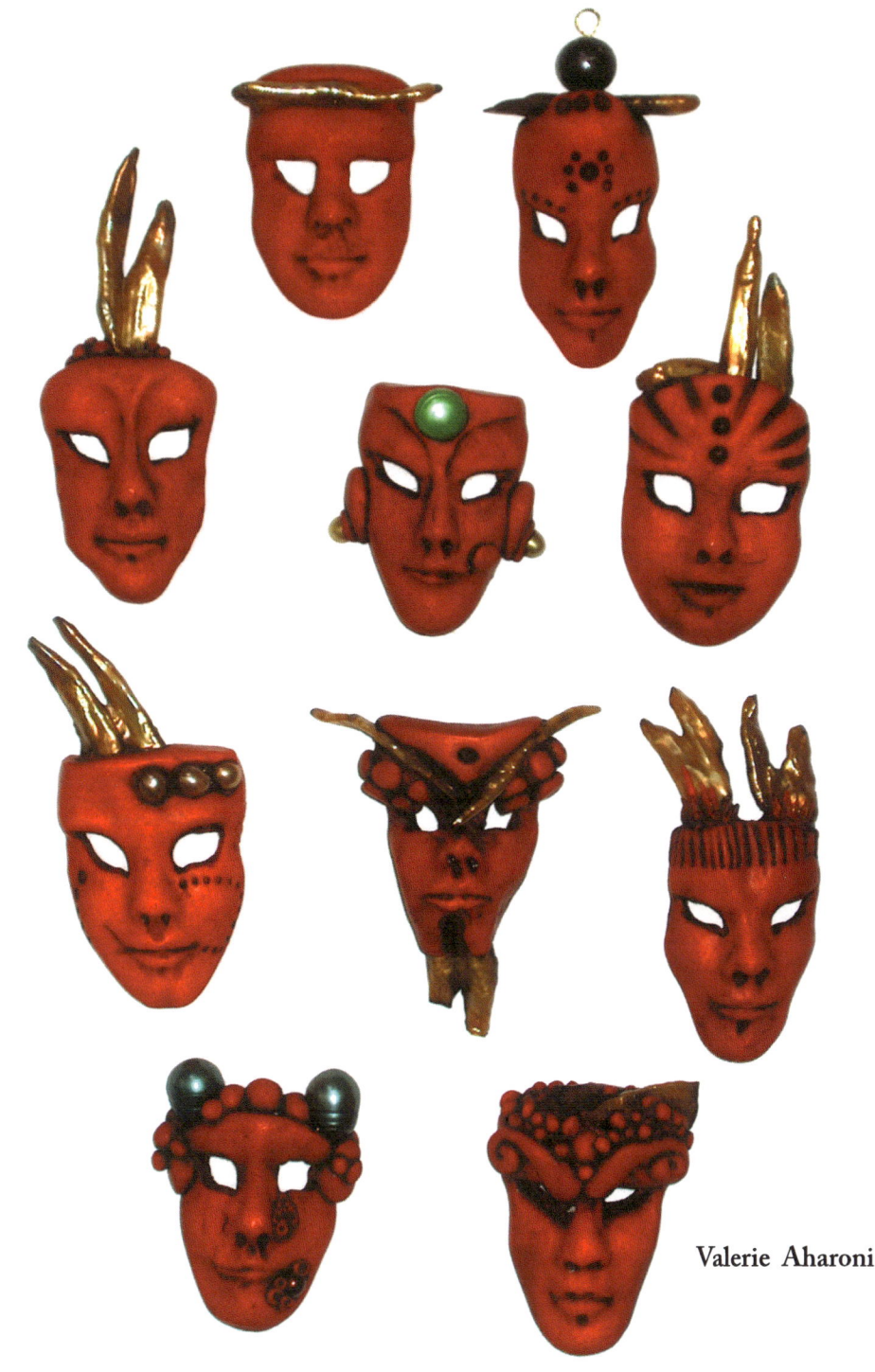

Valerie Aharoni

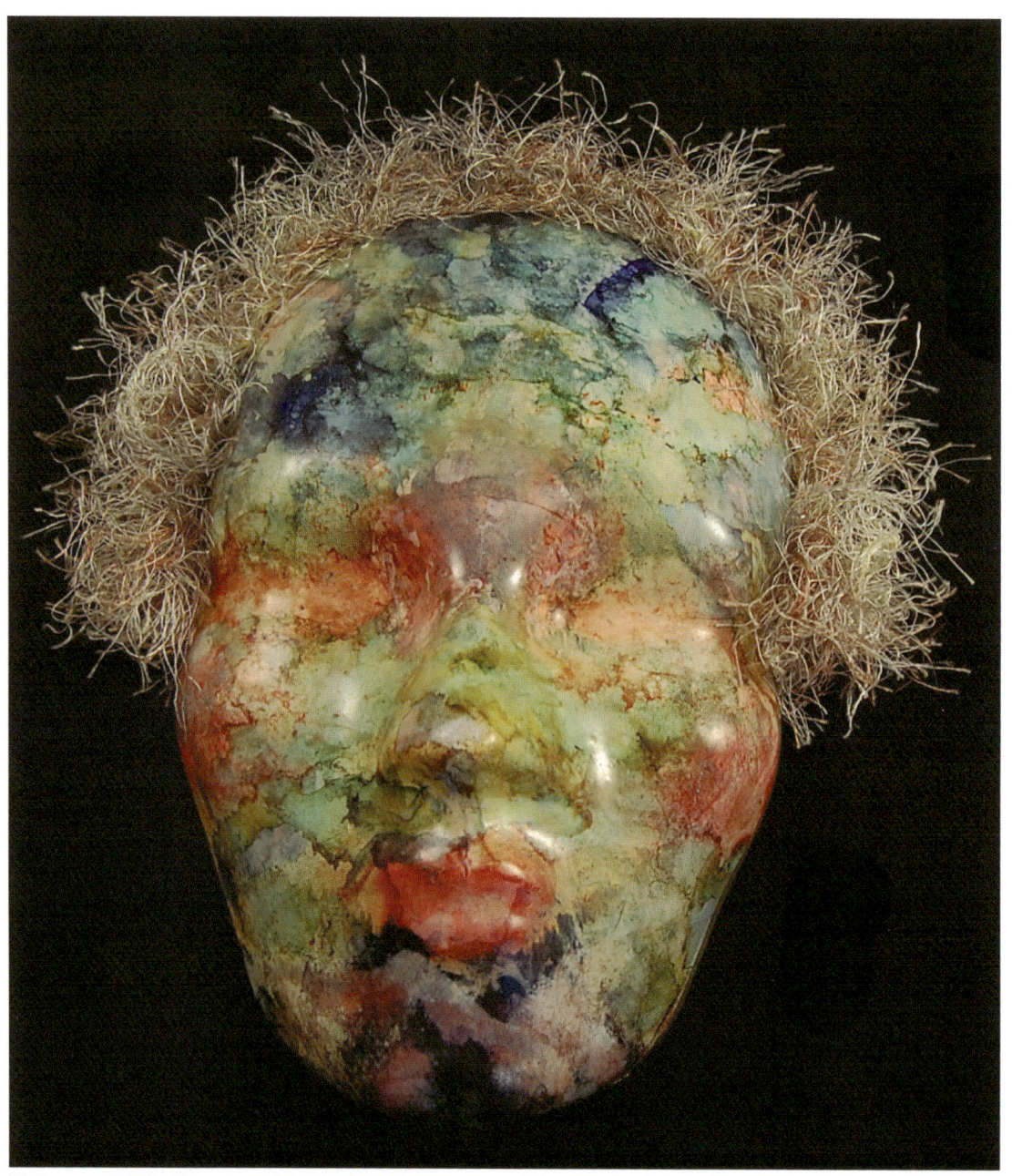

Rebecca Wells Stout   *photo Mark Stout*   8" x 10"

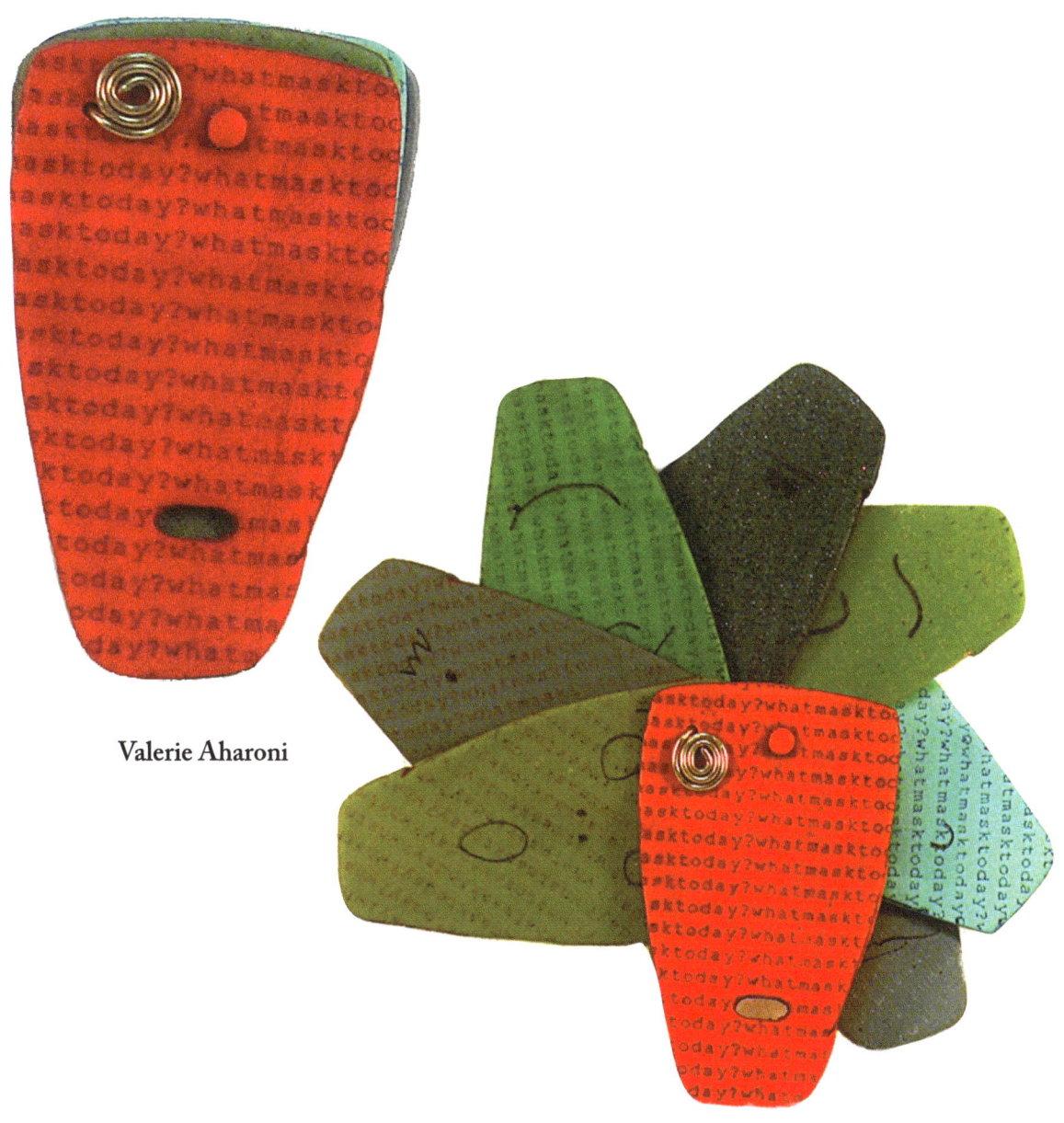

Valerie Aharoni

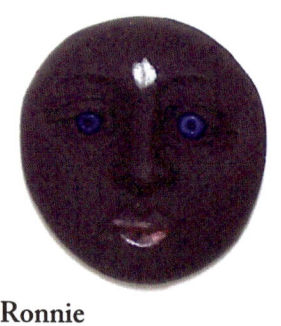

Ronnie

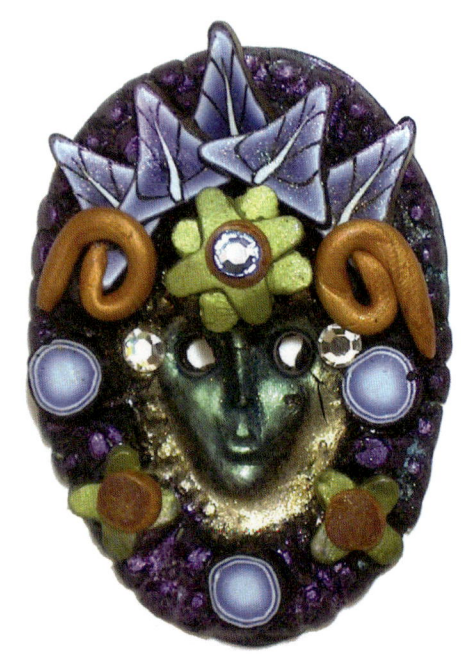

Tracy Callahan

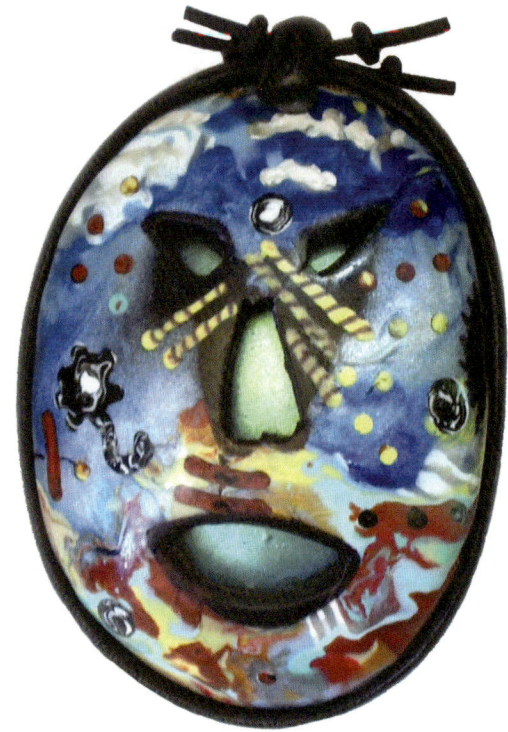

Lashonne Abel

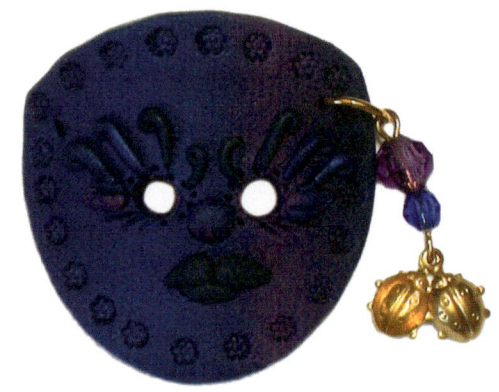

Helen Hughes

A Collection Of Polymer Clay Masks

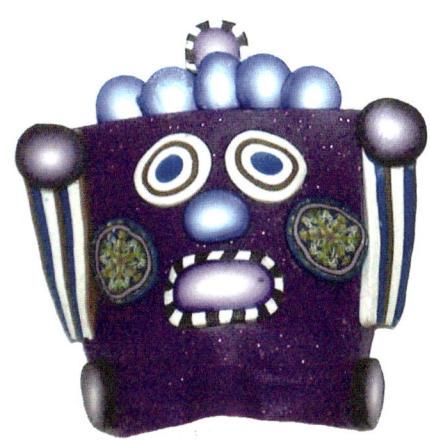

Beth Ackley

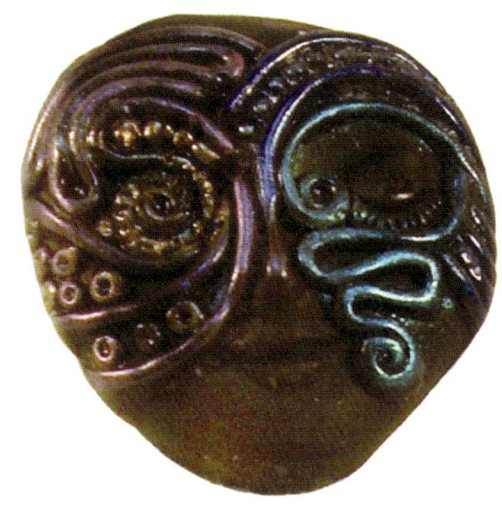

Jenn Dorion

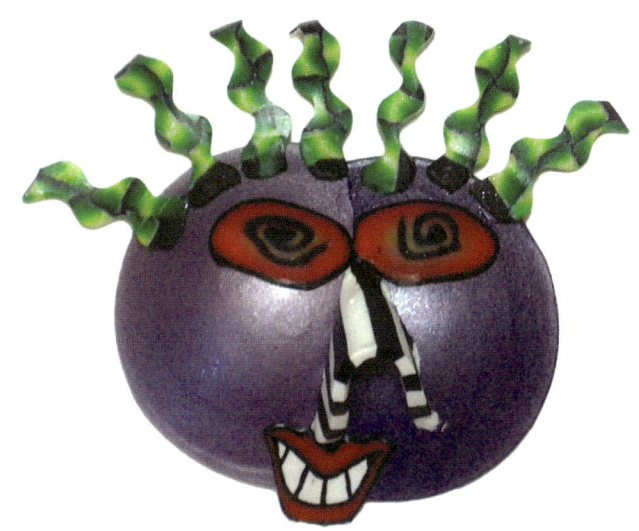

Kathi Briefer-Gose

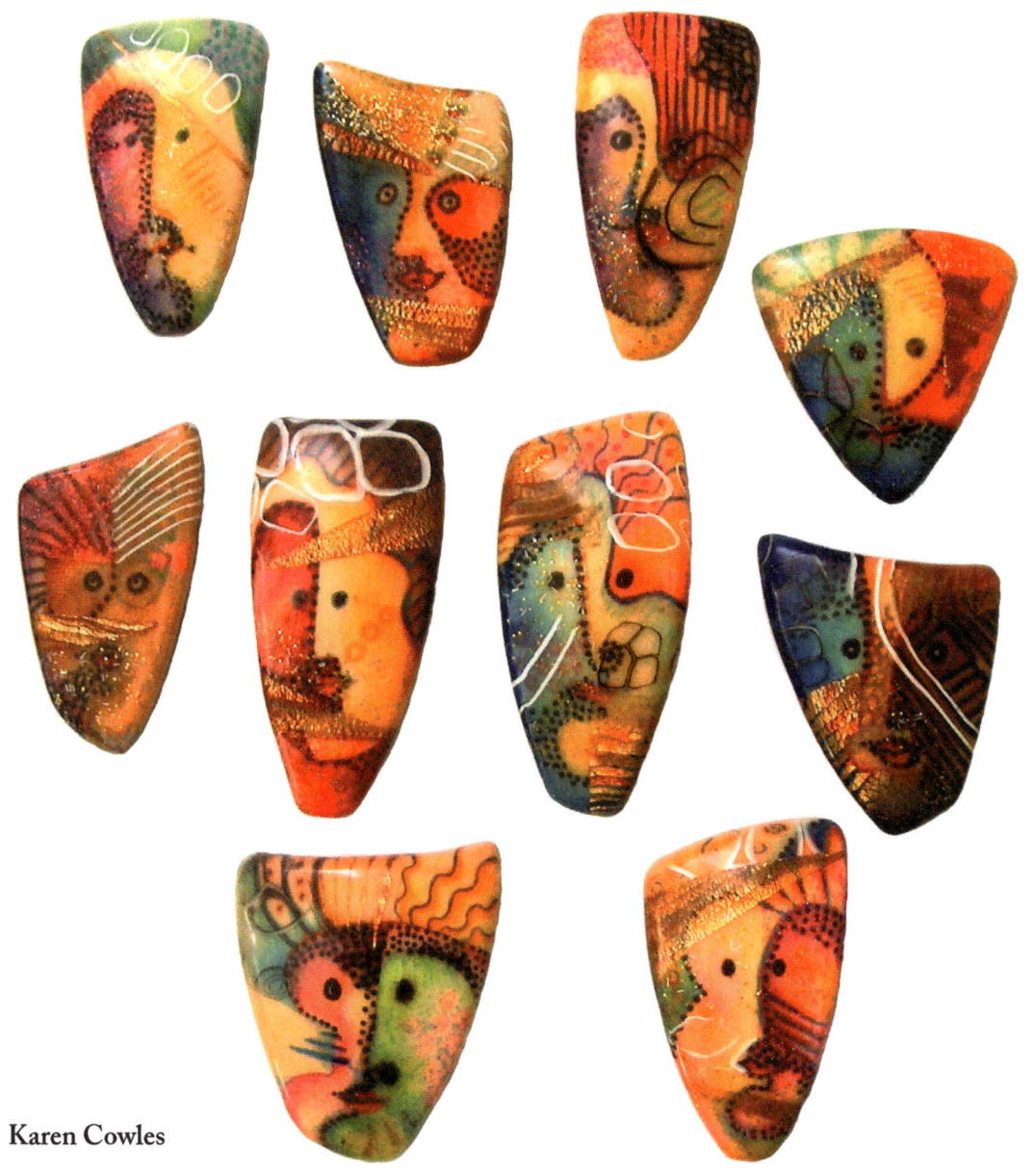

Karen Cowles

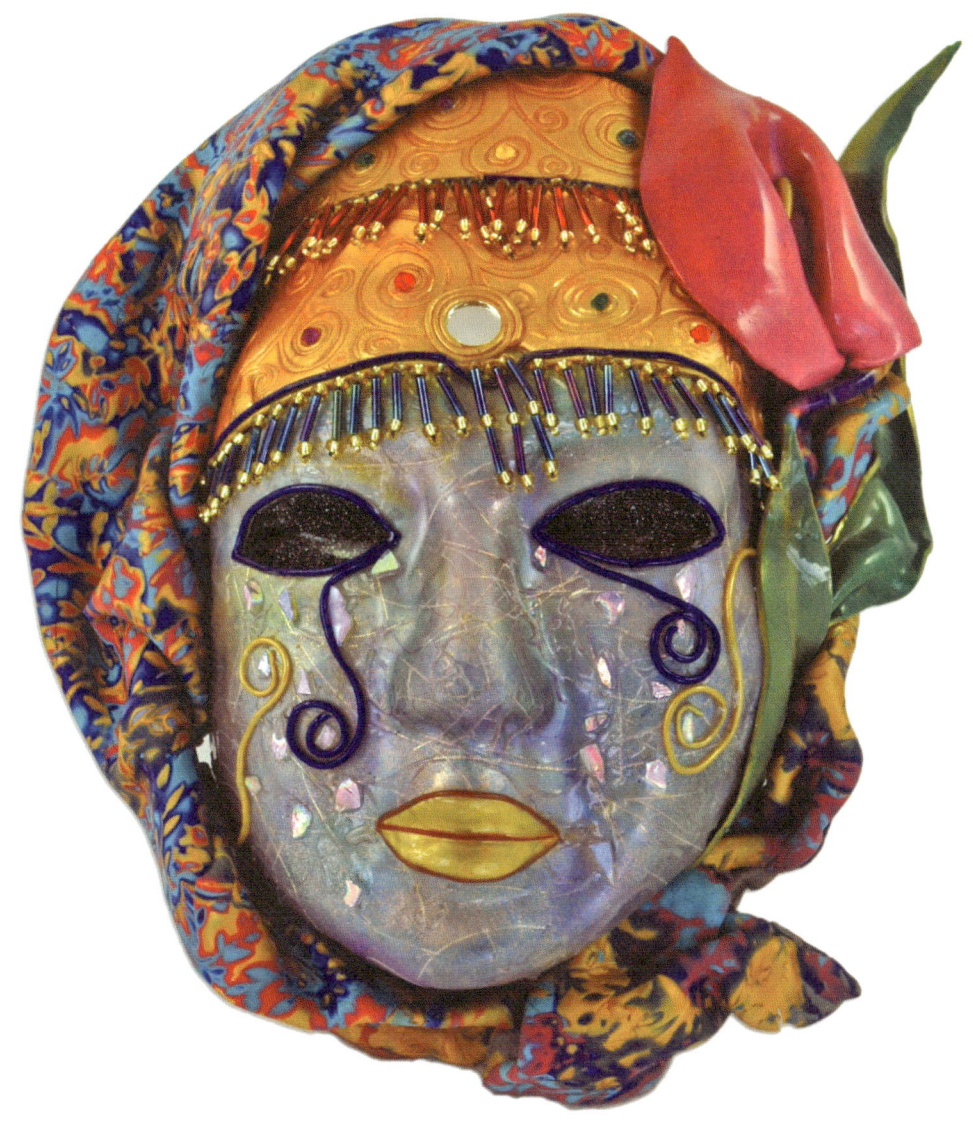

Sheila Furth   *photo Sheila Furth   13" x 8"*

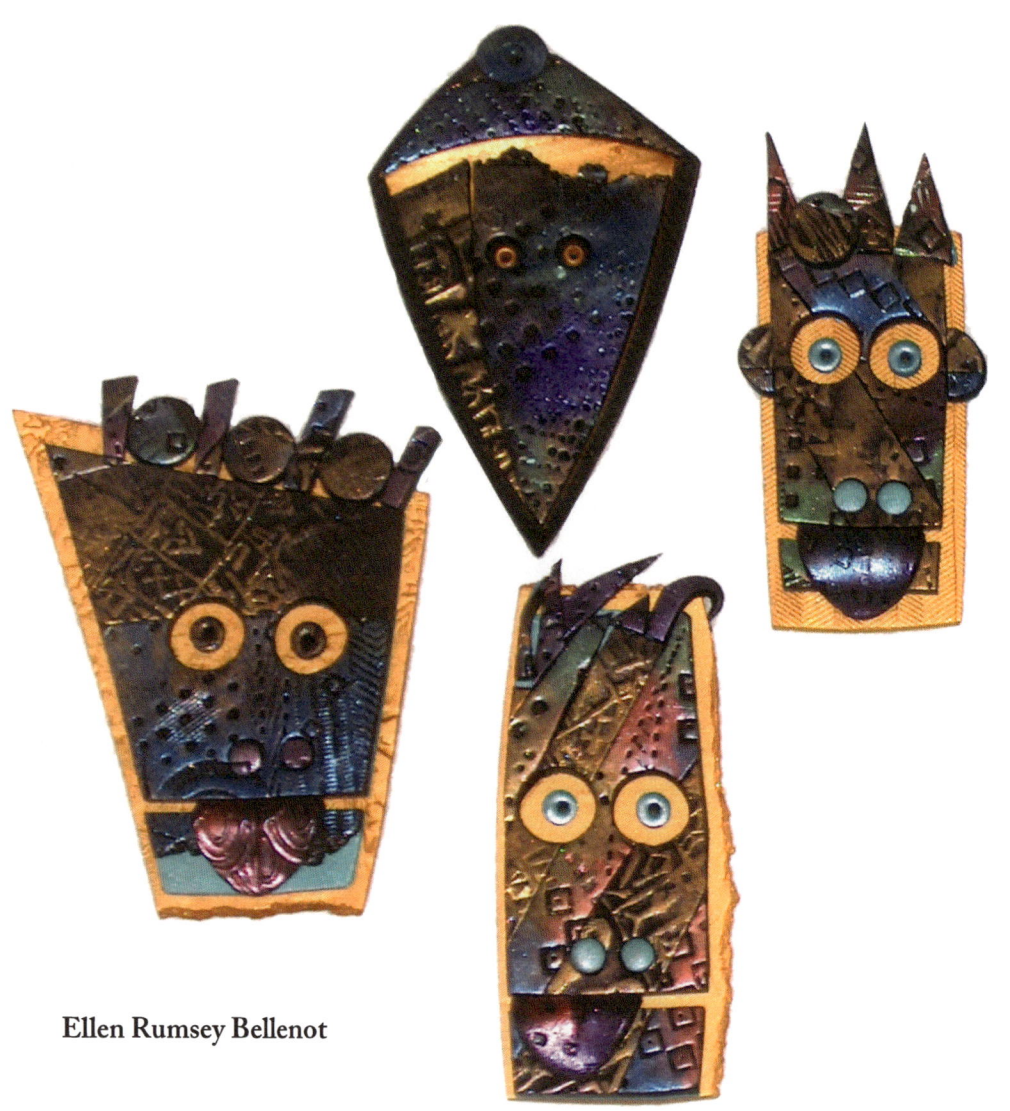

Ellen Rumsey Bellenot

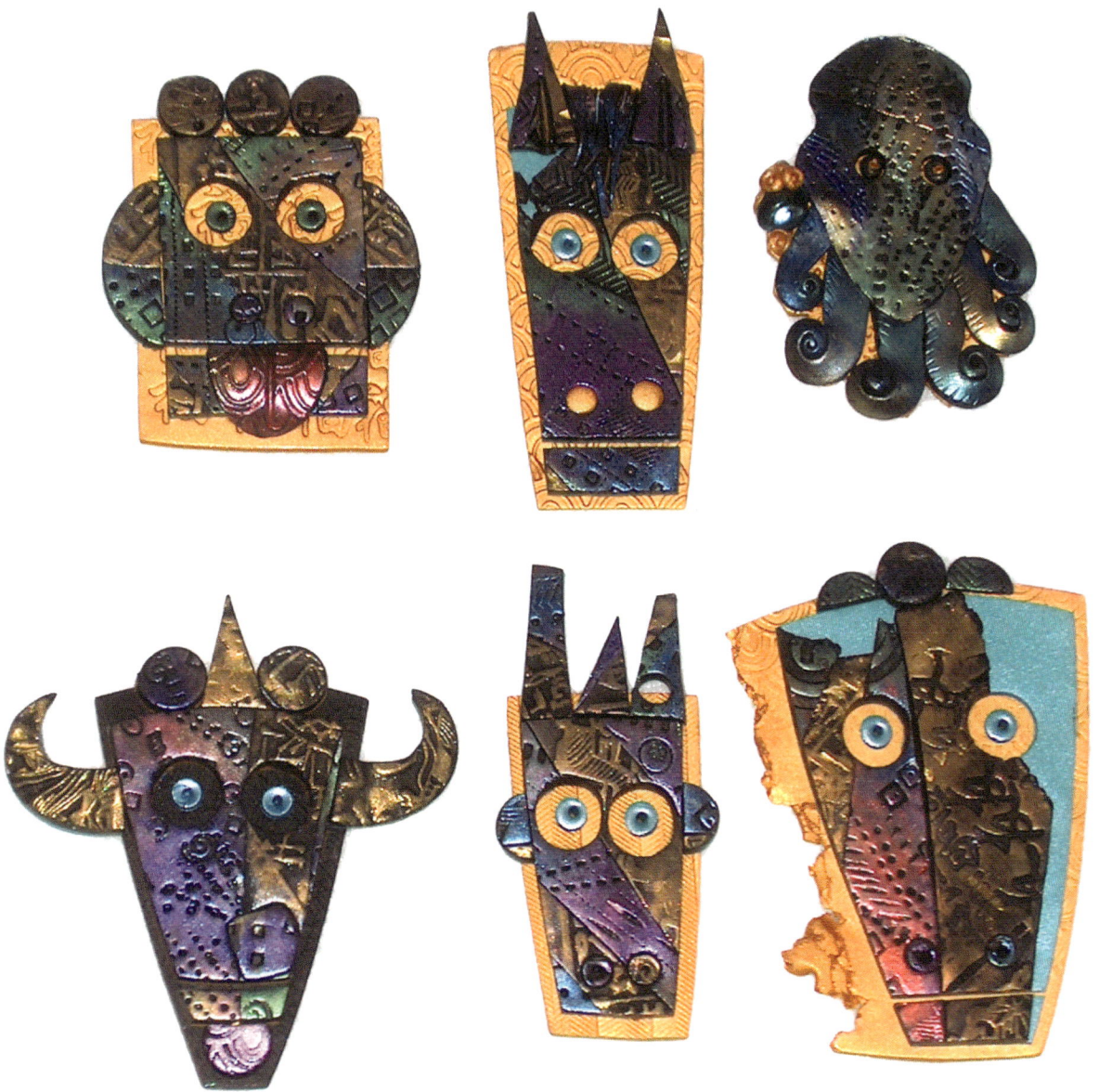

Ellen Rumsey Bellenot

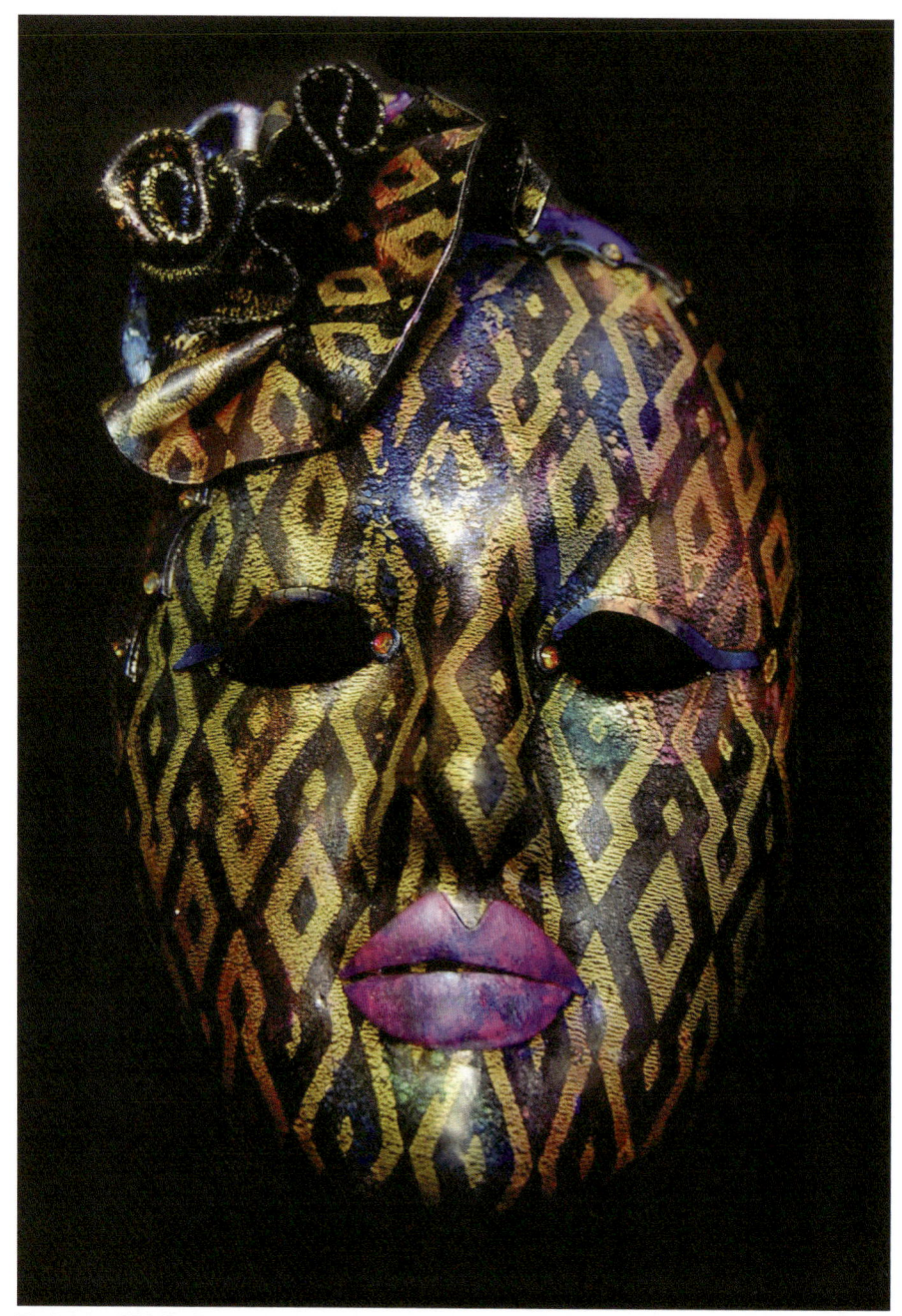

Rebecca Wells Stout   *photo Mark Stout*   5"x 6.5"

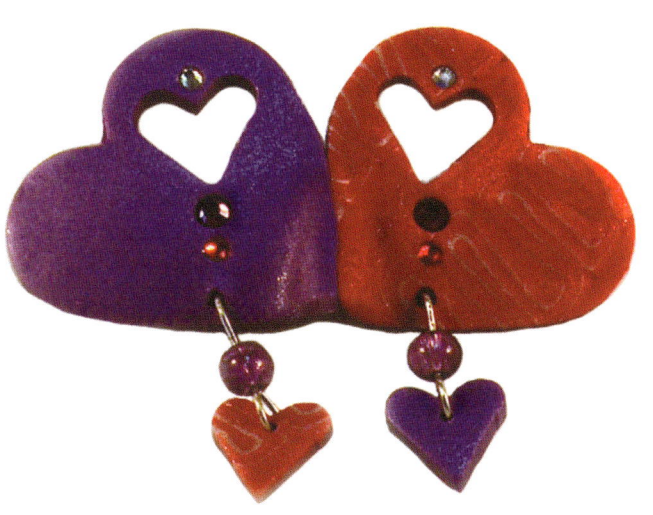

Linda Hess

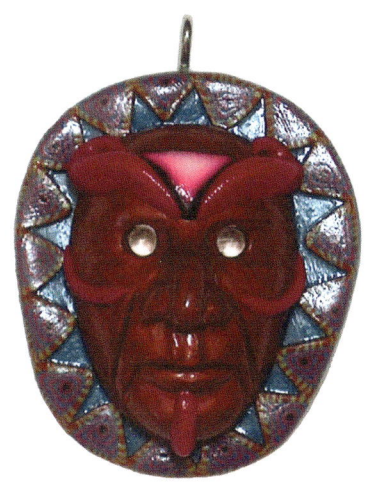

Diane Hobbs

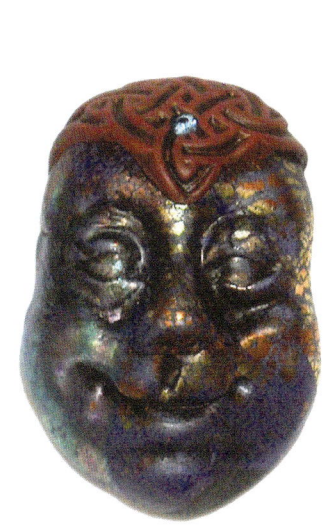

Sarajane Helm

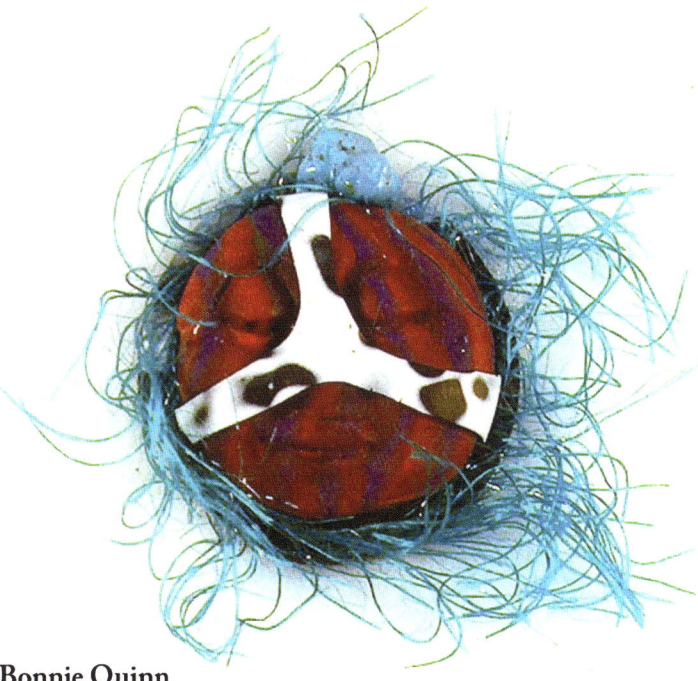

Bonnie Quinn

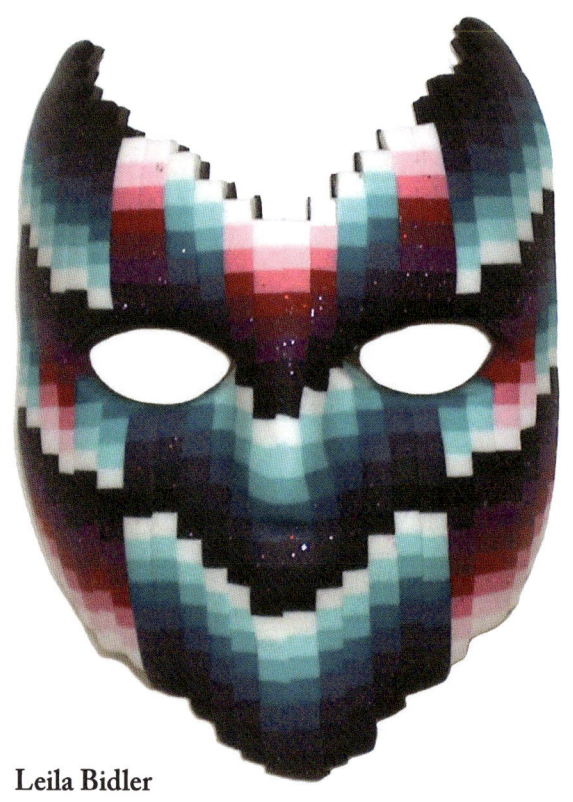

Leila Bidler

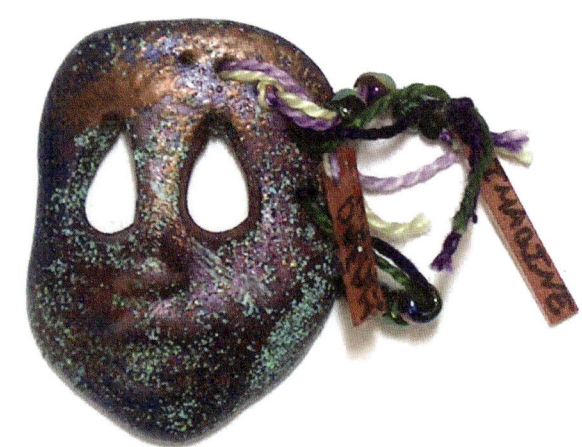

Julie Leir-VanSickle

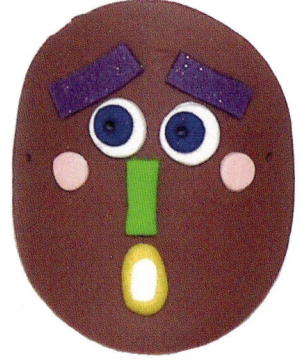

Beth Ackley

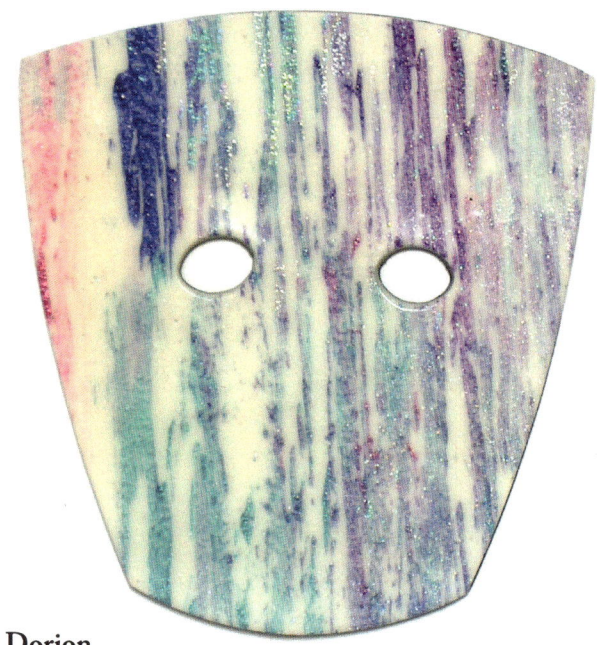

Jenn Dorion

A Collection Of Polymer Clay Masks

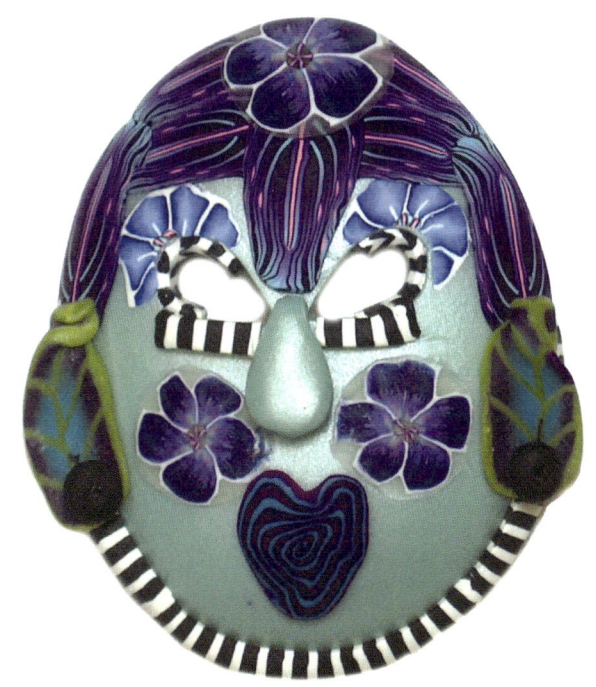

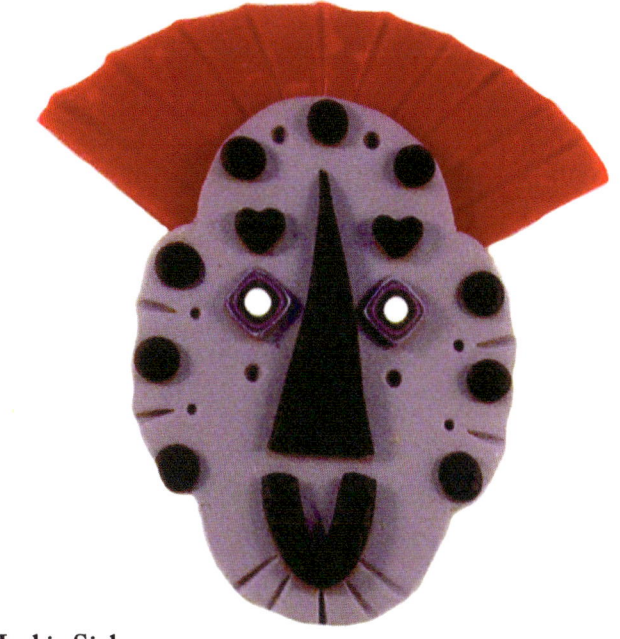

Joyce Miskowitz

Jackie Sieben

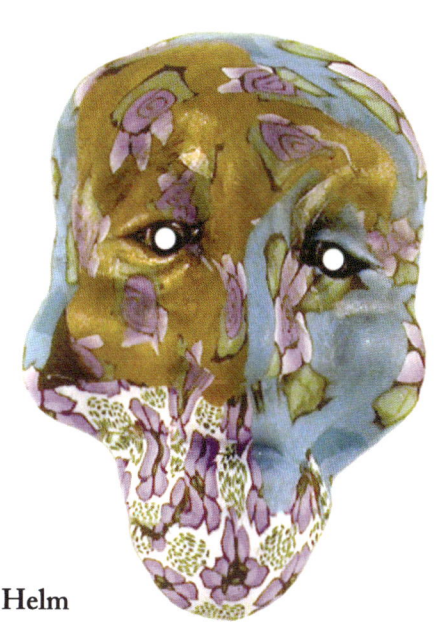

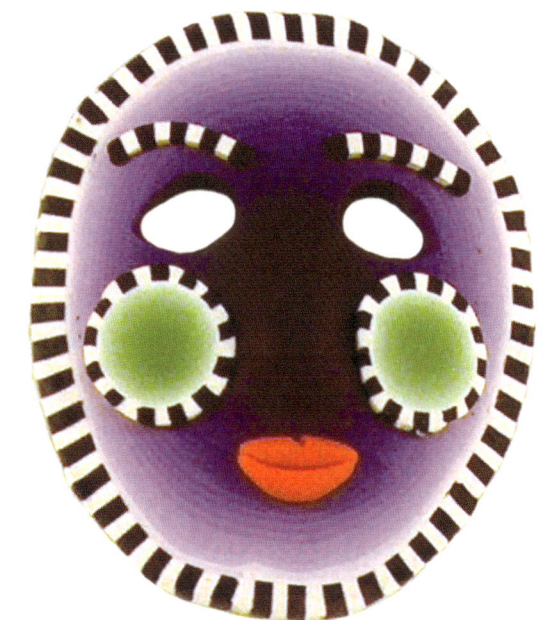

Sarajane Helm

Karen Scudder

PolyMarket Press

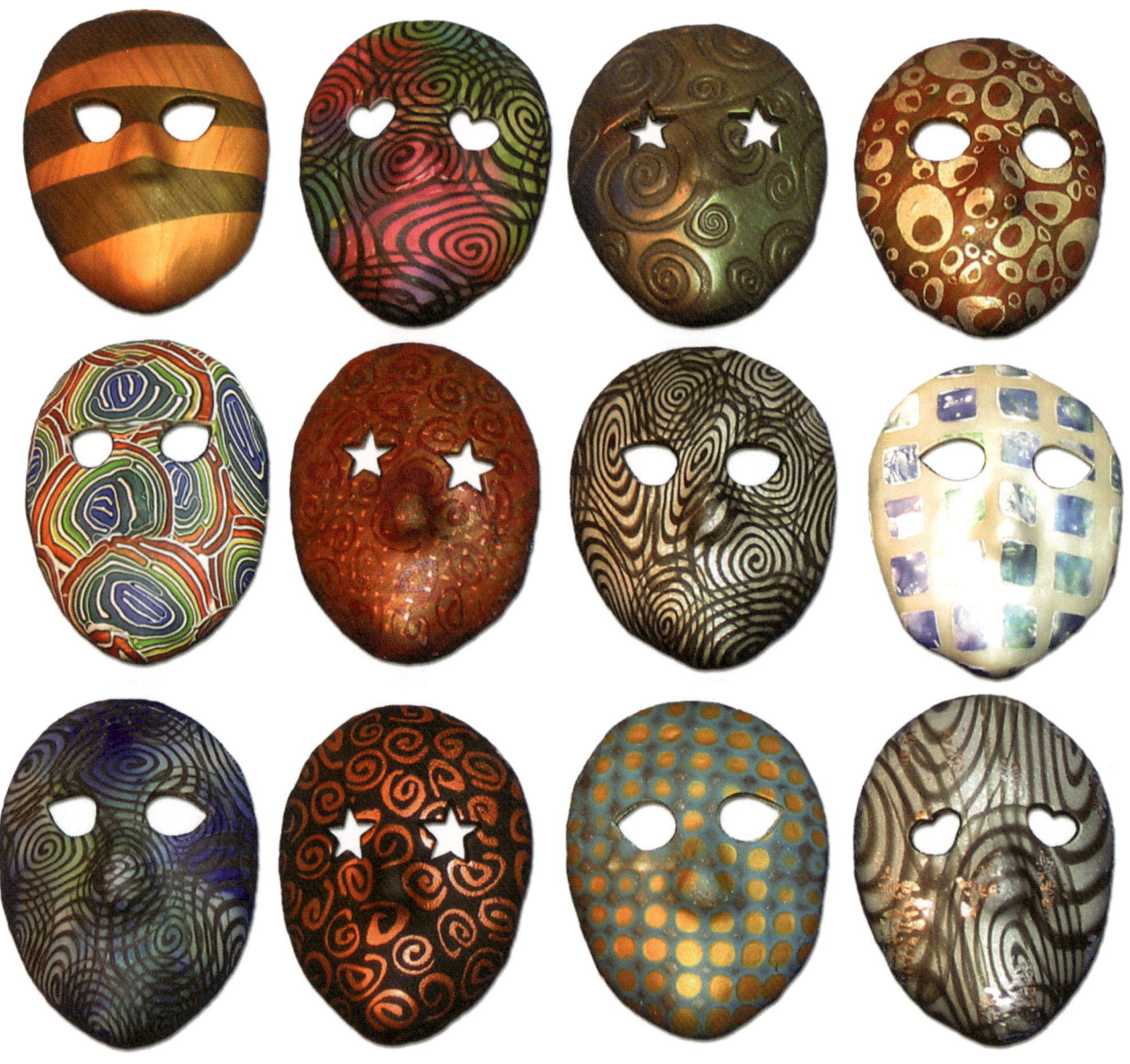

Robin Milne *photo Robin Milne*

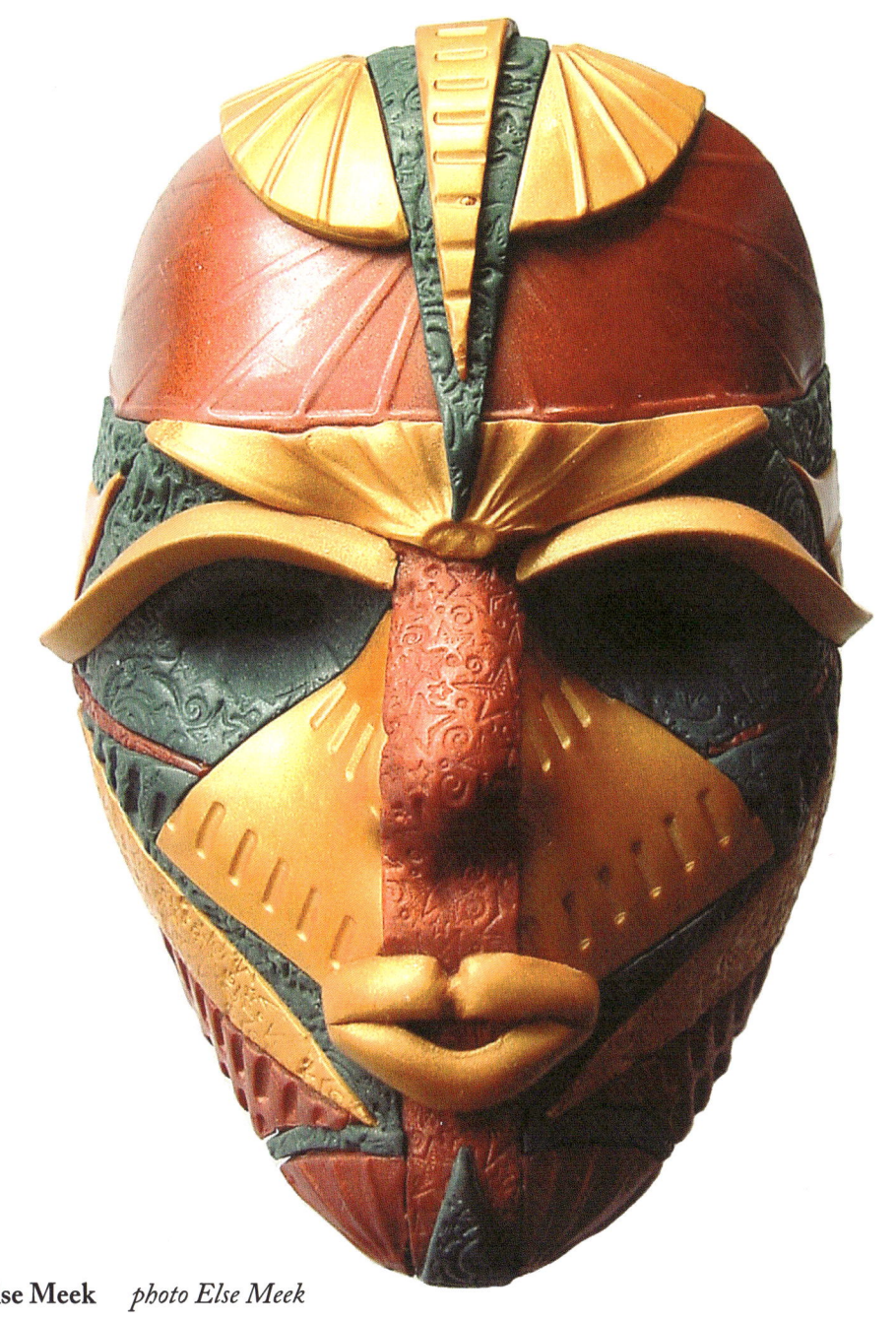

Else Meek   *photo Else Meek*

Kathi Briefer-Gose

Kathi Briefer-Gose

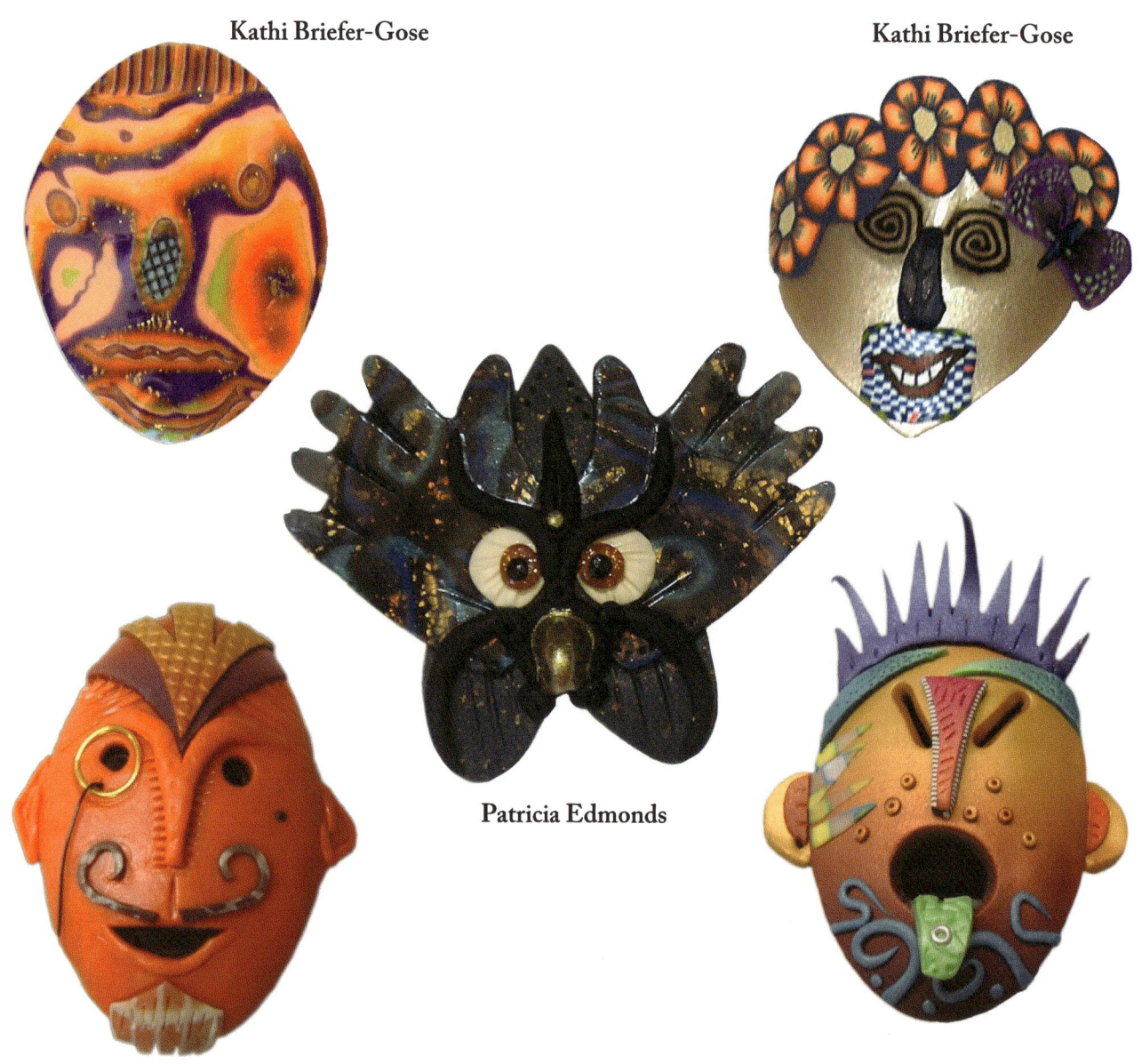

Patricia Edmonds

Dorothy Greynolds *photo Dorothy Greynolds*

Dorothy Greynolds *photo Dorothy Greynolds*

A Collection Of Polymer Clay Masks

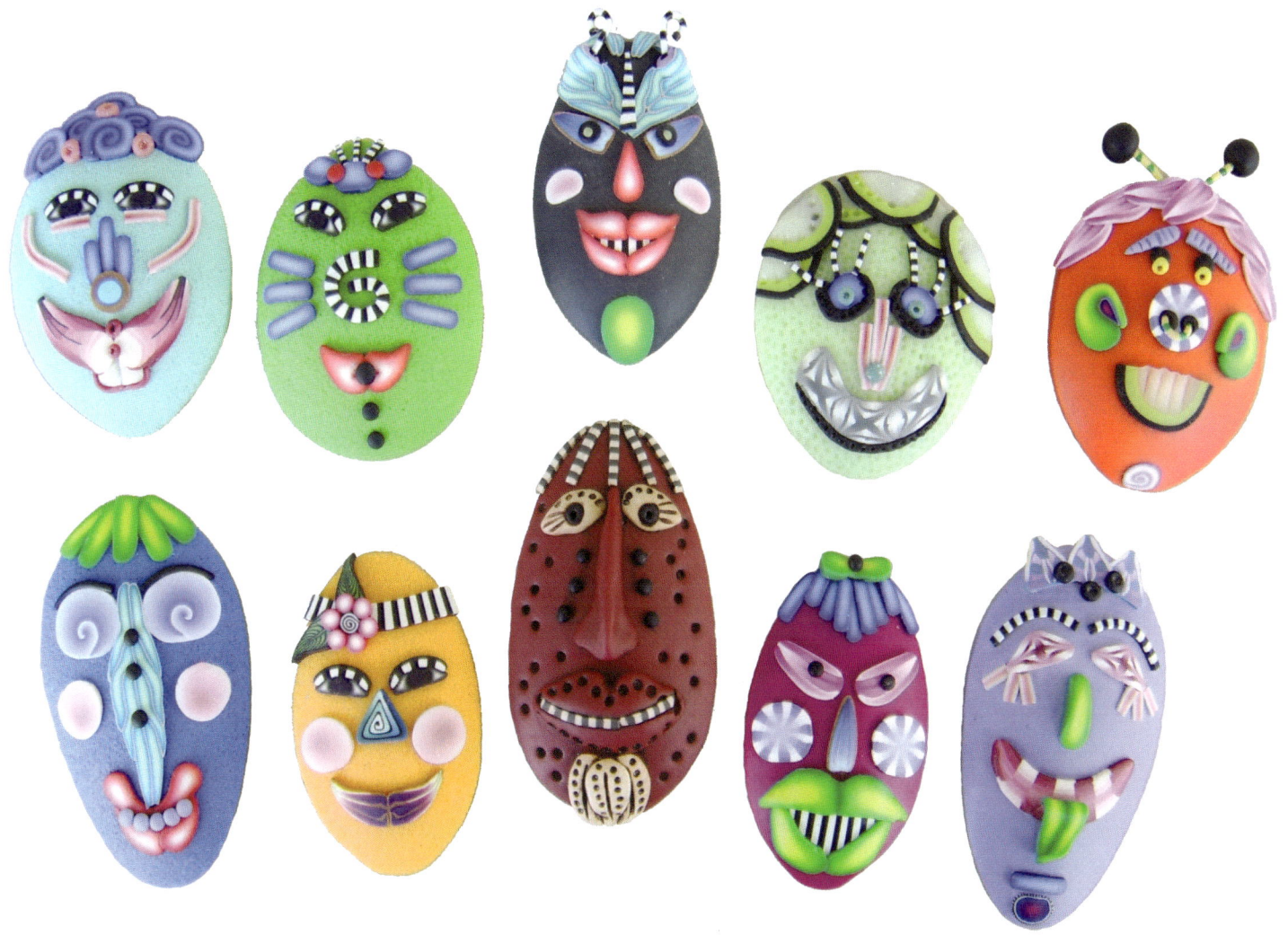

Kim Cavender

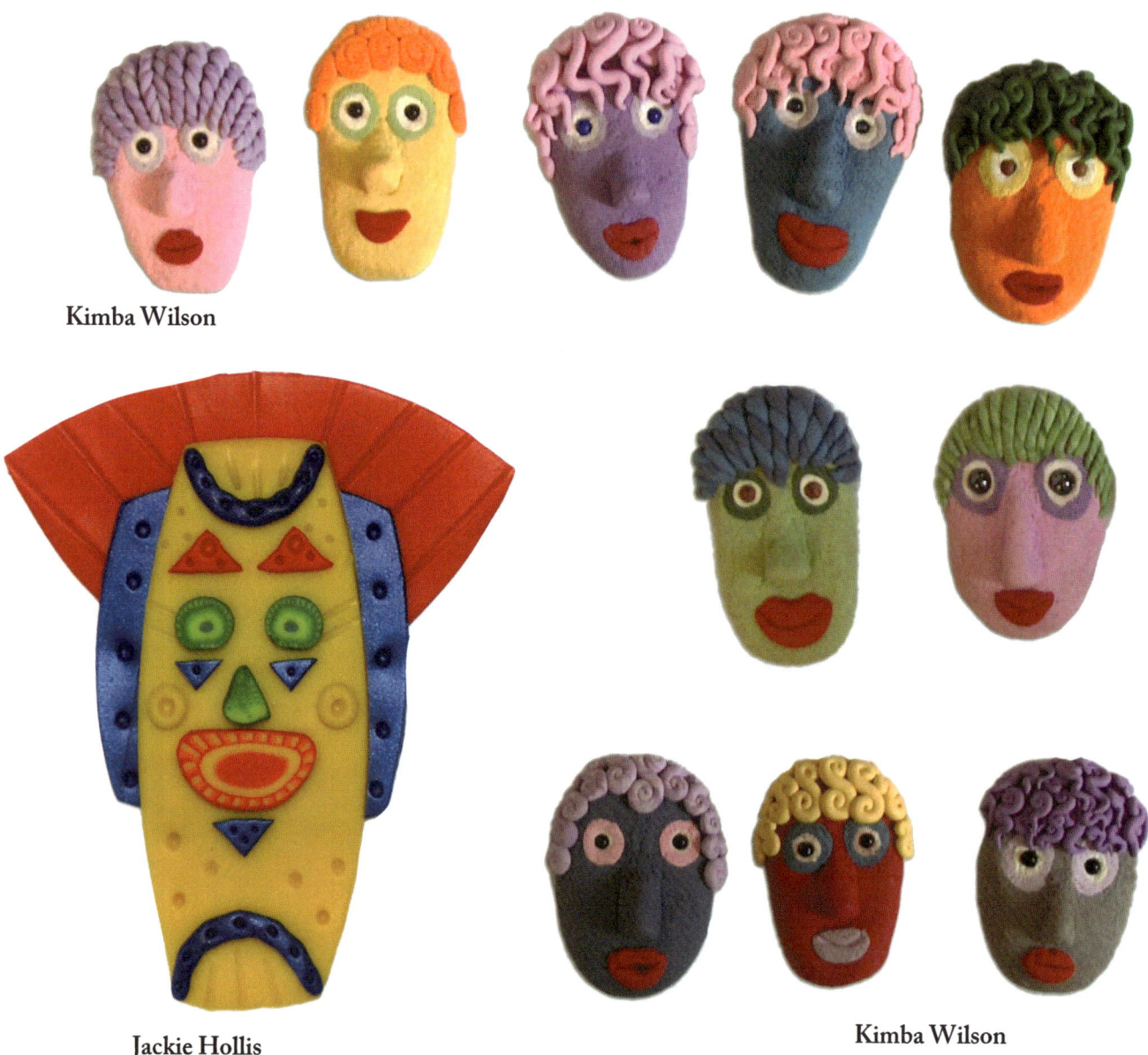

Kimba Wilson

Jackie Hollis

Kimba Wilson

A Collection Of Polymer Clay Masks

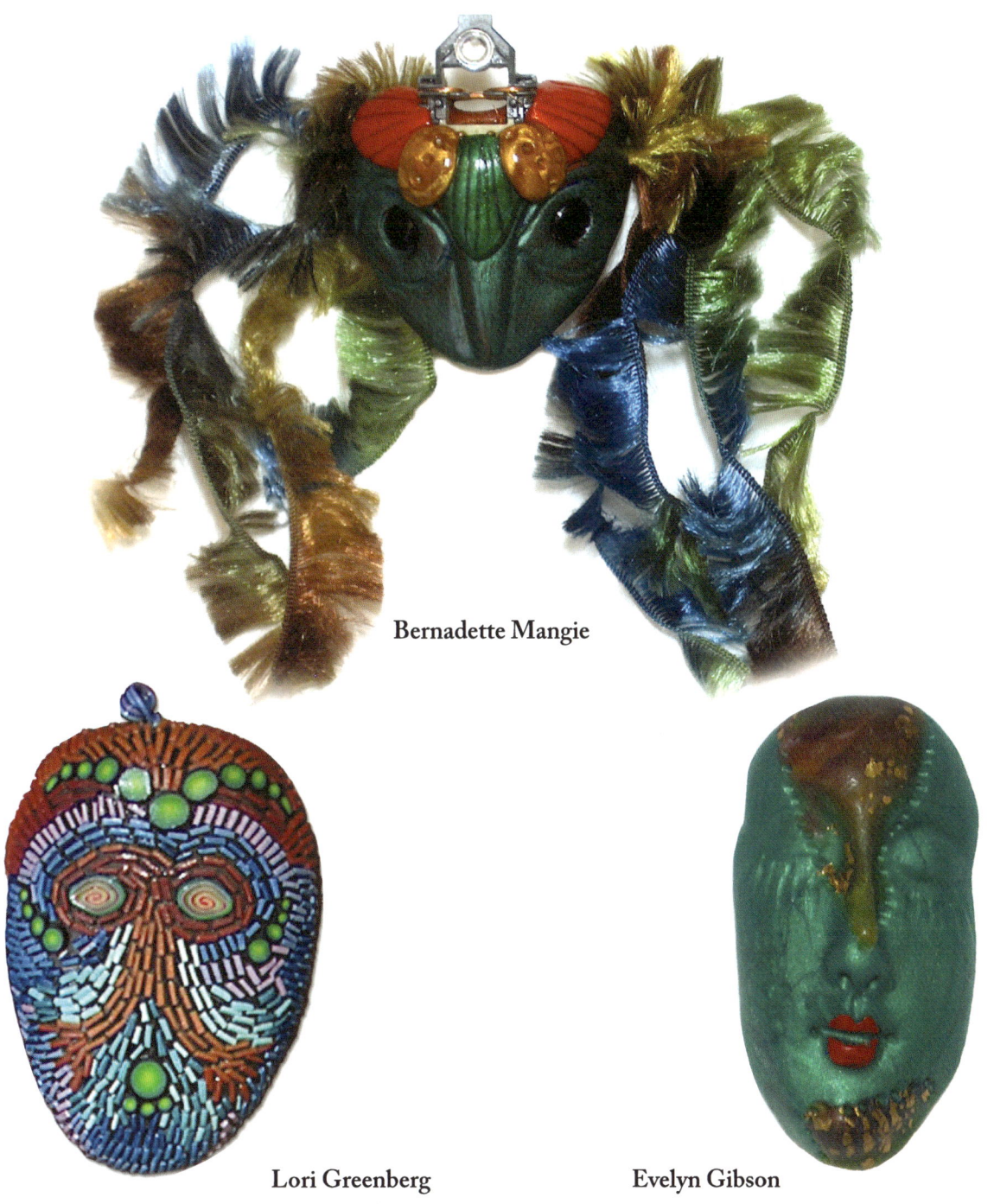

Bernadette Mangie

Lori Greenberg

Evelyn Gibson

PolyMarket Press

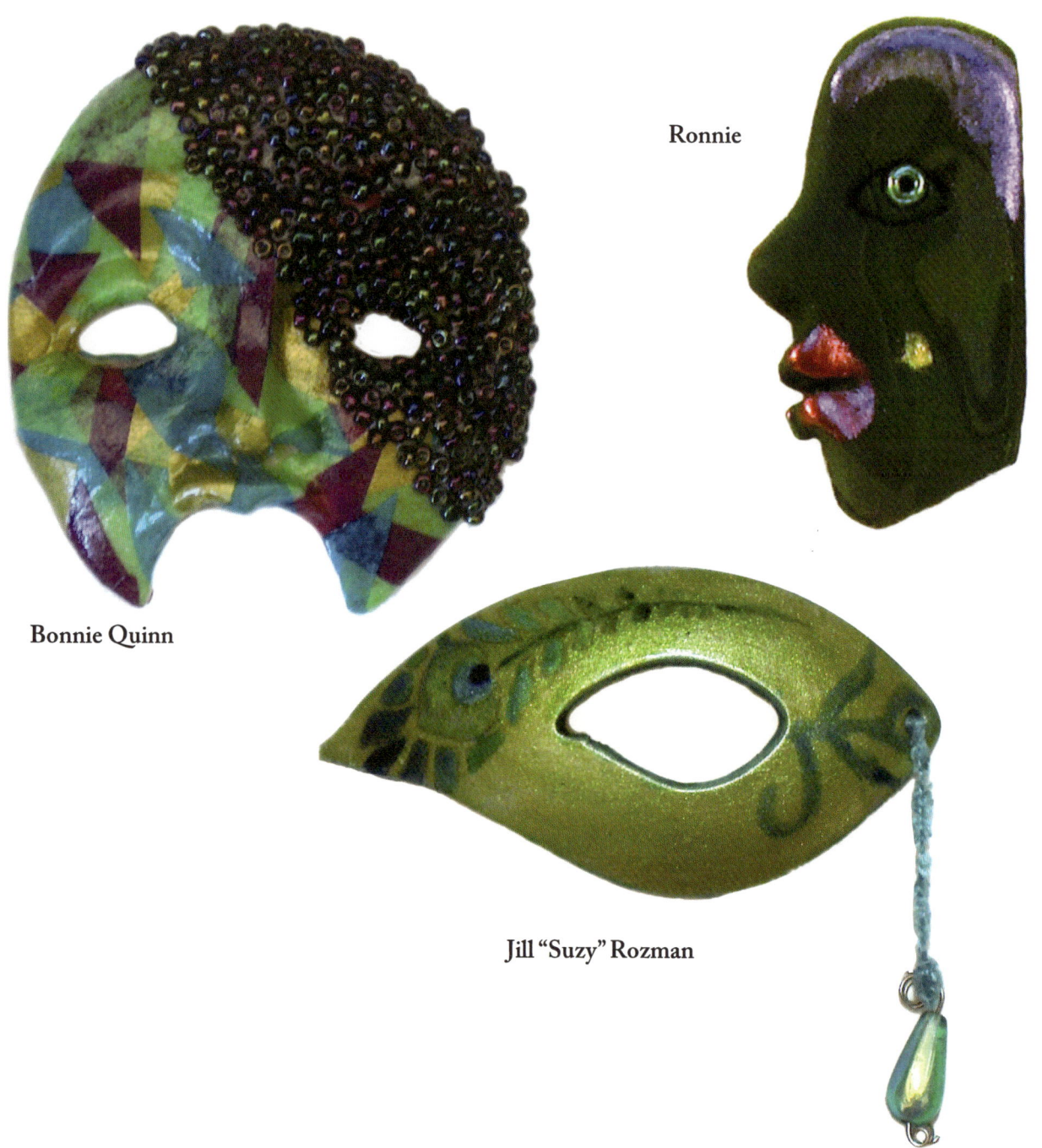

Bonnie Quinn

Ronnie

Jill "Suzy" Rozman

A Collection Of Polymer Clay Masks

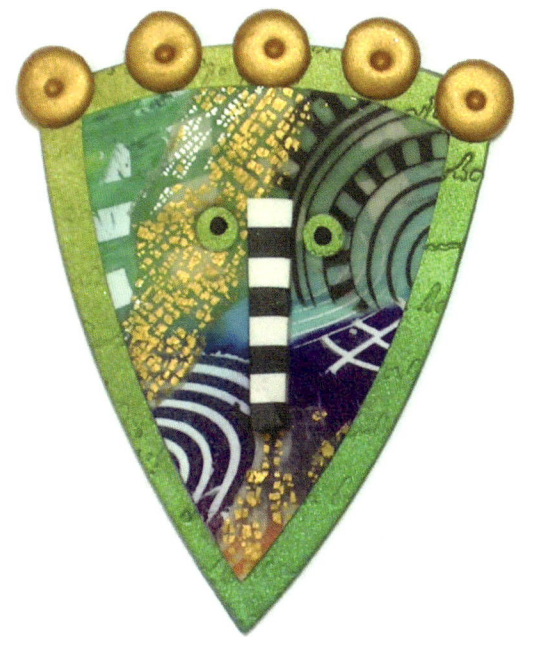

Ellen Rumsey Bellenot

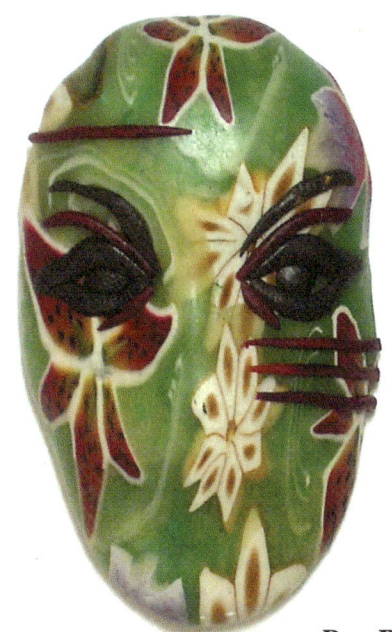

Rev. Byrd Tetzlaff

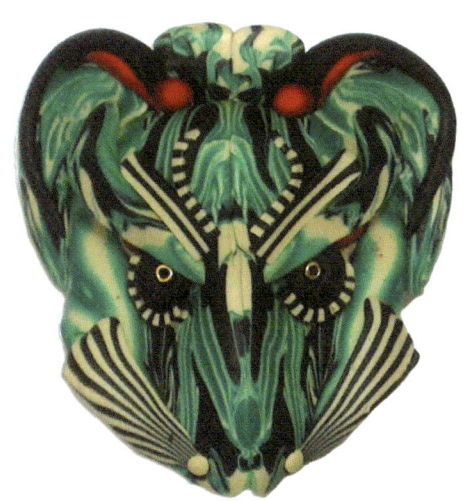

Shane Smith

Robert Wiley

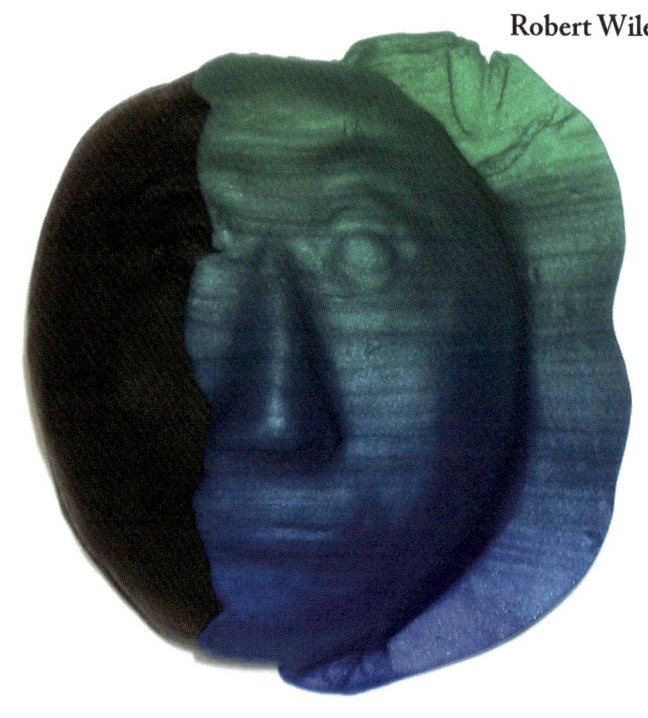

Mary Vanderwood

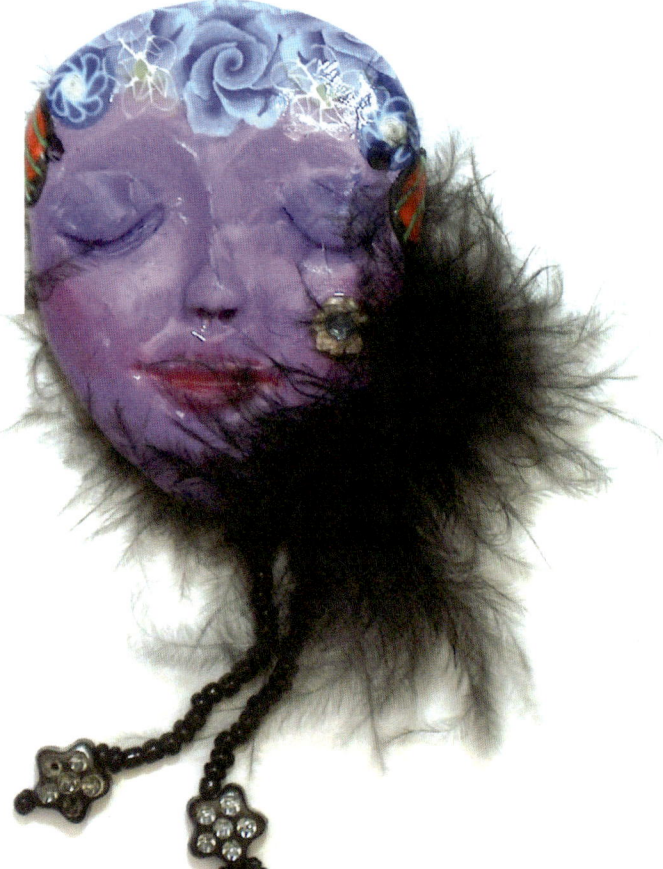

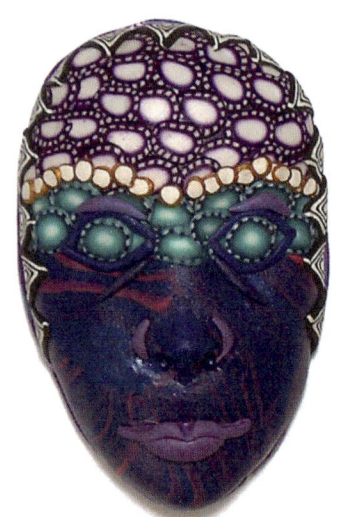

Rev. Byrd Tetzlaff

A Collection Of Polymer Clay Masks

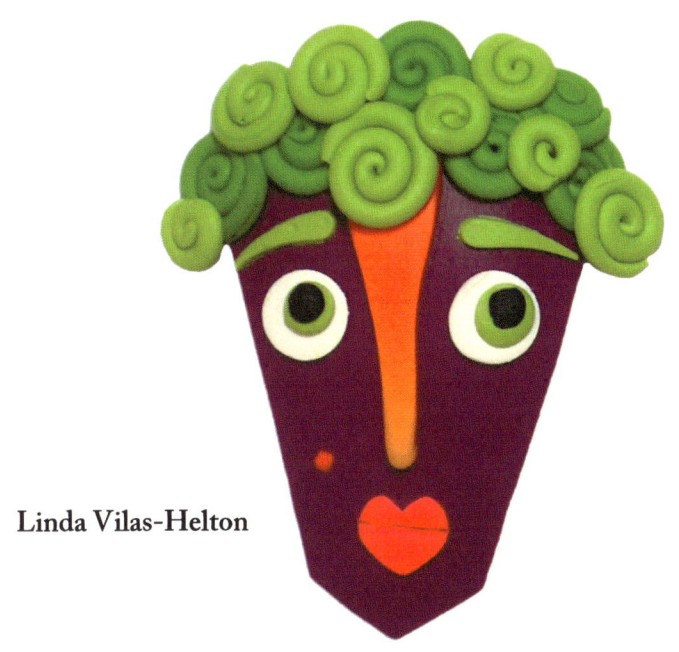

Linda Vilas-Helton

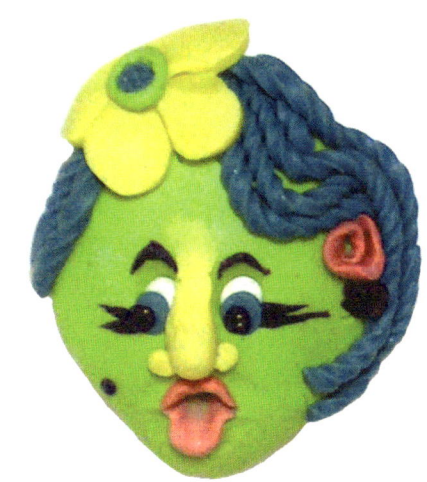

Lynne DeNio

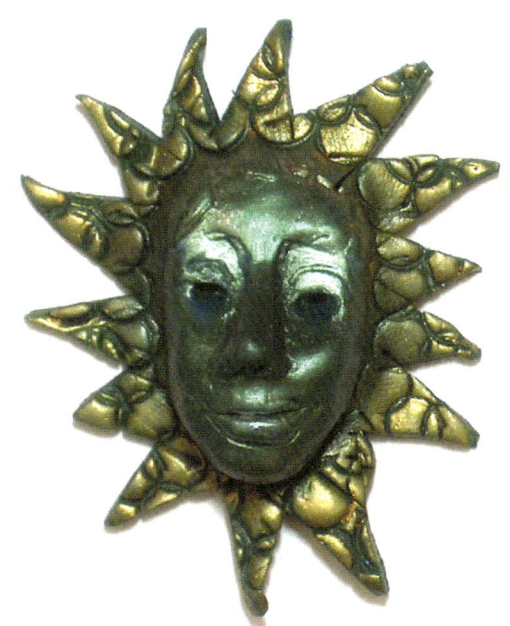

Barbara Valianti

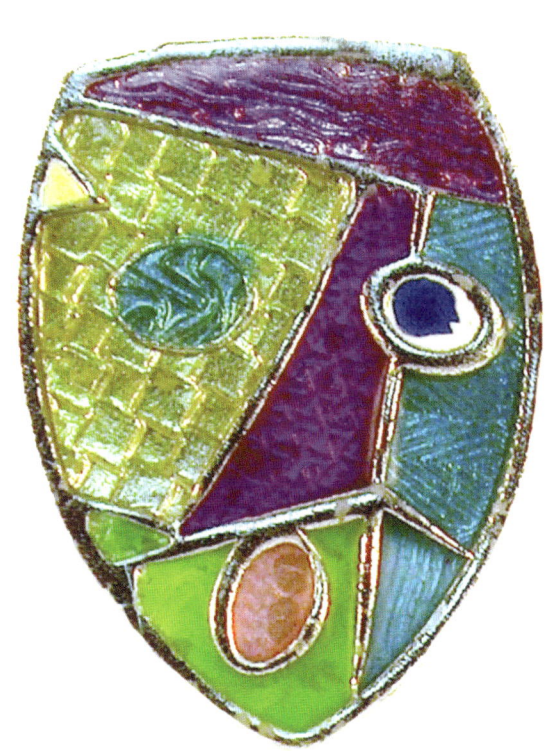

Jenn Dorion

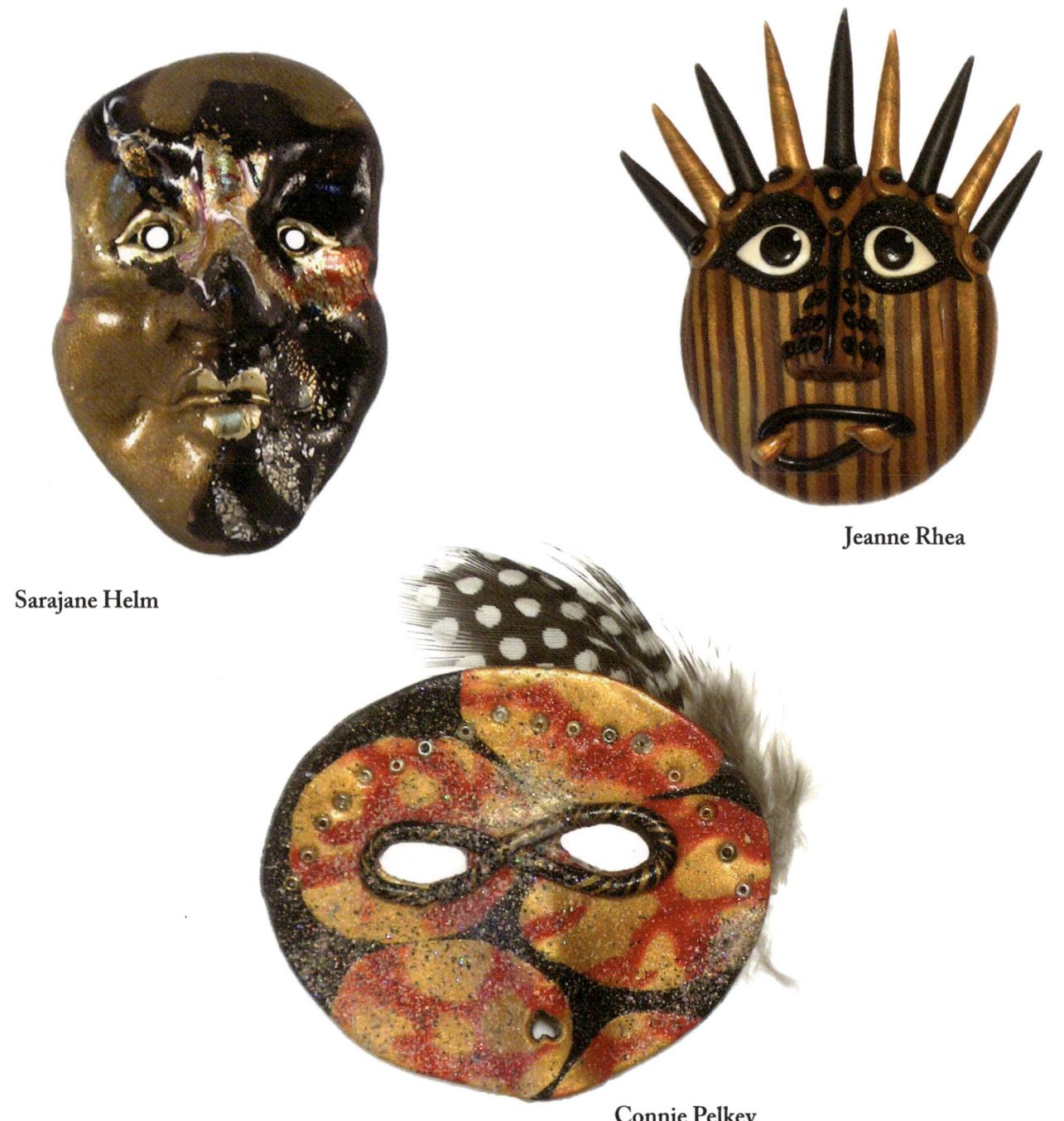

Sarajane Helm

Jeanne Rhea

Connie Pelkey

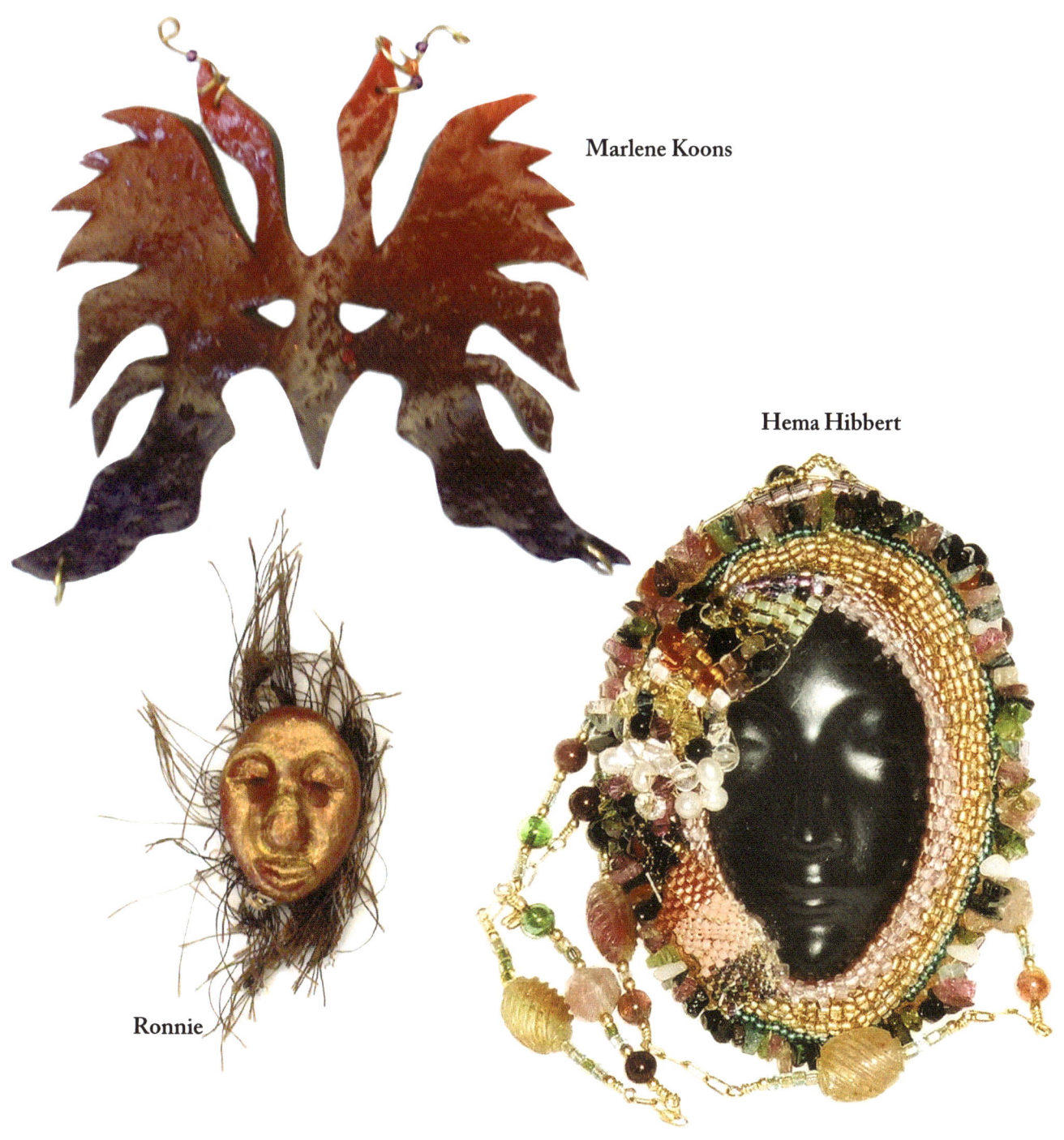

Marlene Koons

Hema Hibbert

Ronnie

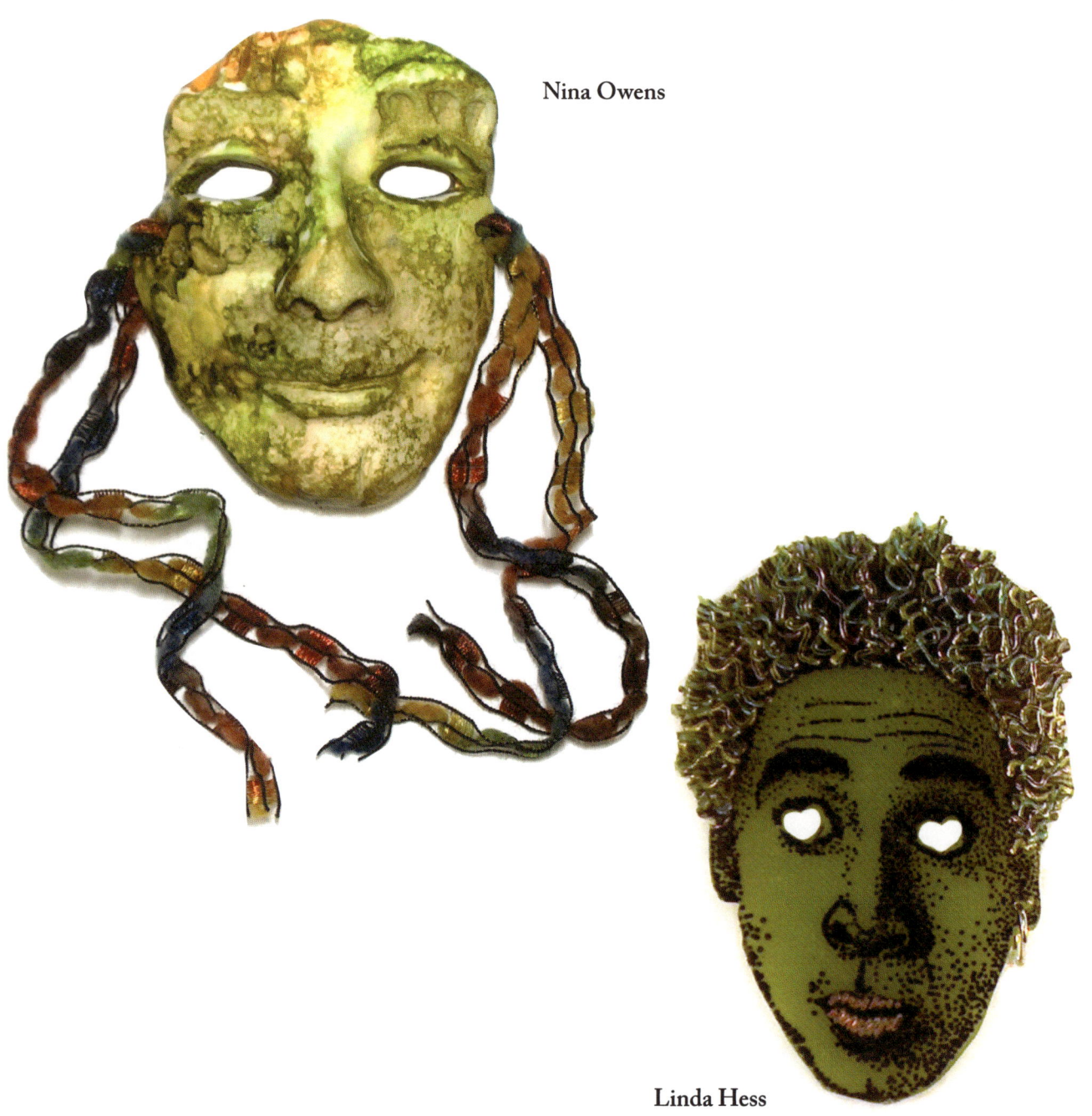

Nina Owens

Linda Hess

A Collection Of Polymer Clay Masks

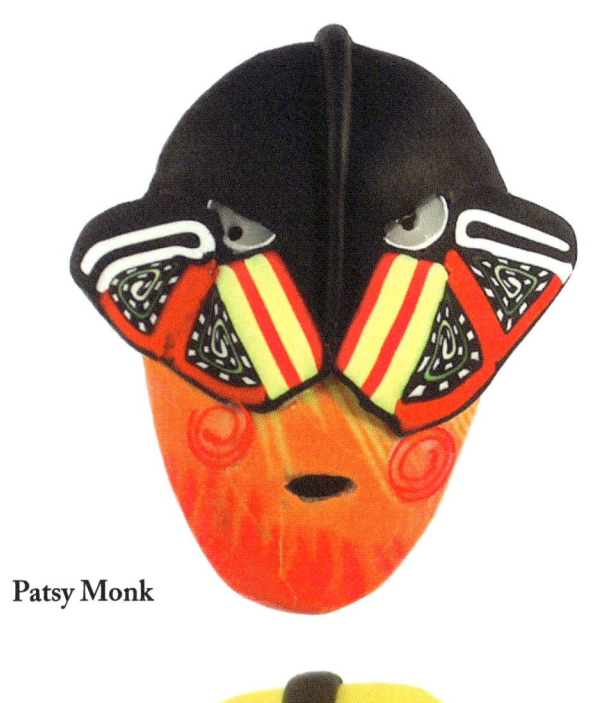

Patsy Monk

Karen Omodt

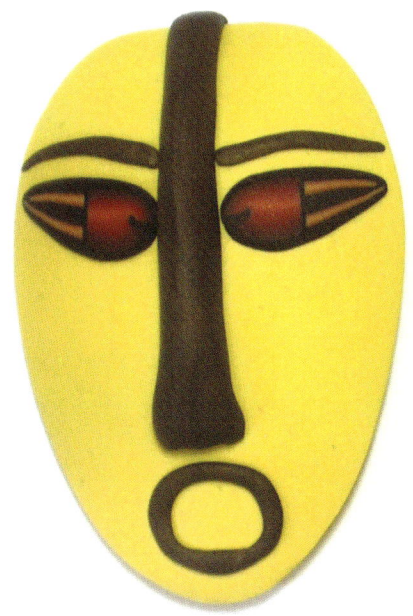

Jackie Sieben

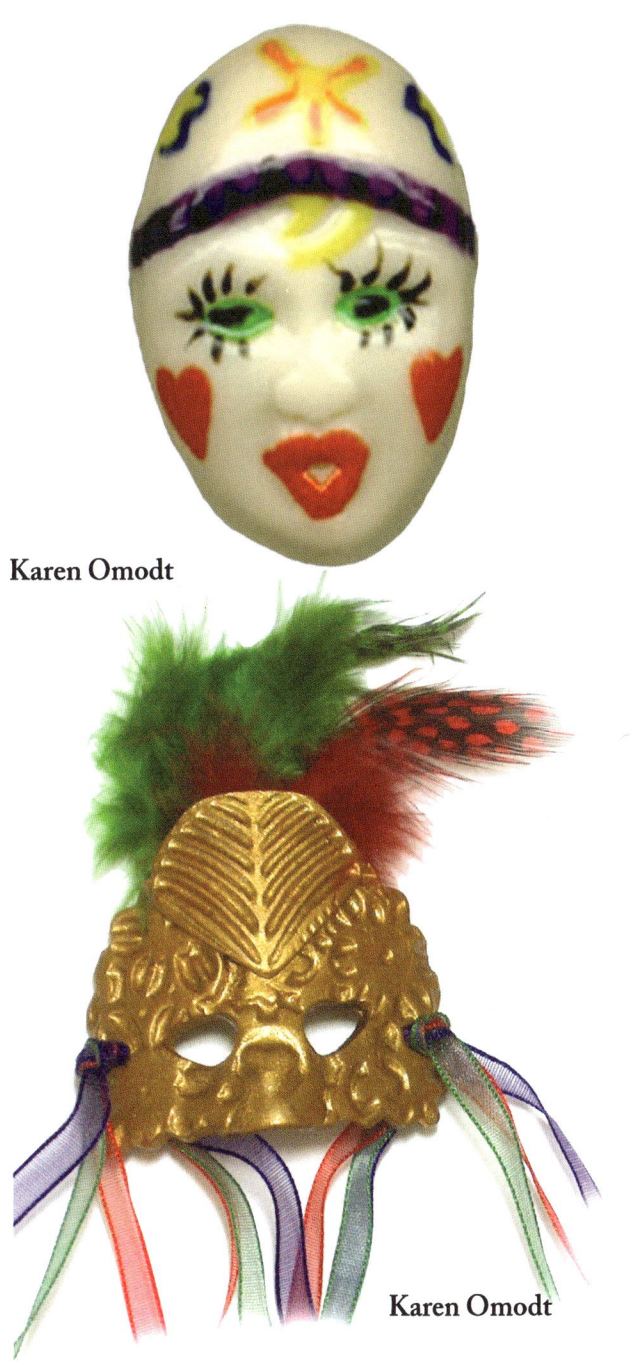

Karen Omodt

PolyMarket Press

149

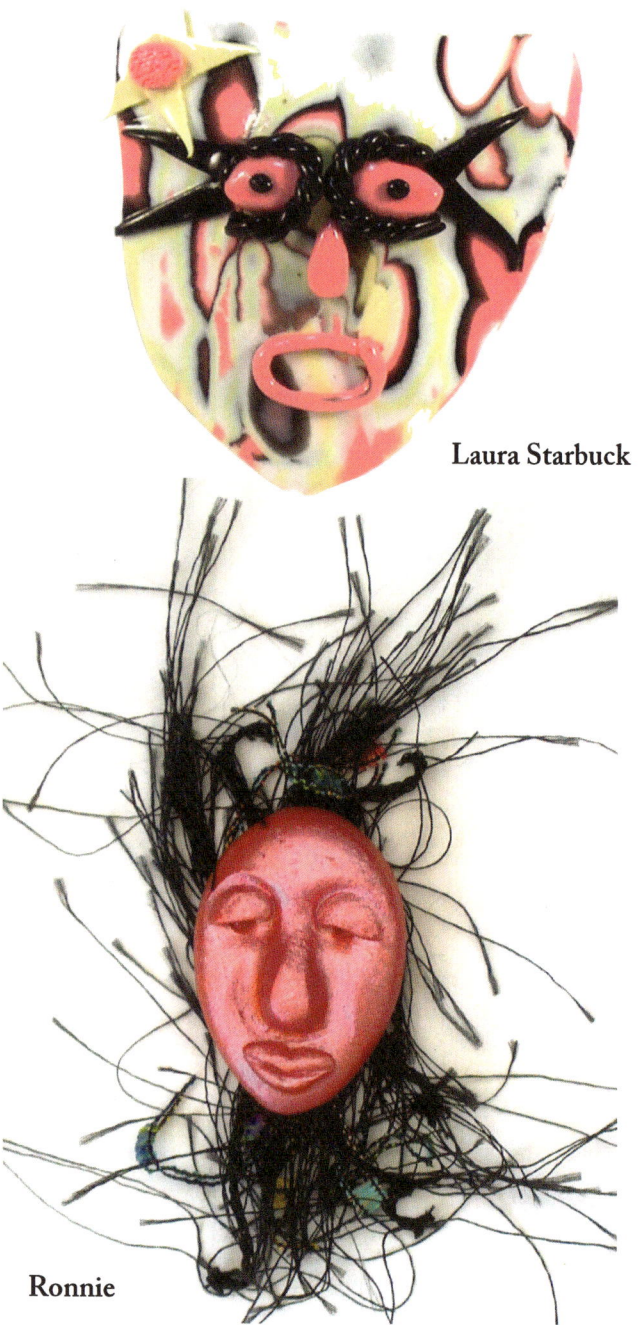

Laura Starbuck

Ronnie

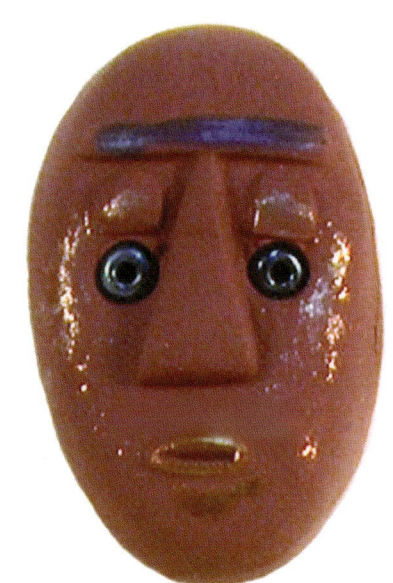

Ronnie

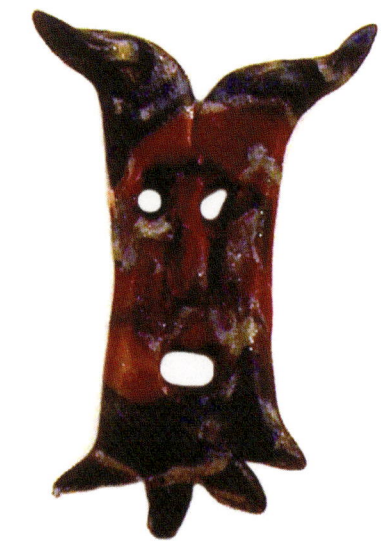

Pepper Mentz

A Collection Of Polymer Clay Masks

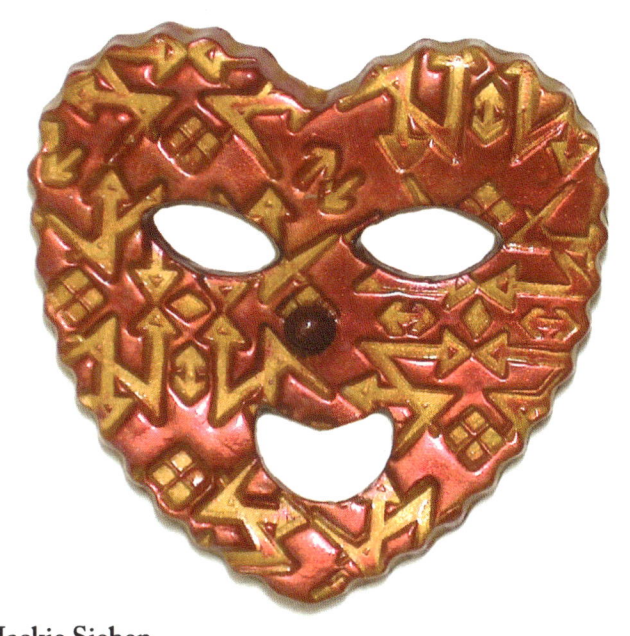

Jackie Sieben

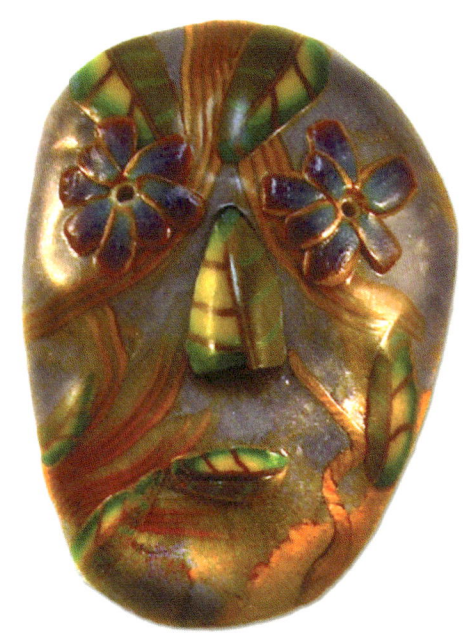

Patsy Monk

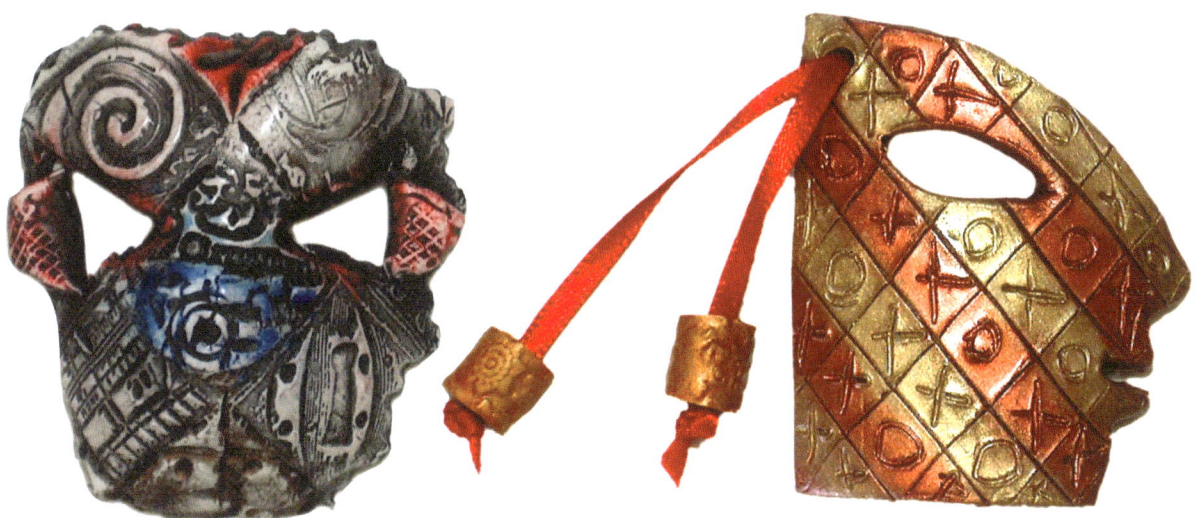

Laurel Steven

Andrea Spatz

PolyMarket Press

Tonja Lenderman

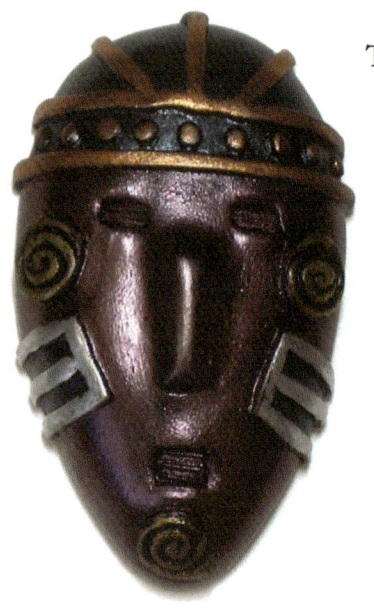

Karen Scudder

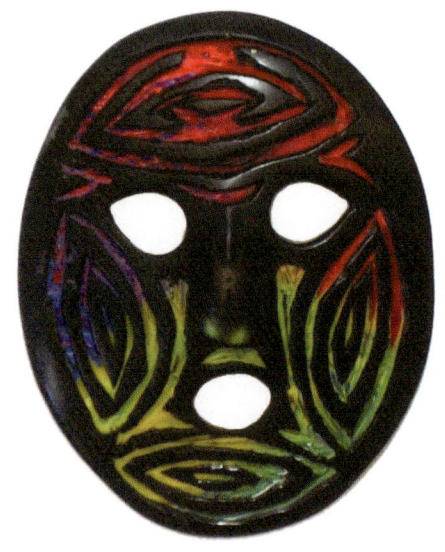

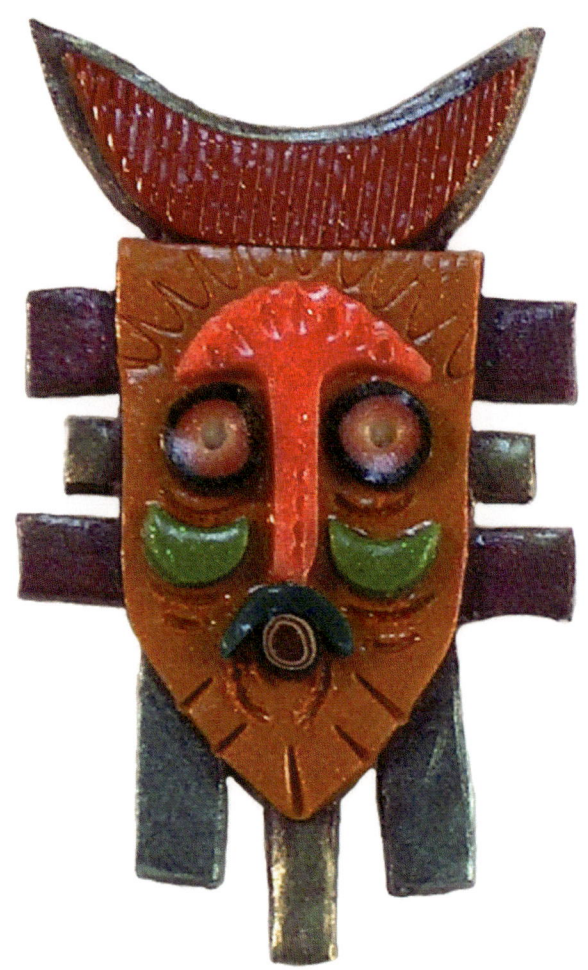

Marlene Koons

A Collection Of Polymer Clay Masks

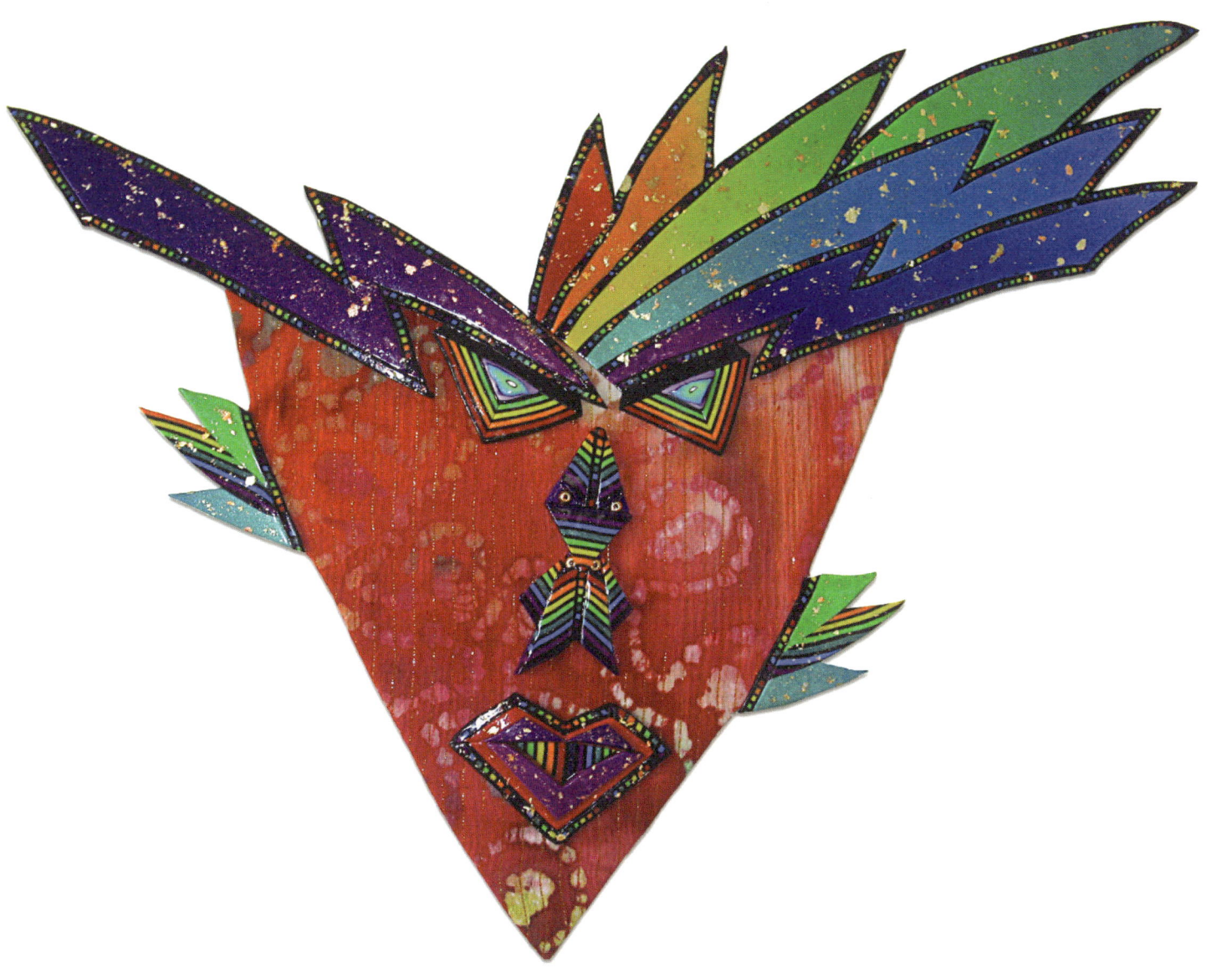

Ann Kruglak   *photo Ann Kruglak*   14" x 17"

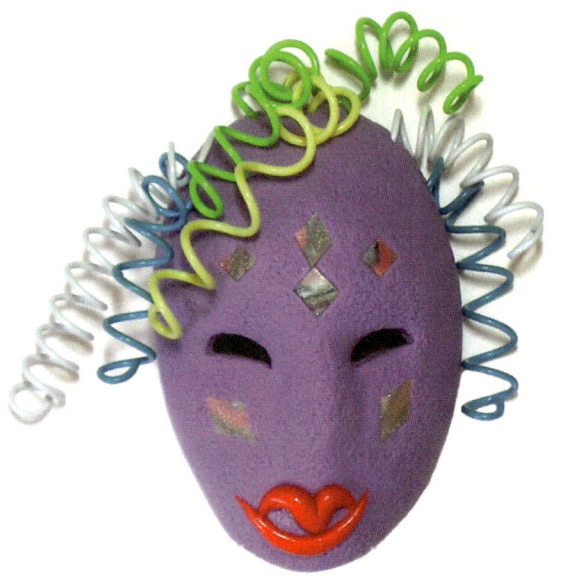

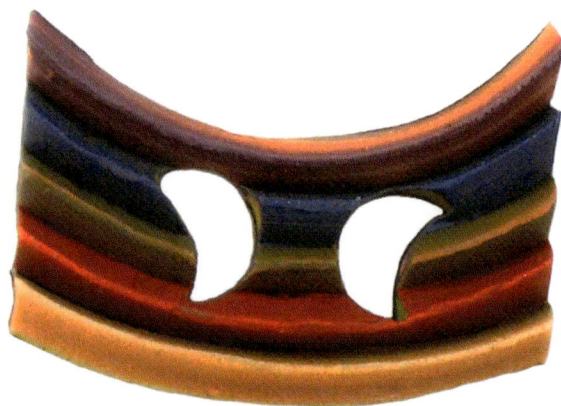

BrendaLea Abbott

Andrea Spatz

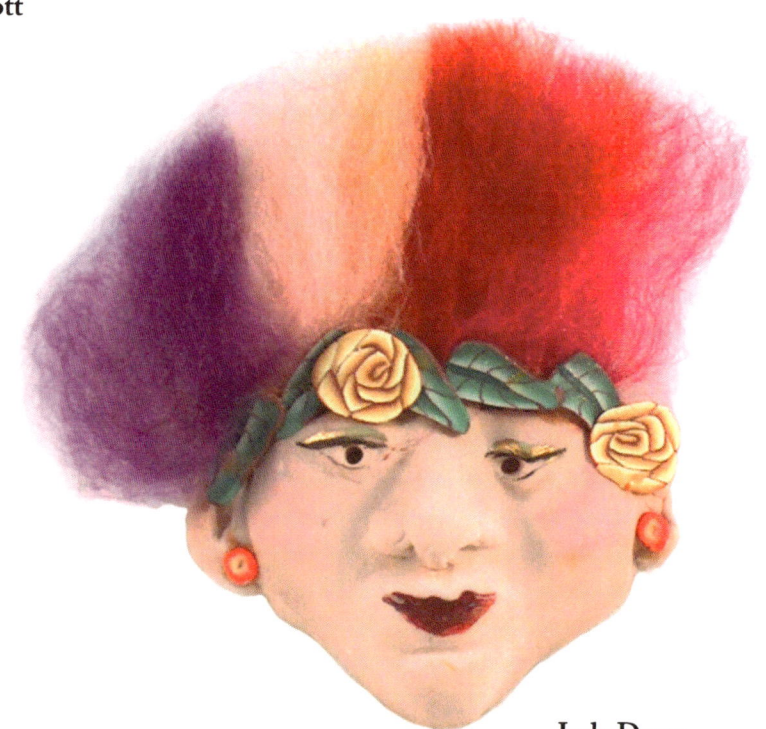

Judy Dunn

A Collection Of Polymer Clay Masks

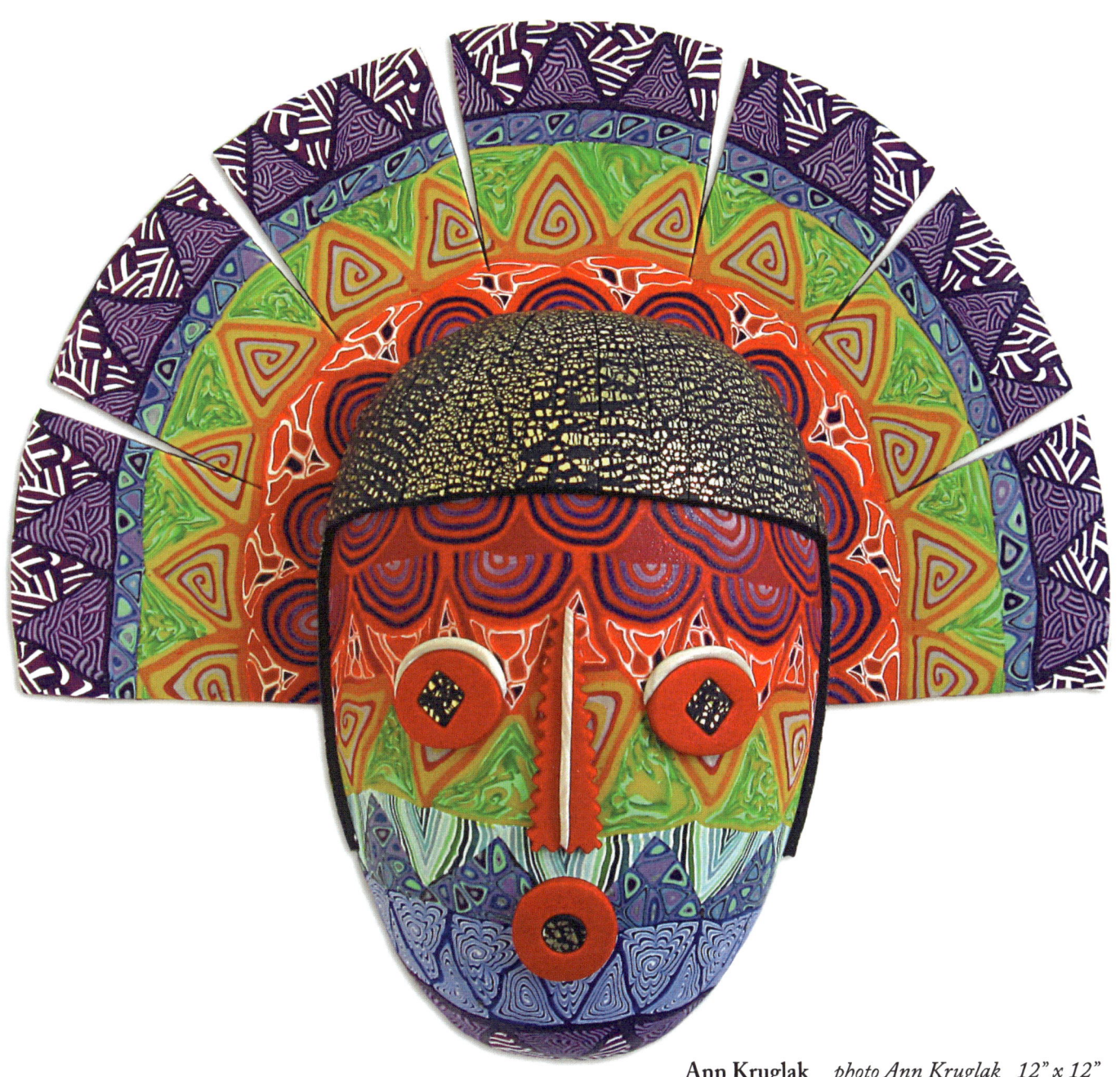

Ann Kruglak   *photo Ann Kruglak   12" x 12"*

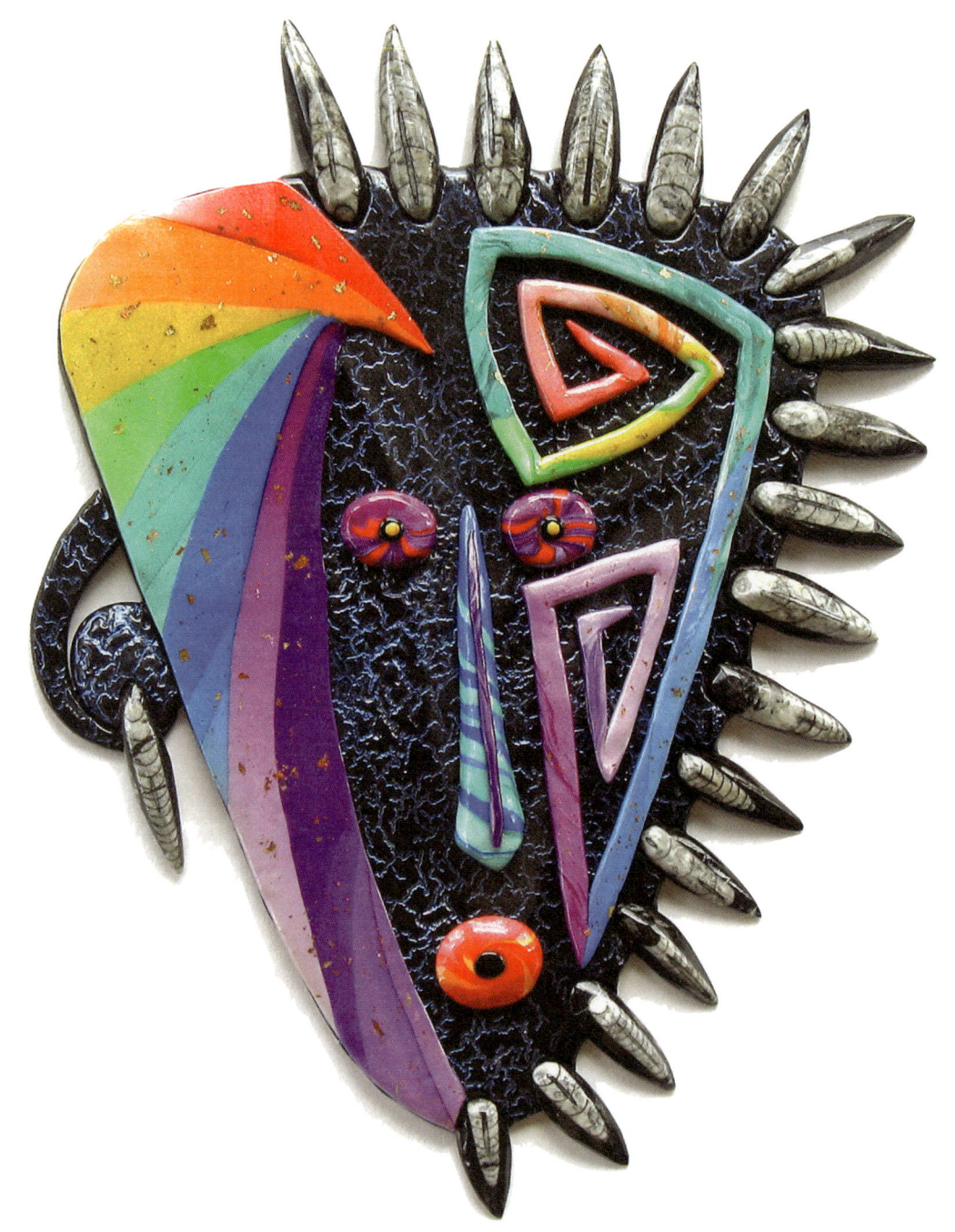

Ann Kruglak   *photo Ann Kruglak*   13" x 9"

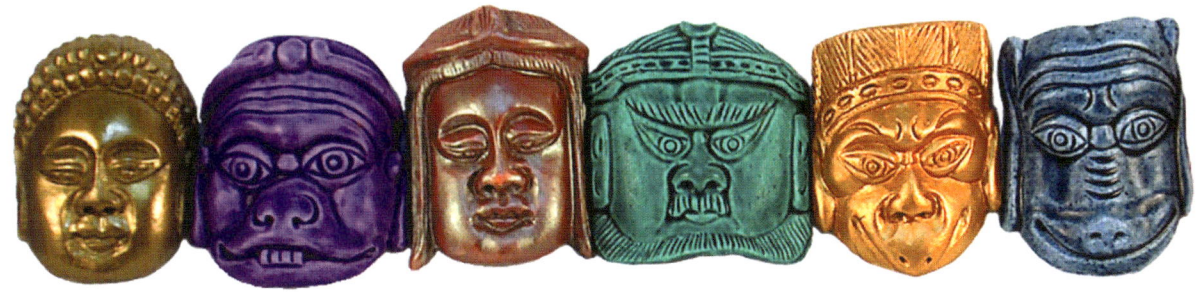

Jeanne Rhea

Index Of Contributing Artists

A

Abbott, BrendaLea 154
Abel, Lashonne 126
Ackley, Beth 53, 127, 134
Aharoni, Valerie 17, 43, 123, 125

B

Bailey, Sherry 8, 34, 64, 68, 86, 96, 98
Baker, Alicia 44, 48, 54, 57, 59
Barnes, Patty 20, 25, 54, 68, 95
Becker, Cynthia 97
Beder, Dawn 96
Bergeron, Sunni 46
Bidler, Leila 134
Biren, Teri 108
Bradley, Helen 67
Briefer-Gose, Kathi 104, 109, 127, 138

C

Callahan, Tracy 43, 96, 105, 126
Camgros, Vicki 46, 52, 81
Carlson, Lisa 23, 86
Cavender, Kim 139
Coller, Deborah 47, 70, 95
Cowles, Karen 63, 78, 79, 128
Cox, Babette 15
Cressman-Reeder, Eileen 80, 88

D

DeNio, Lynne 59, 106, 145
Dewey, Katherine 2, 90
Dorion, Jenn 79, 108, 127, 134, 145
Dunn, Judy 16, 55, 154
Dykes, Dawn 106

E

Edmonds, Patricia 16, 17, 18, 19, 21, 23, 138

F

Fleischer, Beth 107
Follett, Lori O 39, 85
Frankenberg, Marla 53
Fry, Greta 23, 43, 82

G

Geer, Linda 86, 109
Gentry, Sue 19
Gibson, Evelyn 26, 75, 141
Girard, Bill 80, 112
Greenberg, Lori 141
Greynolds, Dorothy 3, 138
Guevarra, Kimberly 97
Gunnell, Tess 57, 80

H

Helm, Ian 70, 74, 75, 76
Helm, Sarajane 2, 4, 5, 22, 27, 45, 62, 63, 66, 73, 75, 81, 89, 90, 91, 109, 122, 133, 135, 146
Hess, Linda 49, 133, 148
Hibbert, Hema 101, 147
Hobbs, Diane 133
Hollis, Jackie 101, 140
Houghtaling, Robert 24, 62, 77, 82
Howell, Tommie 57, 90, 97
Hoy, Janet 60
Hughes, Helen 51, 63, 77, 126

I

Ivester, Suzanne 58, 92

J

Jacob, Helen 36, 50
James, Jeff 122
Jaussaud, Judy 40, 45, 47, 53
Jenkins, Jainnie Cox 105

K

Keyes, Hazel 49, 109
Knauer, Ellen 26, 37
Knoppel, Christopher 11
Kolar, MM 76
Koons, Marlene 147, 152
Kruglak, Ann 69, 111, 153, 155, 156

L

Lehmann, Cecelia 18, 31, 34, 36, 60, 64, 70, 74, 112, 117
Leir-VanSickle, Julie 18, 26, 57, 64, 122, 134
Lenderman, Tonja 28, 40, 66, 84, 95, 103, 37
Linda Weeks 159
Lisa Carlson 23
Loring, Eileen 110
Lowe, J 67
Luppert, Sylvia 89

M

MacCallum, Diane 29, 103, 115
Mackin, Eileen 52
Mangie, Bernadette 25, 74, 141
Mara, Susan 106, 107
Marchiando, Meg 84
Marie-Therese 19
Martin, Rose Mary 109
Martin, RoseMary 51, 60
Martins, Chris 45, 85
McNealey, Marie 46, 48, 64, 112, 117, 122
Meek, Else 83, 137
Mentz, Pepper 50, 150
Mihalyak, Sharon 78, 105
Miller, Amanda Lee 20, 84
Mills, Libby 43
Milne, Robin 136
Miskowitz, Joyce 32, 135
Monk, Patsy 36, 74, 149, 151

N

Newbold, LynnDel 19

O

O'Brian, Ulrika 52
Olson Phillips, Jane 37
Omodt, Karen 21, 82, 103, 104, 108, 113, 149
Ortiz, LaLa 75, 93
Osmundson, Pat 48
Owens, Nina 72, 84, 105, 148

P

Paone, Diane 49
Pelkey, Connie 67, 146
Petelinz, Michelle 99, 100, 101

Q

Quinn, Bonnie 35, 49, 133, 142

R

Reed, Charles 38, 40, 46, 61
Rhea, Jeanne 68, 108, 146, 157
Rheid, Margaret 2
Roberts Daughter 75
Robitaille, Elaine 104

Ronnie 50, 59, 113, 126, 142, 147, 150
Rozman, Jill "Suzy" 142
Rumsey Bellenot, Ellen 57, 74, 103, 120, 121, 130, 131, 143
Rutter, Chris 33, 160

S

Sahlberg, Pörrö 70
Salinas, Esperanza 94, 113
Santoro, Jen 65
Sawyer, Greg 76
Schoubye, Karen 120
Schwarzenberg, Lynne Ann 24, 55
Scichilone, Darleen Bellan 95
Scudder, Karen 34, 35, 65, 78, 103, 135, 152
Seale, Rita 29, 103
Segal, Marie 32
Sheila Furth 129
Sherman, Carolyn 16, 79
Sieben, Jackie 17, 32, 135, 149, 151
Skinner, Judith 29, 63, 67, 70, 113, 115
Smith, Shane 116, 120, 143
Spatz, Andrea 20, 66, 85, 98, 151, 154
Standifer, Denise 35, 47, 60, 62, 86, 98, 106, 113
Starbuck, Laura 150
Steven, Laurel 30, 81, 151
Stout, Rebecca Wells 7, 9, 42, 24, 40, 51, 66, 71, 87, 88, 89, 91, 108, 10, 10
Summer, Judy 12, 13, 14, 119
Sutton, Debra 81
Swartz, Jackie 62, 65

T

Tetzlaff, Rev. Byrd 143, 144
Teunis, Gail 115
Thomas, JoAnn 57

V

Valianti, Barbara 120, 145
Vanderwood, Mary 30, 35, 44, 45, 47, 52, 54, 144
VanDonkelaar, Jan 78, 95
Veldt, Muriel 98
Vilas-Helton, Linda 120, 145

W

Weeks, Linda 76, 86, 159
Wendland, Jeanean 59
West, Melanie 2, 114
Wiley, Robert 33, 50, 55, 144
Wilson, Kimba 28, 140
Wrisley, Susan 21
Wu, Lori 95

Y

Youmans, Christi 30

Z

Zimmerman, Michelle 108

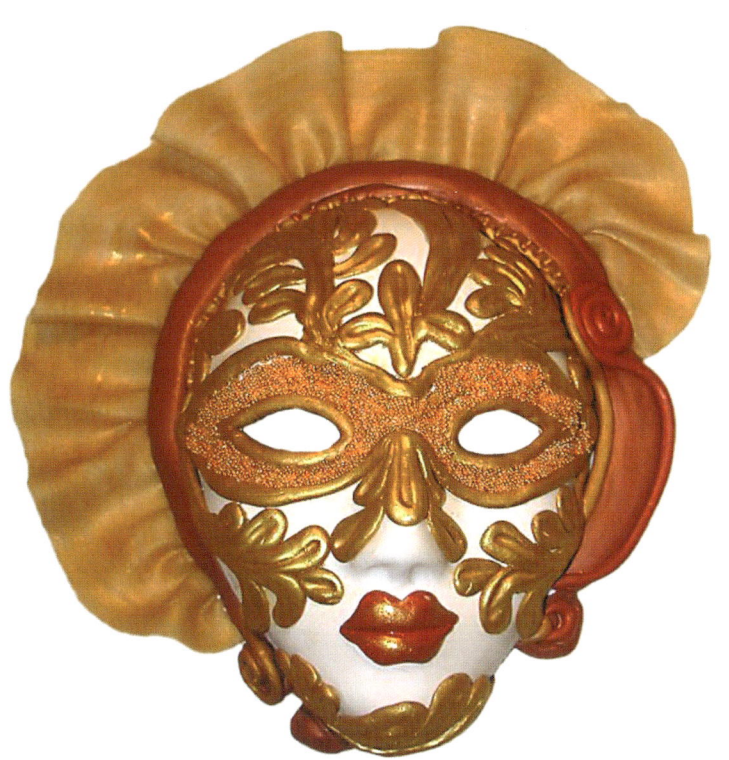

Linda Weeks *photo Linda Weeks*

This book would not have been possible without the cooperation of all the artists involved and the support of my friends and family. I also thank Front Range Community College Professors Deborah Craven and Kate Hagerty for being technically brilliant, patient and endlessly helpful while educating me in the intricacies of Adobe InDesign and Adobe Photoshop.

Thank you!!

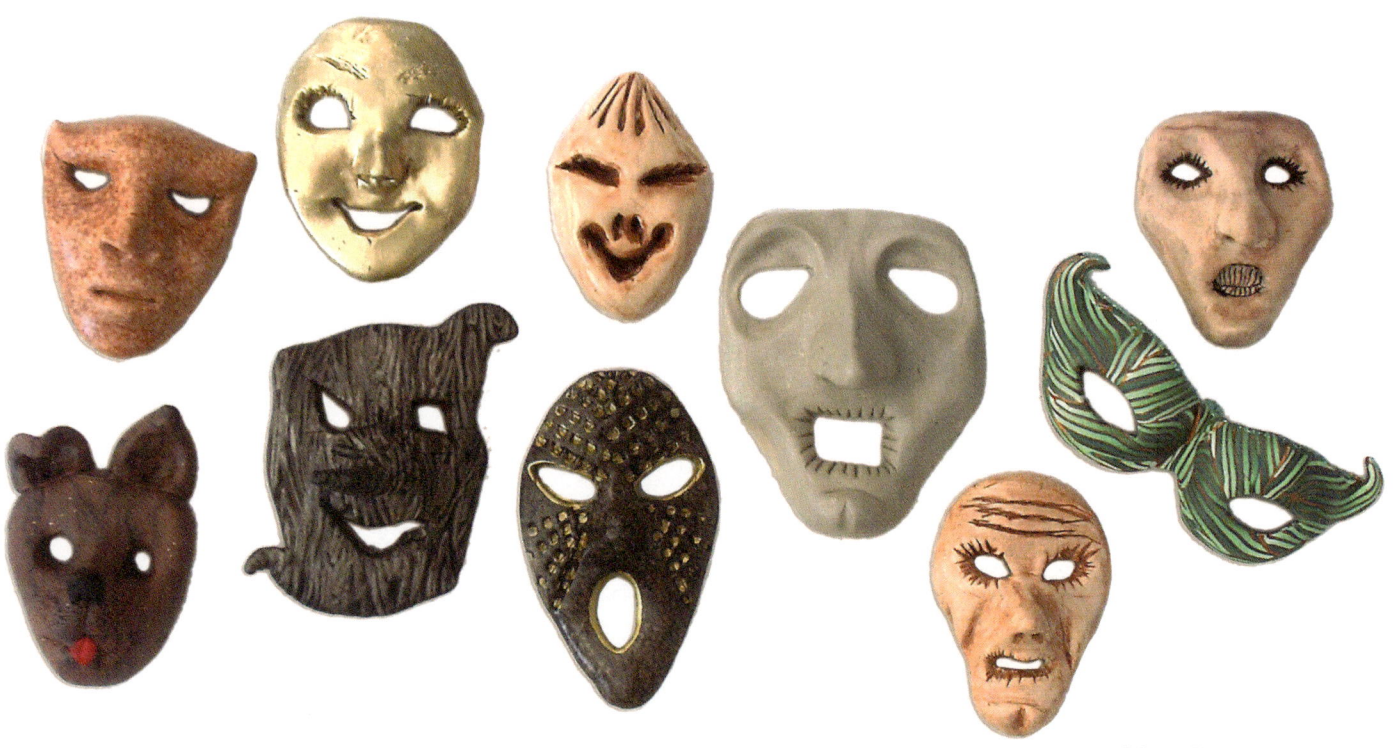

Chris Rutter

CPSIA information can be obtained
at www.ICGtesting.com
Printed in the USA
265031LV00002B